The Story of
ASIA'S LIONS

The Story of
ASIA'S LIONS

Divyabhanusinh

Marg publications

General Editor Pratapaditya Pal
Research Editor Annapurna Garimella
Executive Editors Savita Chandiramani, Rivka Israel
Senior Editorial Executive Biswajeet Rath
Editorial Executive Arnavaz K. Bhansali

Senior Production Executive Gautam V. Jadhav
Production Executive Vidyadhar R. Sawant

Design concept Roma Sinai Mukherjee

Design Execution Marg
Designed by Naju Hirani *based on the concept*

ISBN 10: 81-85026-87-4
ISBN 13: 978-81-85026-87-9
Library of Congress Catalog Card Number: 2008-307093
Price: Rs 1950 / US$ 50

The Gir Welfare Fund will receive 5% of the net sales value of each copy sold.

Published by Radhika Sabavala for Marg Publications on behalf of the
National Centre for the Performing Arts, 24, Homi Mody Street, Mumbai 400 001.

Processed by Reproscan, Mumbai 400 013.

Printed at Thomson Press (India) Ltd., Navi Mumbai 400 708.

For

Asia's Lions
who survive in spite of us

D.D. Kosambi, 1907–1966
Guide, Friend, Teacher, Benefactor

contents:

Pages 2–3, 5 ■ A pride in a grassland, Gir.
Photographs: Divyabhanusinh.

Pages 8–9 ■ Lioness and cubs, Gir.
Photograph: Divyabhanusinh.

Page 5 ■ Portrait of D.D. Kosambi by Jatin Das.
Author's collection.

*Marg acknowledges the generous support
of The Indian Hotels Company Limited, Mumbai
and Oliver Forge and Brendan Lynch Limited, London
in the publication of this book*

preface

THE LION IS so deeply ingrained in the human psyche that the impulse to write a book about this magnificent animal is not unique. However, two additional reasons propelled me to write this one. First, a history of the interaction of the lions of Asia with man over the ages has not yet been attempted fully in English, or for that matter in any other language. Second, my ancestor Vanraj Chavda, the founder of the principality of Anhilwad Patan in north Gujarat in the 8th century, was born in the Gir forest, now the last home of Asia's lions, and was therefore christened "king of the jungle" according to the popular tradition of Gujarat. The suffix to my own name, "sinh", also means lion. It was thus natural that I had a large dose of lion stories in my childhood, far more than most children would have had even in Gujarat where the animal thrives in folklore and literature. Moreover, I studied at Rajkumar College, Rajkot, at a time when M.A. Wynter-Blyth, the pioneer of large mammal census in independent India and an authority on the Gir and its lions, was its principal. This happy happenstance had its own impact on my young mind.

With such antecedents, I should have written about lions much earlier. This did not happen, again for two reasons. First, there was the matter of earning a living, a must for the cadets of small principalities which in any case had disappeared into the cauldron of republican India. Second, the cheetah problem engaged my attention unexpectedly and dramatically, which kept me busy researching the subject from 1984 to 1994 resulting in a book the following year. A vague idea of writing a history of the lion had come to me as far back as the 1960s, when I re-read with fascination the articles on the Gir Forest and its lions by M.A. Wynter-Blyth and R.S. Dharmakumarsinhji in the journals of the Bombay Natural History Society. I started collecting data haphazardly and fitfully from then on but other preoccupations intervened. I have often wondered how differently I would have written the lion story if I had done it more than three decades ago when there were still scores of eyewitnesses who had lived in princely India, experienced lion and other shikar, and survived the upheavals of 1947. It was however only in the 1980s that I encountered the historical lion in a big way, as I dug deep into Indian history's sources for my cheetah work. It was after the cheetah manuscript went to the publishers in 1994 that the lion engaged my attention as fully as is possible for a senior executive in the corporate world, and only after my retirement in 2001 that I finally began writing it all down. Normally, an author should not find it necessary to give such a lengthy background to his work, but after the cheetah book was published, readers wondered how this interloper, neither of the academic world, nor a field scientist or forest officer, came to write about cheetahs. Almost a decade later I find I am still explaining myself.

The sources for the history of the lion are remarkably similar to, and in some cases the same as, those for the cheetah. This helped insofar as collecting research material goes, since my job was partially done during collection of the cheetah data. I believe that there is nothing like visual material to illustrate fine nuances of the past or present; here too illustrations tell their story wherever possible as in the earlier book. And yet there are major differences between the two works. The cheetah is so difficult to find among historical sources and the references are so few that I had to use almost all the material I had unearthed to put the story together. In the case of the lion, the opposite is true. There was often so much material that I was confronted with the dilemma of what I should choose and what I should reject. I beg the indulgence of my readers if I have left out any of their favourite sources or stories. While the size of the cheetah book was limited by the material available, I have deliberately limited the length of this one in order not to make it into an unwieldy tome, for it is possible to expand almost each of the chapters into a book by itself. Besides, the cheetah is dead and gone from India, its story has ended here as far as I can tell. The lion on the other hand has hung on by a thread. The last chapter here deals with the threats it faces from us. I had planned to write two chapters on the subject but soon I realized that this animal and its problems have been the subject of our scrutiny ad infinitum. The Central and Gujarat state governments have initiated some schemes for its preservation, but only time will tell if they have succeeded or have remained on paper as many others have. What is required is not suggestions for solutions – of which there are plenty – but action.

The British period saw crucial developments in the "sport" of hunting the lion as well as in its protection. What is often referred to as the "British administration" or simply "the British" by many an author, consisted of individuals with very different personalities who acted differently and quite often uniquely. It is simply not on to convert the lot into a faceless mass. I have tried to give full names and designations of the dramatis personae of the time wherever possible, also to retain some of the flavour of the past. For the very same reason, I have used place names as they were known then rather than those in use today. The word "Pakistan" appears rarely in the text as lions had disappeared from the area that was to be the new country even before its idea had found political expression and long before it became a political reality.

I must make a special mention of the princely order from whom I am fortunate in having received a fund of inside information. But I have been careful to present the facts – warts and all – for the reader to judge; however, no apology is called for. Persons who have at their command surplus resources and time (Indian princes had plenty of both since the imperial government had taken away from them the bothersome and resource crunching responsibility for external relations of their states) indulge themselves lavishly and often publicly without concern for others' judgements and feelings. It is a pattern of behaviour as old as history itself, and is not unique to the Indian princes. One has only to look at their predecessors and more to the point, their successors – industrialists and politicians – to test the veracity of the statement. It is easy to pass judgement on the past; it is more important however, to build on what the present has inherited from it.

I have adhered to the narrative style and have kept analysis to the minimum to try and make the history accessible and compelling for even the reader with but a passing interest. I have no doubt though, that if a lion could write a history of its relationship with humans and their depredations, it would be very different and illuminating, *the* definitive work.

Suryodaya, 310 Gom Defence Colony
Vaishali Marg, Jaipur
sawaj_cheetah@rediffmail.com

acknowledgements

THE HISTORY OF an animal is somewhat off the beaten track of historical writing. Much information had to be obtained from sources other than the published ones or from archival material. I am indebted to Maharana Raj Saheb Pratapsinhji of Wankaner and Y. Digvijaysinhji for sharing some of their vast knowledge. The latter undertook the arduous task of gathering material from sources in Saurashtra not easily reachable by me because of the compulsions of my former occupation and my physical location away from the peninsula. M. Himmatsinhji of Kutch provided valuable inputs from the region where the memory of lions survives till today. Yudhishthir Khatau gave me information from the *Shikar Diary* of M. Chandrabhanusinhji of Wankaner. Darbar Saheb Jaswantsinhji of Bilkha spent endless hours giving me particulars on lions and their shikar, Maharao Brijraj Singh of Kotah was no less forthcoming with his family's records, Thakur Dalip Singh gave me records of Maharaja Ganga Singh of Bikaner's lion shikar, and Narayan Singh Bhayal obtained information regarding a Gwalior lion from Maharaja Manvendra Singh of Panna. E. Joubert van Ingen, the owner of the world renowned firm of taxidermists in Mysore of that name, gave me free and full access to the company's unique records. Nagendra Singh Hada obtained Junagadh State publications being sold in that town as waste paper. He also sat in the Junagadh District Record Office and took notes from records preserved there as did Rohan D'Souza from the National Archives at Delhi. Shambhuprasad Desai from Junagadh who, as also his father, had been in the state's service, spent endless hours with me discussing the state's and particularly the last Nawab's administration and his times. He was a young officer on the staff of Mahbatkhanji III. His demise a few years ago, has cut permanently one of the very few surviving links of a bygone era of "Soruth" as the state often styled itself. Bhushan Pandya from Rajkot gave me several photographs for use in the book, Ashok Kumar S. Benani from Junagadh gave me postage stamps, revenue stamp papers, and other memorabilia of Junagadh State, while Jitendar Rathore from Jaipur undertook the task of preparing the manuscript for the publishers.

The following scholars gave invaluable advice and direction and made me aware of sources which otherwise would have remained unknown: Professor Helmut Hemmer of Johannes Gutenberg University, Mainz; Dr Julian Reade of the British Museum, London; Dr A.H. Morton of the School of Oriental and African Studies, London; Professor Romila Thapar of Jawaharlal Nehru University, Delhi; Professor Muzaffar Alam of Chicago University; Dr Deborah Swallow of the Victoria and Albert Museum, London; Dr Jeremiah P. Losty of the Oriental and India Office Collections, The British Library, London; Dr Anne Buddle of the National Galleries of Scotland, Edinburgh; Professor John D. Gurney of Wadham College, Oxford; Simon Digby from Jersey; Professor B.D. Chattopadhyaya of Jawaharlal Nehru University, Delhi; Dr Nayanjot Lahiri of Delhi University; Professor S.R. and Dr Renate Sarma of Aligarh Muslim University, Aligarh; Dr T.K. Biswas of Bharat Kala Bhavan, Varanasi; Diane and Geoffrey Ward from New York; P.K. Sen, former Director, Project Tiger, Government of India; Dr K. Ullas Karanth of the Wildlife Conservation Society of New York; and Colonel John Wakefield of Kabini River Lodge, Karnataka. Rishad Naoroji from Mumbai tracked down several references I knew of, but could not find; Bhaskar Khira sent me newspaper clippings from Ahmedabad and he has found a Gujarati translator.

Were it not for the ever generous help and guidance of Dr M.A. Mehendale of Bhandarkar Oriental Research Institute, Pune, the chapter on Ancient India would not have seen the light of day. Dr Asok Kumar Das's encyclopaedic knowledge of Mughal art and artefacts was always forthcoming and his guidance was indispensable. Dr M.K. Ranjitsinhji put at my disposal his unique experience of the jungle, of administration as a bureaucrat, and his equally detailed knowledge of source material as generously as he did earlier for the cheetah book. Dr Mahesh Rangarajan has been a source of unfailing encouragement in my efforts at writing the book and anyone who is interested in this subject would do well to read his incomparable political history of the lion in India. My son Udaybhanusinh, Advocate, Bombay High Court, undertook a long search through stacks of legal tomes to unearth the fascinating story behind the selection of the Ashokan capital as India's national symbol, to which Ashok H. Desai, former Attorney General of India and Senior Advocate of the Supreme Court, put his seal of approval.

I have been visiting the Gir forest for nearly half a century. Several officers of the Forest Department of the Government of Gujarat have given me the help one needs in the field; their support has been invaluable. Foremost among them are Sanat A. Chavan, D.S. Narve, H.S. Singh, S. Tikadar, Bharat J. Pathak, Mahesh Singh, B.P. Pati, N.V. Kataria, and P.P. Raval. Two remarkable *pagi*s of the old school, Abhlabha son of Jafarbha and Bhanabha son of Kathalbha, introduced me to lions and taught me of their ways as no one else could.

My search for the lion through history has been an individual effort for several years which I have pursued with my own limited resources. In its last phase in 2002 though, I was fortunate to receive material support. Amin Ali, Managing Director of "The Red Fort", London readily obtained books for me from the UK and elsewhere, and he and Virginia McKenna of the Born Free Foundation, UK helped me in obtaining transparencies for publication. Harshad Patel of Vanishing Herds Foundation, London; Raj and Diane Singh of Exotic Journeys, New Delhi; and R.K. Krishna Kumar, Managing Director, The Indian Hotels Co. Ltd. extended hospitality and made possible a visit to London in May 2002 to complete my collection of data for the book. Finally, Nina Rao of Saving Wild Tigers Foundation, New York gave me a generous study grant to complete the work at a time when I needed it most, at the behest of Toby Sinclair.

It is a pleasure to record the contribution of my publishers. Dr Pratapaditya Pal read through the text and made invaluable suggestions, while Radhika Sabavala and the Marg team meticulously shepherded the book through every stage to its successful completion. Roma Sinai Mukherjee, who had also worked with me on the cheetah book, left her indelible imprint on the design of the present volume as well.

Our children Uday and Prerna have grown up and away to start their own families, but remain a source of comfort to me. My wife Purnima has given silent but strong support to my every endeavour, and my mother Rajmata Vilaskunverba of Mansa has been the constant source of inspiration throughout my life. To all of them and to several others, I owe a debt of gratitude. They have greatly enriched the result, its failings are mine alone.

CHAPTER 1

Asia's Lions Today

Birds of the Gir
■ The many species of birds include the crested serpent eagle, Indian peafowl, painted sandgrouse, and purple sunbird.
Photographs: Divyabhanusinh.

THERE WAS A TIME when the lion roamed Asia from Palestine in the west to Palamau in eastern India. It was the most visible of the large cats and it struck awe in its human observers as no other animal did.

Yet, today this magnificent animal has become extinct in Asia but for a small population hanging on by a thread in a corner of India. To most Asians the lion survives only in vague memory or in fairy tales. Few of them outside Gujarat are aware of its existence on the continent. How this sorry state came to pass is the story of this book. But first, let us briefly look at the lion's last home in Asia and how lions here differ from those of Africa, and recount some of the close relationships humans have had with the lion which remains an active presence in the culture of Gujarat.

The remote region in which Asia's lions survive is the isolated Saurashtra peninsula. It is bound by the Gulf of Kutch in the north, the Arabian Sea in the south and west, and to the east by the Gulf of Cambay (Khambhat). To the northeast of Saurashtra lie the Little Rann of Kutch and the flat sedimentary lowlands of Nal and the Bhal. Here is a peninsula with a difference, physically almost cut off even on the fourth side from the mainland of the Indian subcontinent. Both human and animal populations have been isolated over the millennia, and among the former, though the language they speak is a distinct dialect of Gujarati, the dress, folklore, and the way of life is noticeably different from the rest of Gujarat even today.

The surface of the peninsula is a sheet of Deccan lava interspersed by trap dykes which are the peculiarities of the region. While most of Saurashtra is low-lying, there are two prominent hill masses. One occupies an area east of Rajkot and much of the middle of the peninsula, with Chotila being its highest peak at 357 metres. The other one is a higher and bolder mass centring on the Gir range with Sarkala the highest peak, at 641 metres. Its eastern offshoot is the Mytiala hill which is 471 metres high, and further east the 498-metre-high Shetrunjay.[1]

The Gir forest, the last home of the Asiatic lion (the term commonly used for Asia's last surviving lion), surrounds the Gir hill system with an area of approximately 1,800 square kilometres, of which a little over 1,400 form the Gir National Park and Sanctuary. Mytiala forest to the east is cut off from the Gir as are the Girnar mountains to the northwest, which are weathered volcanic remains with the highest peak of Goraknath standing at 1,117 metres. The forest is a haven for a variety of flora with 448 flowering plants and 96 tree species being recorded here. *Sag* or teak is the commonest and forms over 31 per cent of the tree cover, followed by *dudhalo*, *khair*, *bor*, and other species.[2] The western area of Gir is dominated by teak whereas in the eastern parts of the forest, *Acacia* species are more prominent. There are areas in the central portion which are thick jungle with semi-evergreen riverine tracts going through the forest. *Khakhro* or flame of the forest trees are a riot of colour at the onset of summer while the stately *vad* or banyan and occasional stands of bamboo are sentinels of the pleasing prospect, interspersed with *bor*, *jambudo*, *sawar*, and many other tree species.

This forest is also haven to some 290 species of birds. From the peacock to the grey partridge, and the crested serpent eagle to the king vulture, it provides them all a habitat to survive and prosper. It has lost only one species of bird in recent times — the grey hornbill which has become locally extinct. The Gir is reputed to have six species of amphibians and 24 species of reptiles, the mugger or marsh crocodile being the largest with a population of some 700 individuals. The forest was at the forefront of the crocodile conservation programme and today it has one of its largest

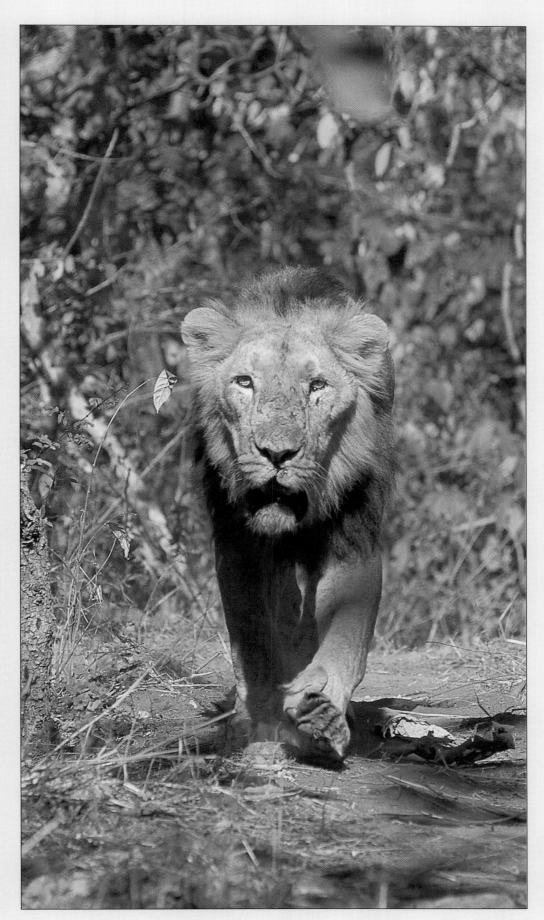

On the road
■ Lions prefer to walk on the soft road surfaces. Here the adult male is heading straight for the photographer, though there is no malice in his expression.
Photograph: Divyabhanusinh.

Some predators of the Gir
(clockwise from right)
■ The rusty spotted cat is rare, and difficult to spot.
Photograph: Bharat Pathak.
■ The jungle cat's small size and nocturnal habits make it rarely visible.
■ The leopard is the second largest predator of the Gir. Very adaptable in its habits, it does not easily show itself.
■ The striped hyena, earlier called the laughing hyena because of its peculiar call, is a carrion eater and a shy animal rarely seen in daytime.
Photographs: Divyabhanusinh.

populations in the country. It is a habitat rich in mammals as well, with 32 species being found there, from the musk shrew to chital, wildboar, sambar, and nilgai which form the prey base for the carnivores which include the tiny rusty-spotted cat which was recorded in the Gir forest for the first time as late as in 1989,[3] jungle cat, jackal, hyena, and leopard, the lion itself being at the top of the food chain.

The forest is studded with human settlements too. There are 14 forest villages and 54 Maldhari nesses (cattle pens of herdsmen) with a total population of approximately 2,500 and a livestock population of 13,000 heads according to the 2004 figures.[4] The three Hindu pilgrimage sites of Tulshishyam, Banej, and Kankai located in the forest cause a human influx during festivals whereas cattle from outside the protected areas invade it annually, particularly during years of scarcity. The forest is important for humans for yet another reason. Four major rivers of Saurashtra – the Rawal, Machundri, Singhavdo, and Hiran – issue forth from the Gir, apart from the Shetrunji whose main source is the eastern Gir and the Ojhat whose tributaries are from the Gir and the Girnar mountains. This then, is the mixed bag kingdom of the *sawaj* – the Asiatic lion, *Panthera leo persica*.

A common question is: how are these lions different from the African lions? One distinguishing morphological feature is the abdominal or belly fold of loose skin which is clearly noticeable both among males and females but somewhat more prominent in the males. This feature is rare among African lions. The tuft of the tail in both males and females is somewhat more pronounced than among African lions but the distinction between the two is not sharp. Male lions have a more pronounced tuft of hair at the elbow than their counterparts in Africa; here too the distinction is not sharp. The male Asiatic lion grows a luxuriant mane surrounding the face, covering the throat and upper parts of the front legs, somewhat halo-like as seen from the front of the animal. However, the mane is not as full or long as that of the African lion and unlike the latter it is not prominent at the top of the head, making the ears of the Asiatic lion very visible. A thin strip of hair grows from the back of the head, past the shoulder blades onto a part of the back of the animal. The skulls of lions collected from Gir often have a bifurcation of the infra-orbital foramen. While this is not a universal feature, it has not been recorded at all in African lions.[5]

Dr Stephen J. O'Brien and his team of scientists who have examined the genetic profile of Asiatic lions have found that their DNA fingerprint patterns are so uniform that: "the Gir lions were all identical.... It was as if they were all clones or identical twins.... The Gir lions had even less variation and were more severely inbred than [even] cheetahs." They concluded that the male lions of Gir who had "dramatically" undersized manes in comparison with African male lions had become "feminized" because of inbreeding caused by a bottleneck which was also the cause of the belly fold and the infraorbital foramen bifurcation.[6]

Lions with manes of different colours are so well known in the Gir that the *pagi*s of old and Maldharis today have a name for each shade of the mane.[7] For example a full grown lion with a light brown mane is called *bhurio*, a lion with a light coloured (yellowish) mane a *pilo*, and a black maned lion a *kalio* or *kamho*. In fact, in the stories and folklore of Saurashtra and Gujarat a lion with a luxuriant mane is called a *kesarisinh*. The Sanskrit word *kesarin* is a name for the lion and means "one who has a mane",[8] whereas *keshwari* is the Gujarati word for mane, of a lion or of a horse.

There is a twist in the tale. In spite of such a range of well defined manes, the lions from India were considered "maneless" for several decades in the 19th century

Prey
■ Chital or spotted deer, and sambar, two of the species which form part of the prey base of the lion in the Gir.
Photographs: Divyabhanusinh.

The Maldharis
■ An old Maldhari walks through the Gir forest in the monsoon.
■ An extended family in a ness in the forest.
■ Women churn curds to separate butter.
Photographs: Bhushan Pandya.

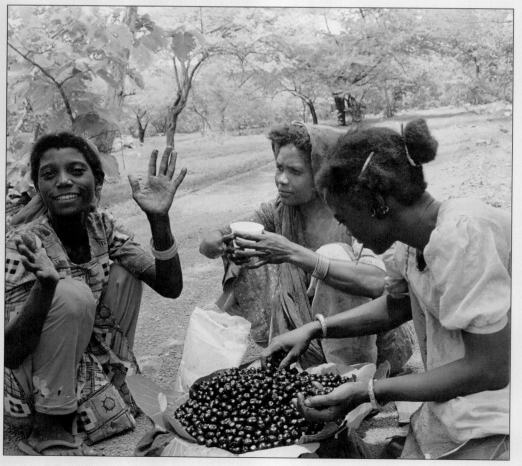

The Sidis
■ Sidi women resting by the roadside with their pickings of jamun to be sold in the nearby markets.
Photograph: Bhushan Pandya.

and in the early part of the 20th. In the 1830s, a Captain Walter Smee described the lions shot by him near Ahmedabad as "maneless", since the manes of these animals were very scanty and did not cover their shoulders.[9] Such lions are indeed known of in the Gir and we have a special name for them, *untio*, but they appear to be very rare with few such specimens seen. In lion populations elsewhere too, maneless or scantily maned lions are not unknown. The Maneaters of Tsavo who played havoc with the railway track layers on the Mombasa to Nairobi railway in Kenya in 1898, were both "maneless".[10] Such lions occur even today in Tsavo National Park, Kenya[11] and they appear to be a variant of the better known forms of the animals from say Kenya's Masai Mara or Tanzania's Serengeti. The "maneless" tag does not apply to the lions of Gir at all.

Unfortunately, in India sufficient data is not available to establish local morphological variations of lions from different regions as they disappeared from the rest of the country before naturalists got down to describing them. Other felines such as tigers and leopards from different regions show noticeable local variations which are well recorded. The cheetahs of India too had three different variations according to Mughal chroniclers: the cheetah of the Deccan, the cheetah of the mountainous regions of the north, and the cheetah of Gujarat – the last-mentioned being the largest and best for coursing antelope. Since cheetahs were used for sport, Mughal chroniclers observed these animals closely and provided this information for the benefit of those who would need to know. But no such descriptions of lions are available.

Even so, the earliest visual records of lions from India which are accurate enough for us to draw conclusions, are those of the Mughals whose paintings do give us a glimpse of what they must have seen. The paintings with lions may be classified as three types: those that depict lions and other animals as part of a story or a fable, those that are studies of lions per se, and those that depict lions as a part of a hunting scene. Some of these paintings are illustrated in Chapter 6, but here we may make some observations on the accuracy of depiction.

The first category of paintings includes the following:

"Noah's Ark" by Miskin, circa 1595.[12] The lion is shown in profile with a thin dark line of a mane around the face and above the head as well. A "smiling" lioness faces the viewer; she too has a dark circle around the face.

"The Raven Addressing the Animals" ascribed to Miskin, circa 1595–1600.[13] The lion listens attentively to the bird along with other animals both real and imaginary. The lion's neck and back are dark brown with barely a suggestion of a mane.

"A Lion's Court" by Farrukh Chela, from the *Anwar-i-Suhaili*, 1595–96.[14] Here the lion holds court from a raised position. All the animals sit below and listen attentively. The lion has no mane but the neck, chest, and front of the legs are rendered in dark brown.

In all the above pictures the animals are accurately enough drawn to be individually recognizable, even the cheetah and the leopard which are often mixed up are distinguishable, but the lions have almost no manes.

In the second category of paintings are the following:

"Animals", circa 1610. This page from the *St Petersburg Muraqqa*[15] is remarkable insofar as it appears to be a collage of unconnected subjects. It has a cat with kittens, a hound bitch with pups, also a urial, nilgai, and other animals. At the top of the painting in the middle, is a lion; at the top left-hand corner is a lion killing a nilgai, while at the top right-hand corner is a lion killing a chital. The lion in the middle is

The Maldharis
- A girl fetches water.
- With a herd of buffaloes at a water trough near a ness.

Photographs: Bhushan Pandya.

The Persian Lion in the Surrey Gardens described by Jardine as *Leo asiaticus*. Adapted from Lear's drawing.

Persian Lion. Drawn from a flat skin in the British Museum.

A Persian lion
■ The one on top was drawn from a specimen living in Surrey Gardens in the 1830s. The other was drawn from a flat skin in the British Museum (Natural History section).
From Pocock, 1930.

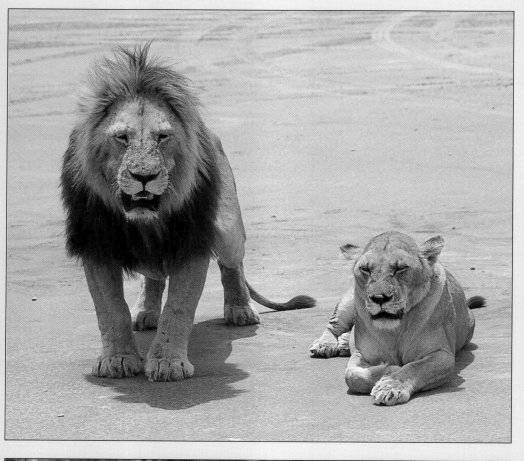

Pair of African lions
■ No bigger than an Indian lion, the male has a far more luxuriant mane which covers its ears and shoulders unlike the Indian lion. This pair is from Ngorongoro Crater, Tanzania, whose population went through a bottleneck some years ago, as had the Gir lions.
Photograph: Divyabhanusinh.

Colourful lions
■ A fully grown lion with a dark brown mane and the same body colour – such specimens are uncommon.
Photograph: Divyabhanusinh.

Hurriana Lion in the Tower Menagerie described by Bennett as *Felis leo bengalensis*. Adapted from the original woodcut.

Gujerat Lion. Drawn from Capt. Smee's skin in the British Museum.

A "Hurriana" lion and a "Gujarat" lion
■ The former was drawn from a specimen living in the Tower Menagerie, London in the 1820s. The British encountered many lions in the environs of Delhi at that time, hence the name. The latter was drawn from a flat skin of Capt. W. Smee's lion in the British Museum (Natural History section). The animal appears to be a sub-adult specimen, hence the scanty mane and the myth of the "maneless" lion of Gujarat.
From Pocock, 1930.

Colourful lions
■ A *kamho* lion. A black-maned lion whose body sports a dark greyish tinge, it could also be called a *jamwo*.
■ A fully grown lion. It has a mane of light brown colour – too dark to be called a *pilo*, but not dark enough to be called a *kamho*.
Photographs: Divyabhanusinh.

A mock charge

■ Disturbed by the photographer's arrival, the lion charged him. Such charges are warnings not usually pressed home. Of note is the abdominal fold, so prominent in Asian lions.

Photograph: Divyabhanusinh.

A pair crosses the Hiran
■ The lion was following the lioness in oestrus and they walked unhurriedly through the stream just below the dam, stopping to drink water. This is virtually unknown lion behaviour in the Gir, as they usually avoid getting wet.
Photograph: Divyabhanusinh.

very realistic as far as its general aspect is concerned. Its mane is dark brown and accurately drawn showing its ears clearly and covering its neck, but somewhat exaggeratedly it covers the shoulder. The tuft of the tail is prominent and a line along the abdomen suggests the abdominal fold. Apart from this rendering the artist has accurately portrayed the action of killing the prey; he has also correctly selected the animals being killed for they are even today the lion's prey.

"Lion Guarding a Leg", circa 1600.[16] This is again an accurate line drawing of the cat guarding the leftover of its kill, the leg of a buffalo. The mane is dark, prominent, accurate enough to show the ears, covers the neck but again somewhat exaggeratedly covers the shoulders. The lion has a prominent tuft on the tail.

"A Lion Drinking Water after Devouring its Kill" ascribed to Nanha,[17] circa 1616. This lion sits by a water body. It is drawn in profile, its mane accurate in all respects even as far as the thin strip of hair going beyond the shoulders, its colour light fawn. It has a prominent tuft on its tail.

"Deux Lions", Aurangzeb period,[18] circa 1670. This painting is of a lion and lioness rendered anatomically inaccurately. However, the mane on the male is prominent on the back of the head though it does not cover the neck.

At a water trough
■ A pride drinks from a water trough near a forest outpost; lions often frequent human habitations fearlessly.
Photograph: Divyabhanusinh.

The third category includes:

"Prince Khurram Attacking a Lion" by Balchand, circa 1640.[19] In this famous incident Khurram kills the lion which has attacked Anup Rai, in the presence of Emperor Jahangir. The animal is made out to be large, but its dark brown mane is scanty. The scene is set in an undulating terrain but it is almost completely barren, and it could have been Bari near Agra where the incident occurred.

"Shah Jahan Hunting Lions near Burhanpur" attributed to Daulat, circa 1635.[20] A lion, a lioness, and two cubs have been cornered. The lion's mane is accurately drawn and it is brown.

"Aurangzeb Hunting Lions", circa 1675–80.[21] Here the emperor hunts from elephantback. A pair of lions has been cornered. The male has a heavy mane but the colour is light brown.

The artists depicting animals in fables are using them to depict an event of the story. They are accurately enough drawn to be identifiable for what they are, the lions are unmistakable, but they are either scantily maned or have a darker colour round the neck and back of the head as if the artists were depicting the mane in name only, because they had to by convention. Mughal artists travelled with the imperial entourage and observed wild animals at first hand. It is possible that in this category of paintings, they were showing animals only as symbols of the story they told rather than depicting them realistically as they would do elsewhere. Inaccurate renderings are certainly not because of ignorance.

But when it came to animal studies or hunting scenes involving the imperial family, the artists were careful enough as a rule to make accurate renderings of lions with proper manes and of different colours. Most of the Mughal hunts of lions are depicted in open country or grasslands, areas which were very easily accessible from the enormous camps which the great Mughals set up when they went hunting. The manes of the lions in these paintings are usually brown.

With the decline of Mughal power, patronage at small courts assumed importance where subsidiary schools of painting developed. This brings us to the paintings of the Kotah and Bundi schools from present day Rajasthan. While they were stylized to a degree, yet they hold some interesting information. All the lion hunts depicted are in jungles as against the open terrain seen in Mughal paintings. The painting titled "Maharaja Ram Singh I of Kotah (1695–1707) Hunting Lions at Mukundgarh", Kotah, circa 1695–1700,[22] has two male lions in it, both with well defined and accurate manes of a dark brown colour. "Rao Bhoj Singh of Bundi Slays a Lion", Kotah, circa 1720, attributed to Kotah Master,[23] has very stylized animals, extremely light coloured, and yet with well defined black manes. A hunting scene attributed to Joshi Hathuwa, 1784,[24] shows Maharao Umed Singh I (1770–1819) hunting lions. There are in all nine lions in the picture within a stockade in a jungle, not one has a mane. The lions depicted appear to be of a pride with lionesses and sub-adult males which would explain the absence of the manes.

There is a striking contrast between the "Kotah lions" and the earlier Mughal paintings. When the Kotah artists painted manes they were usually dark brown or black suggesting a variation in the colour of the lions found in jungles as opposed to

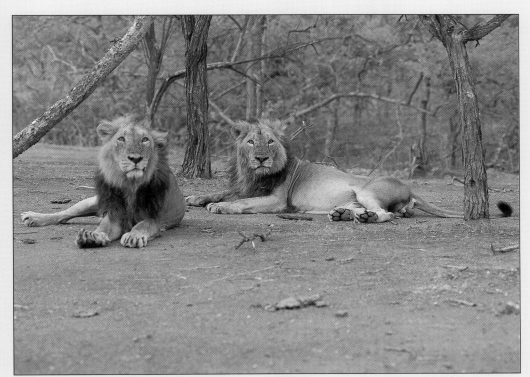

Lions at rest
■ A *belad* of two brothers gets disturbed, they wake up and watch the photographer, then one of them decides to move on. Their body colour has a greyish tinge – such lions are called *jamwo*.
Photographs: Divyabhanusinh.

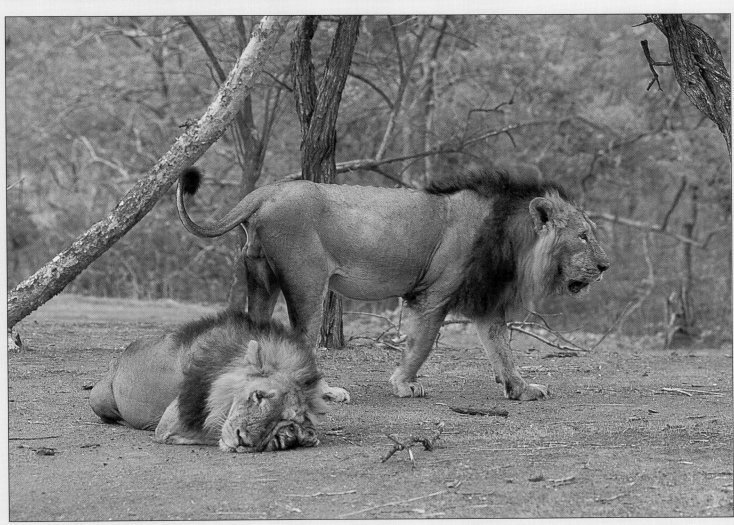

those found in open grasslands. (But some of the darkest maned lions are found in African savannah.) Did the scrubland where the Mughals hunted have an effect on the colour of its lions' manes, or deprive them of some of their hair over the millennia? We cannot say for sure. But the paintings of the Mughal and the Kotah schools must surely be true enough to depict the commonest types of manes of lions seen in their respective regions.

By the time T.C. Jerdon's *Mammals of India* was published in 1867, lions had virtually disappeared from the subcontinent with the exception of Gir and its environs. It was the first "scientific" work of its kind in the empire but it came too late to note local variations in lion populations based on empirical evidence. Jerdon described the animals from hearsay, as is clear from the text.[25]

Apart from the manes of lions, there is the question of their size. The *pagis* of the Gir suggest two variations found in the forest: the short-bodied or stockily built lion known as the *gadhio,* and the lion with a longer body called *velar*. The etymologies of these terms are not clear, they are colloquial and are used among the small band of persons whose traditional occupation was tracking. It appears that the word *gadhio* comes from *gadhedo,* donkey, and hence may mean ass-like, that is short or small in comparison with a *velar* which may well have derived from the "waler" breed of Australian horses from New South Wales which were used by princes in Saurashtra in the first half of the 20th century. Two *pagis* of the old school who had followed their fathers' profession, Bhanabha Kathalbha and Abhlabha Jafarbha, the latter a Sidi of remarkable talent, informed me that the lions of eastern Gir are larger animals. This belief is based on tradition and ocular observation rather than on actual measurement of lengths and weights of animals.

The size of Asiatic lions in comparison with the animals from Africa has also been commented upon throughout the British period and later. The accepted position today is that the average length of the two is the same.[26] But R.I. Pocock, writing in 1930, records that African animals were bigger on the basis of *Rowland Ward's Records of Big Game*.[27] However, this conclusion is based on a very narrow base of information he was working on. After an extensive search in the shikar literature of the British period, journals, unpublished shikar diaries of hunters, and interviews with former hunters, I have been able to compile a list of 73 measurements from Gir and its surrounding areas.[28] While these are hunters' records and are subject to several inaccuracies, they are at least roughly indicative of the length of the dead animals measured. From the present compilation it will be seen that the largest lion (not skin) from India was 10 feet 6 inches long, while the second largest was 10 feet 2 inches. A total of 37 animals were more than 9 feet in length. Captain Walter Smee's lions do not feature among these. It is quite possible that the animals he shot were young lions whose manes had not fully grown. Rowland Ward's records of the twelve largest lions from Africa shows that the largest was 10 feet 11 inches long while the smallest was 8 feet 2 inches long.[29] We may allow for the fact that this record was compiled in 1935 after Pocock's analysis was done and there may have been additions since, which may have shown more lions from Africa at the top end of the scale. In the meantime the method of measuring trophies has changed and we have no comparative data from India.[30] We may still conclude that sizewise, the populations are comparable. It must also be remembered that all the lions from India for whom we have measurements came from one small pocket, as against those of Africa which came from several different areas spread over a vast region, from far larger population bases, and yielded far more measurements.

Many accounts refer to a population bottleneck in the Gir with lions almost dying out in the late 19th century. Several alarming reports were circulating then and one making the rounds was that the total number of lions was as low as a dozen. That there was a drastic reduction in their numbers is certain, but the figure of twelve lions was certainly an exaggeration.[31] There is also the physical bottleneck which usually escapes attention. The Saurashtra peninsula was till about 300 years ago separated from the rest of India by a strait, which can still be traced through the flat lowlands of the Bhal, the large lake of Nal, and the salt wastes between the lake and the Little Rann of Kutch. M.A. Wynter-Blyth was of the view that Saurashtra was possibly almost insular up to the 17th century.[32] What effect this had on the lions over the centuries is a matter of conjecture as there is no database of information. However, a study has been conducted which compares the pure-bred Asiatic lions from the Sakkarbag Zoo in Junagadh, which are descendants of wild animals captured from the Gir, with lions from Serengeti and the Ngorongoro crater in Tanzania. The last mentioned population too had gone through a severe bottleneck in 1962–63 from which they grew to a population of 100 in a restricted area of 260 square kilometres. The study found that the Gir lions had complete genetic monomorphism which had resulted in greater incidence of abnormal sperms (spermatozoa with deranged mid-piece) and lower number of motile sperms (those capable of independent locomotion) in comparison with the two African populations. Asiatic lions had also lower circulating levels of testosterone which could cause reproductive problems. While no such sign was visible in the Ngorongoro population, the Sakkarbag Zoo lions exhibited a similar abnormality. One male which had mated with oestrus females failed to produce any offspring and three of the other tested males produced only single-cub litters or stillborn cubs in 1985–87.[33]

Dr Stephen J. O'Brien and his team have concluded that the founders of the Gir lion population had become separated from the mainland population of the subcontinent as a result of the geographical isolation of the Kathiawar peninsula some three millennia earlier. These deformities are a result of this population bottleneck[34] and not the better known one at the beginning of the 20th century. Though the lion population has grown uninterruptedly from 1985 onwards, these deformities are a matter of grave concern for the long-term survival of this relict population as it would be premature to assume that all is well with the Gir lions.

A unique feature of the lions of Gir is the close relationship that has evolved between them and man. Lions are gregarious in nature and less prone to be shy than tigers; as a result, they have been more closely observed by man over the years. During the princely administration of Junagadh state prior to 1947, the Forest Department shikaris were expected to know the lions in their respective beats and they could recognize particularly males by their size, colour and size of manes, or distinguishing marks such as scars on the face usually acquired in fights. Those shikaris whose tracking skills were honed by generations of observations were unequalled at their job. Hebat of Jambuda ness, a Sidi shikari, was highly respected for his skills even among British hunters.[35] In the 1950s there was yet another shikari Haidu jamadar who was among the last of a long line of accomplished trackers, equally renowned.

A lioness with a cub at kill
■ The mother and her young are on a natural kill of a domestic buffalo. The lioness's stomach is full. Her abdominal fold is noticeable.
Photograph: Divyabhanusinh.

In fact, there was such familiarity between the shikaris and lions that individual animals were given names by them, a practice that continues today.* A lioness who had lost an eye was called Badi, the one-eyed one. Another lioness was called Bandi, the one with tail cut, for she had lost part of her tail in a fight. Yet another was called Khari as she was very short-tempered. A large male lion of the late 1950s was called Tilio because he had a mark on his forehead like a tilak. This lion went on to adorn a postage stamp of India, and his death was reported on All India Radio![36] A pair of lions seen in the late 1960s were named Ubhdo for erect ears and Belio for a drooping ear. In the 1970s two magnificent males were named Akbar and Sultan. In the 1980s two were named Raj and Moti and another two were christened Dharam and Veero, after the Bollywood characters in the film *Dharamveer*. In 1997 a pair of Maldhari twins from Dudhala ness surprised two lions on a buffalo kill. The lions attacked the twins whose cries of distress brought others to the scene and they survived to recount the tale. The two lions were promptly named Natha and Amra after the Maldharis they had attacked!

During the rule of the nawabs, *pagi*s of the Koli tribe demonstrated their skill to important state guests by placing a handkerchief on the mane of a sleeping lion with the help of a stick, while another would go and retrieve it. However, the entertainment came to an abrupt stop when one of the *pagi*s met his end prematurely as the lion woke up in the middle of the proceedings.[37] I have been witness to some astounding encounters in Gir. Once I was sitting on the ground beside the experienced shikari Abhlabha Jafarbha, when Sultan, one of the pair of large lions well known at the time, approached us and sat barely 3 metres away

---

* Large carnivores have been named in the past elsewhere, but not with such regularity. For example, it was only from the late 1970s that several tigers were given names in Ranthambhore National Park, when they became very visible in daylight as a result of strict protection, and individuals became recognizable as a result.

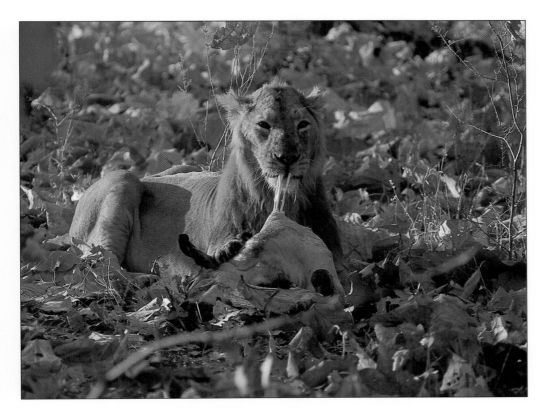

Lion on a kill
■ A young male on a natural kill of a domestic cow which he dragged into the undergrowth to feed on.
Photograph: Divyabhanusinh.

waiting for a handout. On another occasion, one morning in July, on turning a corner in the road I came across two large lions sitting in a clearing. The lions were known to the shikari Bhanabha Kathalbha. Getting down from the vehicle he and I walked up to them and sat down barely 10 metres away. The lions who were full after a kill regarded us with calm curiosity for a while, but soon completely ignored us, lay down, and went to sleep. Once along with the shikaris, I was able to follow a lion on foot as he walked on the road. He moved apparently lazily but actually at fairly fast clip for 6 kilometres as he went along marking his territory. He would look back to make sure that a respectable distance of about 20 metres was maintained between him and us. That aside, he was quite unconcerned and the walk was abandoned only after he moved off into thick jungle away from the road. Even lionesses with cubs but a few weeks old, allow human presence at remarkably close quarters. Being able to watch a relaxed mother with her cubs gambolling around her, from just a few metres' distance, is a glorious experience which remains permanently etched in one's mind.

Such behavioural instances cannot be taken for tameness of lions. The animals are truly wild. In certain parts of Gir they have come to regard humans as no threat to themselves but rather as providers of food, as a result of baits given to them. To take liberties with these animals would be an act of utter foolishness as is illustrated by occasional but repeated attacks on humans in such situations.

The lions of the Gir are very different from wild tigers and leopards. M.K. Ranjitsinhji observes in the context of artificial feeding that, while there are several factors which militate against the practice, it does reveal certain patterns of behaviour of some species in the proximity of human beings. Leopards in Wankaner, Gujarat, and tigers in Dungarpur, Rajasthan, had been artificially fed for four to seven generations in the 1940s and each animal could be individually identified. He records that during darkness and in or near thick cover, the leopard revealed more tolerance, whereas in daylight and in open areas, the tiger was more tolerant. But in no circumstances or with any amount of inducement could the tiger or leopard ever be made to match the "incredible confidence that the Gir lion now exhibits to the close proximity of man on foot".[38]

The Gir lions' behaviour is obviously a result of generations of them having observed humans and what they mean to them. At the same time the lions are sharp enough to spot possible conflict and they react swiftly. On several occasions I have observed lions leaving their location abruptly on seeing or hearing a Maldhari with whom they have continuous conflict, for the latter's cattle form a sizeable proportion of their prey base!

If lions accept people at close proximity in Gir, local culture too accords the animal a central place. The lion is deeply embedded in the culture of Gujarat, and more so in the Saurashtra peninsula where it provides a continuing link with the past. It is interesting to note that there is a typical name for it in the Kathiawari dialect of Gujarati, *sawaj*, which is not known elsewhere even in Gujarat. Colonel J.W. Watson speculated that the word had an Arabic root.[39] This is highly unlikely. The Sanskrit word *swapado* stands for savage, ferocious, a wild beast[40] or a beast of prey and the word appears for the first time in the *Atharvaveda*.[41] The word *sawaj* appears to have roots in antiquity.

Lions are the subject of stories taught in schools or sung in folksongs, and they are immortalized in literature. The state textbook for teaching Gujarati in class 7 has a story titled "Lion's Friendship". It is a tale of a friendship between a local prince and a lion who together endured several vicissitudes, and they were parted only on the prince's death when the lion returned to the forest never to be seen again.[42]

Jhaverchand Meghani (1896–1947) the renowned storyteller and poet of Gujarat, recounted a traditional tale, "Gift of a Lion" in which God took the form of a lion to save the honour of a devotee prince who had promised to give a Charan supplicant any gift he desired. The latter having demanded a wild lion was humiliated when presented with one and he left in shame.[43] Among the most loved poems in Gujarati is "To a Charan Lass" in which Meghani recounts the bravery of a Maldhari girl who tried to save her favourite calf from the jaws of a lion.[44] This local incident has been immortalized in verse and song, and like many others concerning lions is taught in schools and is sung by bards. But lions had made an earlier appearance in Gujarati verse. Arguably the greatest romantic poet of Gujarat was Prince Sursinhji of Lathi (1874–1900) better known by his nom de plume, Kalapi. His romantic poetry born out of unfulfilled love attained a literary elegance unmatched since. His short poem "A Morning in a Forest" describes the peace and quiet of the dawn shattered by a lion's roar. All of a sudden

> A star broke from its moorings in the sky, a cannon ball was fired,
> Red hot streaking the sky it flew,
> River Ganga burst forth from her mountain fastness,
> Lord Ram's arrow flew from his bow string,

---

* Anyone interested in knowing how peaceful the lion–human relationship can be, ought to read the detailed account of Elizabeth Marshall Thomas (1994, pp. 109–86) of the Juwa tribesmen and lions living in the Kalahari where she herself stayed for extended periods in the early 1950s near the Gautscha waterhole. In an area of a few square miles lived a cheetah, a leopard, at least five spotted hyenas, ten lions, and thirty people. In other words there were in all fifty carnivorous creatures who shared the one and only waterhole in the region and hunted the same antelope population.

A pride at rest
■ Three *pathda*, sub-adult males, rest with their mothers near the Hiran dam.
Photograph: Divyabhanusinh.

As the antlered stag jumped across the river in fright.
Standing there was the lion roaring loudly,
Shaking mountains, even the sun was startled turning red like burning coal;
Birds would not flutter or sing, trees vibrated, the earth trembled!
The universe had burst open! Deluge! As if Lord Shiva had blown his conch![45]

The Gir is also sung of in folksongs all over the Sorath area of Saurashtra and elsewhere. The Charans of the forest have sung of the marriage of one hill Ghantulo with another Ghantuli when the rivers Hiran and Sarasvati were part of the bridegroom's party and the hill Vansadhol became the best man, causing happiness all over the Gir![46] One of my most enduring memories is that of a Maldhari performing *arti*, in the four cardinal directions of the earth from his ness where his cattle were penned for the night. When I asked the meaning of the ritual, he replied that it was a prayer to God to protect his wealth in the ness from lions. For beyond it, they were the lion's right!

Such noble sentiments are fast disappearing with increasing pressures on the environment.* The lion is a unique continuing tradition of Gujarat. The most precious gift the state can give to the rest of India and to the world is to allow this prized inhabitant to prosper in its present habitat, as it has done in the past, and also to be reintroduced elsewhere, to ensure its long-term survival.

Both lions and humans having evolved together over several millennia, saw no danger from each other. They scolded each other and stole each other's food, neither one was aggressive towards the other. By the 1980s large-scale farming and livestock breeding in the area changed all that. Farmers and sportsmen started shooting lions, the latter in turn became aggressive towards the former. The first step of aggression was taken by humans, not by lions. There is a lesson to be learnt here by everyone including field zoologists if we are to understand fully the genesis of lion behaviour.

CHAPTER 2

An Oriental Patrimony

PIECING TOGETHER THE PAST is a daunting task for any historian even when the person has the benefit of contemporary language sources. When one moves to proto- and pre-history the task becomes more of a challenge. When zoologists study evolution of species, they deal in millions of years whereas the entire human historical record is about 10,000 years old. It is not surprising that scientists do not agree in interpreting geological ages.

Differences among scientists on "the patterns of ancestry and descent" of species are commonplace. David Macdonald holds that lion-like cats emerged 1.8 million years ago and true lions, 25 per cent larger than today's version, arose 600,000 years ago. Alan Turner points to a much earlier record of lions found at Laetoli in Tanzania, which is perhaps 3.5 million years old. Their range extended to Europe, Asia, and Alaska through North America in the form named *Panthera atrox* which was possibly the same species as modern lions.[1] At any rate glacial and inter-glacial cycles and subsequent human control of the environment fragmented lion populations. By the 20th century, scholars identified eight subspecies of lions spread over Africa and Asia, from the Cape of Good Hope at the southernmost tip of Africa to the Mediterranean Sea in the north and from west Africa all the way to Bihar in India. After a careful analysis of the colour of the skins of lions, the colour and size of their manes as well as the size of the skulls on the one hand, and of the fossil finds at various sites on the other, Professor Helmut Hemmer has grouped the various populations of Upper Pleistocene and recent or Holocene lions into two subspecies: the *spelaea* group of the Northern Holarctic region with *Panthera leo spelaea* in Europe, *Panthera leo ssp.* in Siberia, and *Panthera leo atrox* in America; and the *leo* group of the Southern Palaearctic region with the Ethiopian and the western Oriental region, with *Panthera leo persica* in southwest and south Asia, *Panthera leo leo* in northwest Africa, *Panthera leo senegelensis* in west to central Africa, *Panthera leo nubica* in the broader east African region, *Panthera leo azandica* as an uncertain form between the two last mentioned in the northeast Congo area, *Panthera leo bleyenberghi*, likewise uncertain, in the southeast Congo area, furthermore, *Panthera leo krugeri* in southern Africa, and *Panthera leo melanochaita* in the Cape Province. Hemmer concludes that *Panthera leo leo* and *Panthera leo persica*, i.e. the lions of Africa north of the Sahara and the Asiatic lions "appear as only slightly varied relict forms of lower Middle Pleistocene lions".[2]

Of these different populations of lions, we are only concerned with the Asiatic lions, *Panthera leo persica*.* We must nonetheless examine the interaction between lions and humans as known from ancient Egypt, a civilization at the crossroads of three continents and at the doorstep of Asia, which has left the earliest such records in human history.

The lion was the largest carnivore in ancient Egypt. Its appearance and behaviour were a matter of acute observation and record in those times. Attributes of wild animals which were admired or feared were believed to be connected with divinity, such as the scorpion's fatal sting, the wild bull's power, or the lion's fierceness.[3] Several leonine deities were known and they can be recognized in at least nine

---

* There was another lion population in Eurasia, that is of the European lions. They were recorded by Herodotus in Greece in 480 BCE attacking King Xerxes of Persia's invading army between the rivers Nestus and Achelons in the area today known as Chelkidiki. Strangely the lions attacked only the camels but left the men, horses, and cattle of the army alone (Rawlinson, 1910). According to another source the lions were last reported in Europe in the year 100 CE (Qammen, 2003, p. 25). However, the travails of this lion population are unconnected to the story of lions in Asia.

different forms.[4] The Egyptian cities of Leontopolis and Heliopolis were the centres
of lion cults and in the temple of Amun Ra at Heliopolis live lions were waited upon
by high priests who performed rituals associated with their worship. They were fed
the choicest meats to the playing of sacred music. There was even a law which
decreed public mourning on the death of one of these sacred lions.[5]

Lions were kept as pets by the pharaohs as well. One scene on a golden shrine
shows Tutankhamun (1333–1323 BCE) shooting arrows at waterfowl while a lioness
sits beside him. In illustrations of the Rameses period the lion appears occasionally
running alongside the king's chariot escorting him into battle, and at Beital-Wali in
Lower Nubia, a tame lioness is shown near the throne of Rameses II (1290–1224
BCE) with an inscription "Slayer of his Enemies".[6]

Though the lion was important enough to be worshipped, kept as a pet, and be
sculpted as sphinx with a royal head – the most famous being the one at Giza – it
was also hunted by the pharaohs. While this duality is difficult to explain, initially
the lion and the hippopotamus were hunted as dangerous beasts whose destruction
was essential for human survival.[7] However by the time of the New Kingdom (1550–
1070 BCE) lion hunting had become a favourite sport of the pharaohs and it had
become a royal prerogative. Amenhotep III (1391–1353 BCE) killed as many as 102
lions in the first ten years of his reign according to the records written on the

The hunt of Ashurnasirpal
■ Nineveh, Assyria, circa 860 BCE.
This frieze from Nimrud shows the king hunting lions from his chariot followed by his courtiers. Note the mane of the lion, the growth of hair going up to the abdomen, unlike the Gir lions though similar to the Gir lion in Berlin (see Chapter 13).
Copyright The British Museum, London.

scarabaeus issued to mark the monarch's heroic feats. The pharaoh's hunting could have extended into Mesopotamia where he led several expeditions. Among the methods of hunting lions was to spear them on foot accompanied by hounds. Amenhotep's tally of the lions he hunted is the earliest "hunting record" for the lions, though King Tuthmosis III's (1479–1425 BCE) record of killing almost singlehandedly 120 Syrian elephants for sport and ivory[8] is the oldest "hunting record" in history for a large mammal.

The idea of tame lions adorning royal palaces is plausible enough. As late as the 20th century, Emperor Haile Selassie I of Abyssinia (1892–1975) who was styled "The Lion of Judea" had lions at his court. On state occasions they were kept near his throne, a fact commemorated even in Ethiopian folk art.[9] However tame lions running alongside a pharaoh's chariot in battle is another matter. A carnivore the size of a lion, even if tame, would surely not be on its best behaviour in the commotion and bloodshed of battle. Such an occurrence would have been a unique one, if at all.

As we move east we come to the mainland of Asia where the Euphrates and the Tigris, the two mighty rivers, gave birth to the civilization of Babylon more than 5,000 years ago. The great Assyrian empire came into existence in this fertile land but with the passage of time it passed into oblivion, its monuments crumbled and were forgotten. It was only in the mid-19th century that they were excavated and they came to occupy their rightful place in the history of human civilization. The story of the excavations by A.H. Layard, W.K. Loftus, and others is an epic in itself. However, what concerns us here is the lion.

As in ancient Egypt, the largest predator of the Euphrates-Tigris region was the lion. Wild animals being a threat to the people, a king was obliged to deal with them, particularly with the lion. The earliest record of lions being killed by a king dates back to before 3000 BCE. One authority suggests that lions were not numerous enough to be regarded as common vermin, and as early as circa 1750 BCE lions had become royal game and only the king could hunt them.[10]

In Mari, a small kingdom of the middle Euphrates and an important city in the

3rd and 2nd millennia BCE, a lion was found in the granary of a house. An official
serving the king dashed off a missive to his royal master:

> A lion has been taken in the granary of a house in Akkaka. If this lion is to remain
> in the granary until the arrival of my lord, let my lord write to tell me so; if on the
> other hand, I ought to have it brought to my lord, let my lord write to tell me that.

Unfortunately for him a reply was not forthcoming and so the hapless official had to
take a decision himself:

> Now I have been awaiting letters from my lord, and the lion has remained five days
> in the granary. A dog and a pig have been sent in to him that he may eat. I said to
> myself: "Perhaps this lion will get away!" I was afraid. I have had the lion put in a
> wooden cage, loaded on a boat, and sent to my master.[11]

Hilarious as these letters may appear, they speak for the strictness of the
injunction against the killing of lions by commoners. Ashurnasirpal II the Assyrian
king (884–859 BCE) had chosen Nimrud as his administrative centre. His vast palace
and throne room were replete with carved panels depicting the life and times of the
king. The panels closest to his throne show him hunting lions and wild cattle. The
king no doubt was proud of his exploits in the field, for his annals recount:

> The gods Nimurta and Nergal, who love my priesthood, gave me the wild animals
> of the plains, commanding me to hunt. 30 elephants I trapped and killed; 257 great
> wild oxen I brought down with my weapons, attacking from my chariots; 370 great
> lions I killed with hunting spears.[12]

That lions caused havoc among the farming population from early times is
testified by the fact that endless seals and carved bowls have scenes of lions
attacking bulls.[13] It was therefore necessary for the king to eliminate the menace.
King Ashurbanipal (669–631 BCE) who ruled from Nineveh was even more specific
about the importance of the task at hand. He records:

> Since I took my seat upon the throne of the father that begot me, Adad has sent his
> rains, Ea has opened up his fountains, the forests have been thriving exceedingly,
> the reeds in the marshes have shot up so high there is no getting through them.
> The young of the lions grew up therein, in countless numbers.... They became fierce

and terrible through devouring of herds, flocks, and people. With their roaring the
hills resound, the beasts of the plain are terrified. They keep bringing down the
cattle of the plain, they keep shedding the blood of men. As if the plague had
broken loose, there were heaped up the corpses of dead men, cattle and [sheep].
The shepherds and herdsmen weep.... The villages are in mourning day and night.
Of the deeds of these lions they told me. In the course of my march [campaign]
into ... their lairs I broke up....[14]

The king's exploits also mention another situation where "in the plain a wide
expanse, rag[in]g lions, a fierce mountain breed, attacked [me, and] surrounded the
chariot, my royal vehicle". The confrontation between king and lions was important
enough to depict such face-to-face combat on Neo-Assyrian imperial seals.[15]

While hunting lions in the wild was a matter of the king's duty to protect his
subjects and their cattle wealth, Ashurbanipal also hunted purely for pleasure. His
hunts near Nineveh included lions brought in cages for the purpose. The hunting
scenes from the friezes of Ashurbanipal's palace, now in the British Museum, show a
caged lion being released by a boy before the king. Above is a small cage for the boy
to take secure shelter on releasing the lion from its confinement.[16] These were
encounters under controlled conditions and the king uses epigrams such as "while I
was enjoying myself" or "while I was carrying out my princely sport".[17] Such activity
may only be explained as demonstrations of the king's prowess for the benefit of the
populace, an assurance that they would be safe from the depredations of wild beasts.
Assyrian kings also kept lions as pets, a fact which can be ascertained from the
depiction on a frieze of a lion and a lioness in a garden.[18] There is however no record
of lions going into battle with their royal masters, nor did lions become objects of
worship as was the case in Egypt. However, Nana the Babylonian (Sumerian)
goddess, the mistress of beasts, rode a lion. She was considered the same as the
Akkadian as well as the Assyrian goddess of hunting, Ishthar. One of the conceptions
of Ishthar was that of a mother goddess to whom the lion was sacred. It was a
symbol emphasizing her warlike character. The goddess was also similar to the
Persian goddess Anahita, the mistress of beasts.[19] The Kushana king Kanishka whose
kingdom flourished in northwest India in the 1st century had coins struck with a
goddess identified as Nana riding a lion.[20] It is quite possible that the Bactrian
Greeks or the Shakas were to some extent responsible for introducing Anahita
(Ishthar-Nana) to northwestern India.[21] She was the forerunner of the Hindu
goddess Durga, who rides a lion to this day even in Bengal, the heart of "Tigerland".

A close examination of lions of the time of Ashurnasirpal II shows them to be
"brutish, massive and overpowering in appearance", whereas by the time of
Ashurbanipal this "stylistic" depiction of lions has been replaced by a "naturalistic
tendency" in the rendering of these creatures.[22] There is also the black obelisk from
Shalamaneser III's time (859–824 BCE), which has two lions, one standing and the
other leaping to attack a stag.[23] Neither of these is accurately drawn since the lions
have bushy tails! Such a rendering is surely not the result of ignorance of a lion's
appearance.

The rendering of lions in the sculptures from the palace of Ashurbanipal II in
Nineveh, preserved in the British Museum, are amazing. They show the great hunt
of the king, so most of the lions are in the process of being dispatched or are already
dead. The friezes show an attention to detail which is remarkable. The outlines of
tails extend beyond those actually carved, indicating that the royal patron or one of

King Ashurbanipal's hunt
■ Nineveh, Assyria, circa 645 BCE.
Top: A boy releases a caged lion for the king to hunt.
Middle: A courtier distracts the lion and the king grabs it by the tail.
Bottom: The king pours libation over the dead lion.
Copyright The British Museum, London.

King Ashurbanipal kills a lion
■ Nineveh, Assyria, circa 645 BCE.
The king kills a lion on foot by stabbing it with a sword, grabbing the animal by the throat with his left hand. This method of hunting was practised up to the 19th century, the left hand being padded for protection.
Copyright The British Museum, London.

Tame lions

■ Nineveh, Assyria, circa 645 BCE.
The pair here are shown in a garden, an
indication that lions were tamed during
the time of King Ashurbanipal.
Copyright The British Museum, London.

his high officials corrected the dimensions outlined by the stone carver so that the size of the tails would be in proportion to the body of the animals.[24] Here is a clear indication of the hunter's knowledge of his quarry's anatomy. The carved lioness pierced with arrows dragging herself away with agony on her face and the lion sitting on its haunches with pierced lung and blood spewing from its mouth would evoke pity from the most hardened casual observer. Of interest here is the lion's mane. It is luxuriant around the face, goes beyond the shoulder and forearms with a very marked ventral mane. These features from the sculpture tally fairly accurately with R.I. Pocock's study of the last century as also Helmut Hemmer's examination of a skin of a Mesopotamian lion in Vienna though the colour of the ventral mane was whitish-greyish which can be described as a "strong extention of stomach hair as in the case of Barbary lions".[25] A Gir lion now living in the Berlin Deer Park in the eastern part of the city also has developed a ventral mane, a phenomenon not seen in the warmer Gir itself (see chapter 13). Dr Julian Reade states that it was "genuinely possible" for a monarch to stab a lion standing on its hind legs, "because the Mesopotamian lion, now extinct, was smaller than the African variety with which we are now most familiar".[26] A.H. Layard describes a male lion which he owned around 1850 at Hillah near Babylon as being taller and larger than a St Bernard, and like the lion "generally found on the banks of the rivers of Mesopotamia, was without the dark and shaggy mane". He does go on to add:

> I have however, seen lions on the river Karoon, with a long black mane. The inhabitants of the country make a distinction between them and the common maneless lion; the former are kafir, or infidels, the others Mussulmans. By a proper remonstrance, and at the same time pronouncing the profession of faith, a true believer may induce the one to spare his life, but the unbelieving lion is inexorable.[27]

Black-maned lions were recorded in Syria in ancient times by Pliny (23–79 CE) as well[28] and such animals were obviously the preferred objects of royal hunts, as is testified by the sculptures of the Assyrian kings, for they too would be considered more ferocious. The Arab belief noted by Layard would only imply that the "kafir" lions were more difficult customers to tackle in a chance encounter with man.

It appears that "maneless" lions or probably lions with scanty manes were quite common in the regions of present day Iraq and Syria. Emperor Probus of Rome (276–282 CE) who was known for his beast shows is reputed to have shown on one occasion in the year 281, 1,000 ostriches, 1,000 stags, 1,000 boars, gazelles, ibexes, wild sheep and so on. On one day he showed 100 maned lions as also 100 Libyan and 100 Syrian maneless lions.[29] However, these reports of different looking lions are a record of local variations of the species in a vast geographical area. Such variations could have been caused by environmental or other factors. It is pertinent to note that tigers and leopards from different parts of India show noticeable local variations too.

The lion also finds a place in the Old Testament. It appears as a powerful beast whose subjugation required divine intervention. Thus in the story of Samson (probable date circa 1150 BCE) "the spirit of the Lord came mightily upon him and he rent him [the young lion] as he would have rent a kid, and he had nothing in his hand". Similarly when Daniel was thrown into the lions' den by King Darius the lions could not kill him for "My God hath sent his angel, and hath shut the lions' mouths, that they have not hurt me".[30] The prophet Ezekiel had a vision of God who gave him a stern warning for the rebellious children of Israel, specifically the princes of Israel, in the form of the story of a lioness and her cubs. The lioness brought up a cub, he learnt to devour prey and ate men but he "was taken in a pit" so the lioness brought up another one of her cubs which too learnt to catch prey and he devoured men:

> And he knew their desolate places, and he laid waste their cities; and the land was desolate, and the fullness thereof, by the noise of his roaring.
>
> There the nations set against him on every side from the provinces, and spread their net over him: he was taken in their pit.
>
> And they put him in chains and brought him to the king of Babylon: they brought him into holds, that his voice should no more be heard upon the mountains of Israel.[31]

Lions were trapped in ancient times to adorn Egyptian pharaohs' palaces or for royal hunts in Assyria. The Old Testament records the method, surrounding a lion by nets and catching it in a pit. It may be noted that nets were used for hunting lions in India as late as the Mughal period.[32]

With the rise of Persian power under Cyrus the Achaemenid king, a new political force came to dominate the region from 540 BCE onwards. In time to come Babylon itself came under the sway of these conquerors from the east. The lions however fared no better, for over the centuries newer methods of hunting them came to be devised. They were also used for hunting. For instance some 500 years later Apollonius of Tyna who recorded a hunt, states that the Persians had a preserve at Babylon where lions, leopards, and bears were kept for the hunt. They used "beaters" to "beat'" the animal out at the predetermined place[33] where a lion or any other animal could be dispatched at will by the hunter. This method was used in India and elsewhere almost to the present day.

To the ancient Persians too, lions were an important part of life, but they are best represented in art forms or rituals rather than in the realism of the hunting ground. Astronomical observations of the constellations of Leo and Taurus and their connection with the annual cycle or calendar were not confined to Persia. Thus we have the Lion and Bull combat on a relief from Persepolis as also the earlier Assyrian bronze disc of the 8th century BCE from Khorsabad with the same motif.[34] Persian kings appear to have maintained tame lions as well, as evident from a lifesize statue of a lioness with a chain round her neck found at Persepolis dated to the 5th century BCE and now preserved at the National Museum in Tehran.[35]

The lion came to symbolize royal power in Persia too, as in other regions. A rhyton in the form of a golden lion preserved at the Metropolitan Museum of Art, New York and the royal seal of Darius I (521–485 BCE) preserved at the British Museum, depict the lion with great delicacy of touch. The latter shows the king in his chariot shooting an arrow at a male lion who stands up on his hind legs in a position of attack while another lion lies pierced by an arrow, inert below the chariot horses.[36] This royal seal is in the same genre as the earlier Assyrian seals. More than a thousand years later in 590 CE, Bahram Gur is believed to have seized the throne of Persia, retrieving the crown after defeating the lions guarding it. There is an interesting painting by Sultan Muhammad from the *Khamsa* of Nizami from Tabriz painted between 1539 and 1543, depicting Bahram Gur hunting a lion which was itself in the process of killing an onager.[37] The lion, along with the rising sun, as a symbol of royalty survived the onslaught of Islam for centuries in Iran but was ultimately snuffed out in 1979 when it became an Islamic Republic. This may well have been on account of its pre-Islamic associations of royal power.

Empires came and went across Asia and fortunes changed beyond recognition. It is tempting to quote the words of Omar Khayyam who uses metaphors of a fox, a lion, and a Persian wild ass, the last two being important large mammals of Persia which were also predator and prey, to drive home his point of the ebb and flow of royal splendour:

> A Palace gorged in by gigantic Bahram
> The vixen whelps there and the lion nods.
> Bahram who hunted none but onagers,
> Lies tumbled in a pitfall called the grave.[38]

But even though Bahram Gur went and empires were reduced to dust, the lion continued to be relentlessly hunted through the ages. In medieval times the Arabs pursued the lion in the desert, river banks, and marshes, and devised several methods for the lion hunt. A lion would be induced to give chase to a rider on a horse. The horse, being swifter, remained out of reach until the lion was tired of running, whereupon the horseman would turn around and shoot an arrow into the lion's foot. This would

Lion attacking bull
■ Greek marble relief dated to the last quarter of the 6th century BCE. Soon thereafter the lion became extinct in Europe, but lives on in art and culture to the present day.

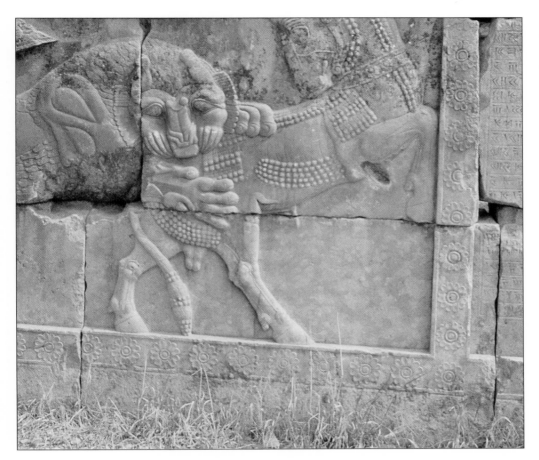

Lion attacking bull
■ Palace of Darius, Shiraz, Persia, 6th–
5th century BCE.
This Achaemenian bas-relief is
symbolically related to the spring
equinox. The lion represents imperial
power and might.
Courtesy Khojeste P. Mistree.

infuriate the lion and the chase would be repeated until the lion was riddled with
arrows and died. Such a method of hunting required training of horses to face the
lions. Some rich persons kept caged lions in their palaces and the horses were
trained to get used to the lion's sight, smell, and roar. The horses were fed daily in
front of the caged cats until they lost their fear of the carnivores. Sometimes a
wooden dummy would be made and covered with a lion skin. It would then be
moved around by manipulating strings and horns would be blown to produce roar-
like sounds in the stables.[39]

On occasion two men would track down and hunt a lion, one working as a decoy
while the other surprised the lion from the left and pierced its heart. Or, a group of
men would form an ever-decreasing circle around a sleeping lion in the midday sun
and then spear it. To hunt a lion a man would carry a spear and a double-edged
sword in his hands, and daggers in his belt. If attacked he would plunge the spear in
the lion's throat and would try to strike it with the sword in the rear legs. Then he
would jump back, and if the lion pursued him, he would thrust the sword through
one of the lion's eyes into the mouth, or stick a dagger in its throat. The hunter
would then stand aside and watch the lion in the throes of death.[40]

Yet another method related by Arab writers was of a hunter approaching a lion's
den. The lion would be lured out by creating a commotion. The hunter would thrust
his left arm, padded securely in woollen cloth, towards the lion. As the animal
lunged at it, the hunter would plunge his sword into the lion's flank. A.H. Layard
who was in Mesopotamia in the middle of the 19th century reports this method of
hunting as well – with one difference in technique. Instead of covering the hand in

woollen cloth, he mentions hard wood sharpened at one end in one hand which would be thrust into the lion's mouth at the critical moment.[41]

Apart from being an object of sport, parts of the lion were used in traditional medicine in Arabia. Two grains of a lion's brain dissolved in an ounce of milk was an antidote for grey hair. An epileptic child was supposed to be cured of the malady if it was made to wear a piece of lion skin suspended from a hair round its neck. The gall bladder and fat of the lion were specially sought after, as anointing the eyelids with the lion's gall was supposed to give piercing eyesight while applying dry gall powder to a sword wound would help it heal speedily.[42] Such beliefs only added to the lion's woes.

Lions continued to be kept as pets till not so long ago. Henry Creswicke Rawlinson, orientalist and soldier who deciphered the Persian cuneiform, lived in Mesopotamia in the middle of the 19th century. He had a pet lion which was very attached to him. It followed him about like a tame dog and ultimately died of a disease at his feet.[43] General Omer Pasha the Turkish Governor of Hillah, presented a full-grown lion to A.H. Layard, which moved around the thoroughfares of Hillah near Babylon harming no one. Only the butchers had a tough time, for the lion would help himself to their meats until satisfied, whereupon he would lie down in the sun and "allow the Arab boys to take such liberties with him as in their mischief they might devise"![44]

There is one intriguing miniature painting in the *St Petersburg Murraqqa*.[45] It is a painting of the Isfahan school of the late 17th century, attributed to 'Ali Quli Jabbadar which shows the Shah, probably Sulaiman (1666–94), out hunting with lions. The Shah with a nimbus around the head is pictured towards the right-hand side of the painting astride a white horse, with a servant carrying a golden parasol for him. In the left foreground is an attendant with a hawk on his right hand and two dead birds in his left. Further left a lion has caught a wild boar, one attendant has sunk a dagger into the boar with his left hand while the right hand tries to restrain the lion. Another attendant approaches the lion with a chain as if to fasten it to the lion's collar and take it away. In the left middle portion two Asian elephants with their mahouts watch the proceedings. They have cages instead of howdahs, which were presumably used to bring the lions to the hunting grounds. In front of them a collared lion attacks another boar while further in the background a mounted hunter is about to spear a stag. It may be noted that the lion in the foreground has a dark brown colour on its neck and partly on the face, which is barely the suggestion of a mane, whereas the animal at the back has no such colour differentiation and therefore may be a lioness.

This is the only known painting of lions being used for the hunt and therefore merits some scrutiny. Dr A.H. Morton opines that hunting with lions was never a normal practice in Iran. He goes on to add that though Muslims would not eat the flesh of boar, it would not prevent them being killed in a hunt. He feels that wild boar would as a rule have been excluded from hunting scenes because of their unclean nature.[46] According to Dr Morton, the scene could have been set somewhere in the Caspian provinces where the Safavids had palaces. The miniature may not be entire fantasy as the likeness of the Shah and other courtiers is real enough. Morton goes on to add that training lions may be an experiment which may not have been much of a success and what one needs is confirmation from some other source.[47] The most intriguing part of the painting is that two keepers are trying to draw away one lion from the boar it has caught, just as a cheetah would be separated from an

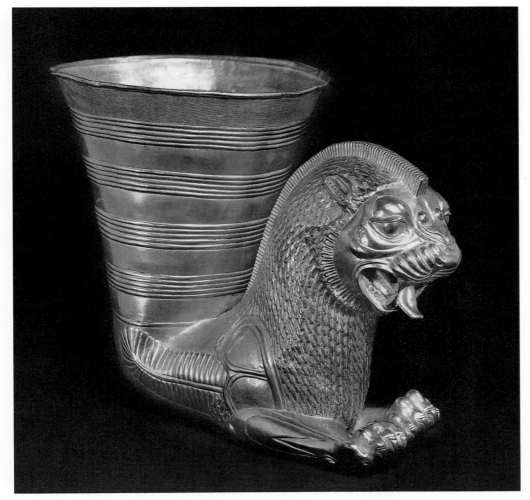

antelope in order to perform halal on the latter to make it fit for consumption by the faithful. Since a boar was in any case not permissible food, what was the need to remove the lion? Why not let it eat the boar? However, the focus of the painting is on the trained lions hunting boars, so obviously the event was important enough for such a rendering, and not all fantasy. Thus the question were lions ever used for hunting, has no definite answer.

It appears that lions had already become extinct in the Trans-Caucasus region as early as the 10th century where these animals were not incidental "but rather an important member of the fauna".[48] As European powers extended their reach in continental Asia, records of local rulers gave way to those of conquering armies from across the oceans which give us more accurate information. According to recent sources, lions were still found in the northern and easterly direction of Tashkent around the 1880s and they were "heard" of in the hilly areas around Kabul in Afghanistan about the same time.[49] The last reported sighting of lions in Baluchistan at Bolan Pass was in 1921.[50] In Iran a lion was sighted in the southwest some 40 miles from Dizful in 1942,[51] and a British administrator, J. Trench reported seeing lions in 1943 on the border of Afghanistan.[52] Outside of India, the maximum number of sightings and reports of lions in Asia in this period was from Iran. And yet, almost no material remains by which the lion of Iran can be described – "no skin, skeletal material, photograph or detailed description" as noted by Fred A. Harrington in his

Bahram Gur hunting lions
■ By Sultan Muhammad, Tabriz, Persia, 1539–93.
A much later depiction of the king who was a very keen hunter, from the *Khamsa* of Nizami. Here the lion itself is hunting an onager while being attacked by the king.
By permission of The British Library, London, MS Or. 2265 F202b.

authoritative work on the mammals of Iran. The painted picture of the lion in Harrington's book[53] appears to be drawn from a likeness of a lion of Gir. The Mammals section of the British Museum (Natural History) London, has the skin of a lion from Iran in their collection. R.I. Pocock drew a picture of a Persian lion on the basis of a flat skin in the British Museum, presumably the same one.[54]

In Iraq the Turkish governor of the Ottoman empire at Mosul had two pet lions taken from the Khabur river in 1914, but by 1917 lions were believed to be extinct in the region. In 1920 the British Expeditionary Force who were asked to report lion sightings, found none.[55] In Syria, a dead lion was brought to Damascus around 1880 and the last report of the lion's existence in the region was around 1891 when Sir Alfred Pease reported that they were still to be found there.[56]

These first glimpses of interaction between lions and human beings reveal that the lion's fate was sealed from very early on in human history. The ancient Egyptians worshipped them. But they and the ancient Assyrians both tamed lions and hunted them for sport. In Assyria they were also destroyed because they were a threat to the human population. The Persians too were relentless in their pursuit while the Hebrew Bible gives us an account of how the lions were trapped, a method which continued into the 16th century in India. Though the lion was considered royal game in ancient times and it received some protection as a result, such was not the case in the middle ages when persons of means hunted them at will in Arabia. This practice continued up to the 19th century in the Ottoman empire.

The lion evolved as a large predator over several millennia, its ancestors' remains dating back 3.5 million years. In Asia as in Africa it lived off a diverse and large food base. It thrived in an extremely varied environment. It is recorded in human history from the semi-arid lands of Palestine, in the riverine tracts of the Euphrates and Tigris in present-day Iraq, in the oak forests of the Zagros mountains and the riverine forest of Kuzestan in Iran, and the mountain regions of Afghanistan. From the dawn of human history we have a record of the depredation of the lion's environment and prey base to which human beings laid siege to meet the ever-increasing need of sustaining and developing their culture and civilization. In addition, they relentlessly pursued the lion to tame it, hunted it for sport, and in many cases eradicated it simply as being a nuisance to themselves.

It only took 3,000 years of human domination of the environment to destroy Asia's lion. The blueprint for its destruction was evolved long before we encounter the lion in its full blown form in the Indian subcontinent in the 3rd century BCE. This is the patrimony of the last remaining lions of Asia which survive today in the Gir.

CHAPTER 3

A Search through Antiquity

A lion handle
■ Found at Taxila this piece is dated to either the late Harappan or post Harappan period.
After Schwartzberg 1978.

INDIA IS THE ONLY COUNTRY outside of Africa where lions still live, and its history provides a long record of the interaction between lions and humans. Often it is not as detailed or unbroken as one would wish, but one can monitor the dwindling fortunes of the animal through the ages as it was confronted by different human cultures from time to time. Our earliest civilization is 5,000 years old and it is to these and older records that we must look to take the story forward.

At several sites in the Indian subcontinent, archaeologists have studied faunal remains among their finds from the Holocene period onwards. Among the animal taxa identified at Langhnaj in Gujarat are wolf, mongoose, rhinoceros, wild boar, chital, hog deer, swamp deer, nilgai, blackbuck, and "undetermined bovine species". But no *Panthera* cats were identified. At Bagor and Tilwara in Rajasthan among others, animal taxa of wild boar, buffalo, blackbuck, gazelle, chital, sambar, hare, mongoose, and cattle were found.[1] At Ganga valley sites, the presence of large animals such as gaur, wild buffalo, elephant, and rhinoceros, even hippopotamus have been found.[2]

It is of interest to note that remains of *Panthera* cats, i.e. in this case tiger and leopard, have been found at two Chalcolithic sites at Inamgaon and Walki in Maharashtra, of tiger at two Neolithic (dated between 2500–1000 BCE) sites, Loebnar and Aligrama in the North-West Frontier Province, and of both at the Early Historic site of Atranjikhera. At various other sites, remains of several species of the prey base of *Panthera* and other cats apart from some other carnivores including representatives of *Felis* cats have been found, but none of *Panthera* cats.[3]

The picture that emerges from these sites is quite incomplete insofar as an area as large as the Indian subcontinent cannot be adequately portrayed from a few dozen locations. Additionally, the identification of a species from a bone or a fragment of it, is a Herculean task with the possibility of error in identification. As far as the lion is concerned, the only conclusion that can be drawn is that its *remains* have not been found at these sites! There is one interesting report of a fossil lion (*Panthera* cf. *leo*) and spotted hyena (*Crocuta* cf. *sivalensis*) being found in Bankura district of West Bengal among Pleistocene deposits. The report goes on to point out that though the lion is well represented in Indian mythology, there has been no definite fossil find in India even from the Shiwalik group which is well known for its fossil mammals. Apart from the Bankura find, there is only one record of an upper premolar and limb bones of a doubtful *Panthera*, either *tigris* or *leo*, from Pleistocene deposits of the Kurnool caves in Andhra Pradesh.[4]

The lion's range extended from Baluchistan up to Bihar and present-day Jharkhand, the last one being encountered there in Palamau in 1814,[5] whereas there is no record of a spotted hyena in historical times from the Indian subcontinent though both these animals inhabit the same environment in Africa. There is one more report of a fossil lion tooth from Sri Lanka[6] but there were no lions there in historical times.

The Indus civilization which dates back to circa 3000 BCE was among the oldest and largest in the world. Its cities, fortified establishments, ports, and river stations were spread over Sind, Makran, Punjab, Rajasthan, and Gujarat in the Indian subcontinent. We turn to their artefacts for our enquiry.

The most startling representations of a variety of fauna are from the Indus seals. There are many composite animals, but those that depict "normal" animals are remarkable for their accuracy. Among the wild animals we find the elephant on 55 seals, the tiger on 16 seals, and the rhinoceros on 40 seals. Some animals are sometimes depicted with troughs in front of them. Among the reptiles, the gharial has pride of place being represented on as many as 49 seals.[7] The frequency of representation of a species of animal can only be indicative of the importance of the motif and no more, and it is always possible that representations of a hitherto unrecorded animal may be found given the new discoveries constantly being made at various archaeological sites.

It is rarely realized that some artefacts do have the lion motif on them, for instance a gold goblet found at Quetta. The animals are anatomically accurately rendered except for their tails which are not even lionlike, but bushy like that of a fox[8] or squirrel. They appear to be composite animals and are very similar, particularly in the depiction of their tails, to the lions found on the "black obelisk" of Shalmaneser III of Assyria (circa 825 BCE) preserved in the British Museum.[9] The goblet could have reached the find site from West Asia. At Sibri near Mehrgarh, representations of a lion facing a bull or pouncing on it have been found on cylinder seals[10] which again are not typical of Harappan culture and could have come from West Asia. At Taxila a lion handle was also found which was of the late Harappan or post-Harappan period.[11] The animal representation is highly stylized and its provenance would be difficult to ascertain. There is however one Harappan terracotta of two lion heads.[12] But, Gregory L. Possehl concludes that there were no clear representations of lions in Harappan finds, nor were any bones or teeth found at such sites. While there are representations of felids which may have been lions they could also have been other cats as there was nothing to distinguish them as such.[13] Given that lions were present in Sind till the 19th century, they may well have lived in dry areas inland. The tigers remained around the Indus valley up to the early part of the 20th century. What is evident is the presence of the tiger in Harappan culture; the lion on the other hand was an oddity.

This brings us to the famous Harappan seals of man-animal fights. Whereas the animals in West Asia are lions, here they have been substituted by tigers. Asko Parpola argues that there are many Harappan seals which depict a manly hero holding a tiger by the throat. In Mesopotamian art the animal was either a lion or a bull in similar representations. The substitution by the tiger in Harappan seals only reconciles the scene with the fauna of the Indus valley.[14]

There is weight in the statement insofar as the tiger, elephant, and the rhino are all animals of thick jungles and tall grasses that one sees today in what is left of the Terai. This is not the preferred habitat of the lion which is an animal of grasslands and dry deciduous forests. Even so, if lions were found in the reed beds of Mesopotamian rivers, why would they not be in the reeds of the Indus? Were they deterred by the other large predator which was more at home in thick cover, the tiger? Were lions not found further afield away from riverine vegetation where the Indus civilization had spread? There are Indus seals of wild goats and urial[15] which lived in the mountainous regions away from the Indus. And yet there are no seals of the lion. The proximity of lion-knowing cultures would explain an occasional object with a lion motif, but the point really is of the frequency of human contact and familiarity with the lion. This appears to be missing.

The period of the Harappan culture ends around 1400 BCE. It has been long held by some scholars that climatic change caused its demise. This theory has been challenged recently and other causes have been advanced for the Harappan culture's

Lion capital
■ Sarnath, 3rd century BCE.
The most famous of Emperor Ashoka's symbols crafted by "Perso-Hellenistic" tutors in a "foreign heraldic style", India's national emblem.
Courtesy Archaeological Survey of India.

end. However, drought did occur over prolonged periods, with the Lunkaransar lake in Rajasthan starting to dry up around 2000 BCE and the Sambar lake just 200 kilometres away, similarly drying up only a thousand years later.[16] It is difficult to reconstruct what happened to the environment around this time in the region from Baluchistan to the banks of the Ganga, which was to be the range of the lion in historical times. Did recurring drought open up large swathes of land to grassland and scrub thus making it fit for lion habitation and causing a spurt in the lion population over the centuries? Did the river Indus no longer remain a barrier? Did the lions inhabit its environs and cross it to populate the regions which they occupied until the 19th century? There is another factor which could have had an impact. As human settlements were already established in the Indus region from about 3000 BCE, the use of fire, presence of cattle, and clearing of large tracts over the millennia may well have opened up habitats which would have helped edge species like the lion to prosper and proliferate in the region from, say, the 3rd century BCE. Suffice it to say that lions were prominent in Persia in the 1st millennium BCE and by the time of the Mauryas (4th century BCE) the animal assumed sufficient importance in India to take centrestage in Mauryan monumental art. Some of the findings of John Irwin, who studied the Mauryan pillars extensively, may be summarized here briefly. Of a total of forty pillars which are known to have existed from historical records, only two pillars survived the ravages of time in situ. The others which were excavated were broken or buried. On the basis of the design of their foundations, Irwin concluded that four pillars – those at Rampurva with a bull capital, Sankisa with an elephant capital, Kausambi without a capital, and Vaishali with a lion capital – were pre-Ashokan or even pre-Mauryan. The first two were of an indigenous Indian style whereas the sejant lion of Vaishali was carved in a "foreign, heraldic style" inspired by Achaemenid art of the 5th century BCE. According to Irwin, the pillars at Sarnath, Topra, Lauriya-Nandangarh, and Gotihawa, and the Rampurva pillar with lion capital, were all erected by Ashoka and all their surviving "emblems are lions carved in a foreign heraldic style". The most important was the pillar at Sarnath, the creation of which was guided by "Perso-Hellenistic tutors" from Iran. To Irwin the pillars of Ashoka were an older continuing tradition of the world axis or axis mundi, that which separates the earth from the heavens. The elephant and the bull were symbols of Indra, the god who separated heaven and earth. The lion was a symbol of royalty and if Vaishali was the earliest lion pillar, it may well have been during the period of the Nanda dynasty (about 360–324 BCE), and inspired by motifs from western Asia. In Egypt the lion had served as a royal symbol as well as a symbol of the sun, a divine being. The lion is the king of beasts and in the human world it is associated with kingship as the counterpart of its strength and nobility.[17]

While Irwin's conclusions have not found universal acceptance, he certainly brings into perspective the sudden appearance of the lion on the Indian subcontinent. The lion capital at Sarnath topped a pillar which proclaimed a royal message. The aspect of the lions suits "a mood of isolation and majesty".[18] Ashoka's lions were proclaiming the majesty of *dhamma*, though one can debate whether it was the *dhamma* of the Buddha or Ashoka's own version of it.[19]

The expression on the face of each lion on the Sarnath pillar is mysterious. Professor Helmut Hemmer has pointed out that the face has its mouth open with the lips drawn back baring the teeth, and the tongue protruding over the lower incisors

The Sarnath lion's expression
■ A careful look at the face shows the "flehmen" expression typical among cats, though during flehmen the eyes are almost completely shut.
Courtesy Archaeological Survey of India.

Jain devotees with symbols –
triratna and lion.
■ Pediment of an image from
Kankali Tila, Mathura, circa 2nd
century CE.
Courtesy State Museum, Lucknow.

with its tip hanging out. This expression approximates to the leonine "flehmen"
except that the lions' eyes are open instead of being almost completely shut. A lion
or other felid adopts such an expression when it encounters the scent of a lioness in
oestrus or any other strong or strange smell. The lion holds its body absolutely
motionless and appears totally calm, as if it has "turned away from the outside world
concentrating on something of its inner experience". This impressive sight is
different from all the animal's expressions of rage or fury, it is not a threat, it shows
absolute peace. Professor Hemmer suggests that it could be in conformity with
Ashoka's philosophy of peace.[20] However, such expressions are also found on Hittite
finds of the Bronze Age of Asia Minor.[21] Of particular interest to us is the gold rhyton
from the Achaemenid period circa 500 BCE and the lion capital on the Vaishali pillar
both of which have similar expressions. The sejant lions' faces from the Sanchi
capital are mutilated and hence the expressions are lost.

It is significant though that the arrival of the lion in Mauryan monumental art
was not to the exclusion of other animal symbols. The elephant was central to
Buddhist symbology from very early on. It played a role in the Buddha's nativity and
it remained of importance to Ashoka as the elephant carved at the site of Dhauli and
the elephant likeness etched in stone at Kalsi testify. The inscription at the latter site
includes the word Gajatama, meaning the "supreme elephant", an appellation of the
Buddha himself.

It is evident that lion symbolism gains importance in India only in the second
half of the 1st millennium BCE and in all probability the concept came from Persia or
maybe even further west. However, Irwin suggests two other possible reasons for its
sudden arrival on the Indian scene. One was that the Indra cult was in decline by
the 4th century BCE "at least as far as metropolitan cults are concerned". With the
decline of Indra would also decline the importance of the bull and the elephant, the
two animals associated with Indra. Secondly, the Nandas and the Mauryas may have
chosen the lion in preference to the bull and the elephant because it was not
associated with any cults prevalent then, hence lending itself as a symbol without

any association with another religion or faith for the new concept of royalty.[22] Irwin adds:

> Although the Nandas and the Mauryas may have paid lip service to Indra as king of the gods and therefore as their divine patron, the real model of Indian kingship had become more worldly than celestial: in part at least it was the sovereignty of the Achaemenids, who ruled the largest and most powerful empire the world had ever known, and whose edicts (and even the actual wording) scholars have long recognized as having influenced the style of Asoka.[23]

Cities of Harappan culture had both the bull and the elephant along with the tiger as important, possibly cult symbols. Irwin points out that the lion may have remained largely "unsymbolic" until the second half of the 1st millennium BCE and as Professor J.C. Heesterman put it, the animal was "conveniently available for use as a symbol of a new conception of royalty".[24]

Two new religions took root in India in the second half of the 1st millennium BCE. Vardhamana, better known as Mahavira, was born around 540 BCE. His mother was the sister of the Licchavi chief Chetaka. His quest for salvation took him to the Nirgranthas, those who were free from worldly bonds, a group founded 200 years earlier by Parshva who later came to be recognized as the 23rd Tirthankara, or Great Teacher, by the followers of the Jain faith. Mahavira who had taken to the life of an ascetic around 510 BCE, was the last Tirthankara. Each Tirthankara has a symbol of an animal (a snake in the case of Parshvanatha), known as *nishan, chinha,* or *lanchan.* Among the symbols are the bull, elephant, horse, monkey, crocodile, rhinoceros, buffalo, deer, goat, fish, tortoise, etc. There is no cat other than the lion and this is the symbol of Mahavira, the Great Teacher belonging to the second half of the 1st millennium before Christ, which is when the lion had begun assuming importance as a symbol.

Siddhartha who became the Buddha, the Enlightened One, had a similar background. Son of a Shakya chieftain born around 560 BCE, he too renounced worldly pleasure to seek salvation. He attained enlightenment around 524 BCE and lived till 480 BCE to preach his Path. He is known as Shakyasimha, lion of the Shakya tribe, and his first sermon at Sarnath is known as *Simhanada,* the roar of a lion, as he raised his voice to preach the new doctrine.

Both Mahavira and Buddha came from a part of eastern India which was an ideal habitat for the tiger, the dominant cat of the region. Both of them spent their lives preaching their faiths in this region. The spread of Jainism into other parts of India started 200 years after Mahavira's death. In the case of Buddhism too, the faith started to spread in India and elsewhere centuries after the founder's death. When Ashoka refers to the Buddha in the rock inscription at Bhabra (Rajasthan), he does not use any title signifying a lion.[25] Neither of the teachers in their lifetime would have been associated with the lion. The animal assumed symbolic importance for the first time with the Vaishali lion pillar whose heraldic sejant lion in all probability drew its inspiration from West Asia and may be dated to 360 BCE or later. The association between the two teachers and the lion is obviously posthumous. Irwin arrives at a similar conclusion though from a very different route.[26]

The lion's journey to prominence in Indian culture took it from pillars to coins. In Asia, the first off the mark was Pantaleon the Bactrian king circa 185–180 BCE, who struck coins with a female deity in oriental costume holding a flower in her right hand on the obverse and a statant lion on the reverse. He was followed by

Addorsed sejant lions
■ Sculpture on the southern torana of the Great Stupa, Sanchi, 3rd century BCE – 3rd century CE.
Though these lions are reminiscent of the Sarnath capital, they are stylistically different, more indigenized.
Photograph: Gary Michael Tartakov.

Three rampant lions
■ Panel on the west gateway pillar of the Great Stupa, Sanchi.
Photograph: K.B. Agrawala.

Agathocles circa 180–170 BCE, who also struck coins with these motifs.[27] According to one authority the date of Agathocles is 175–165 BCE. A coin of Agathocles with a similar motif has been identified as a cheetah.[28] That the Indo-Greeks were the first to use the lion as a symbol was surely not an accident, as it was a familiar animal for them. Equally naturally the first representation of a lion on tribal punch-marked coins dated to the 1st century is from Taxila.[29] The lion symbol probably travelled south into India at about the same time. The Western Kshatrapa king Aghudaka's coins had the winged Nike, Greek goddess of victory, holding a wreath on the obverse with a lion-wheel standard on the reverse. His son and successor Bhumaka's coins too, have a similar lion motif.[30] By the 2nd century CE, the statant lion had appeared on the Satavahana and Western Kshatrapa coins found in the Krishna and Godavari districts.[31]

We must now ask the question why the lion assumes importance in the second half of the 1st millennium BCE. Heesterman (quoted by Irwin) states that the lion was a free agent waiting to be adopted. Irwin argues that its meteoric rise from a symbolic nonentity to stardom was inspired by the great empires of West Asia with

Warrior with a shield fighting a lion
■ Panel on a pillar at Stupa 2, Sanchi,
2nd century BCE – 1st century CE.
Photograph: K.B. Agrawala.

whom the early Indian monarchies of the Nanda and Maurya dynasties had contact
and whose grandeur inspired them. To these two explanations we may add one
more. A large cat, gregarious in nature, noisy with its frequent roars, diurnal in
habit, easily observable in open country, and often unafraid of man, the lion allowed
itself to be seen as the king of the natural world by man very distinctly, unlike the
tiger which inhabits thick jungles that hold many terrors for man. The lion symbol
lends itself easily and naturally to a monarch, lord of his subjects, rather than to
shepherds, cattle herders, traders, or food gatherers, and producers or their
oligarchies. The lion had therefore to wait until the rise of large, expanding, and
powerful kingdoms in India to acquire symbolic importance here. This was not a
one-shot step but a protracted process.

It will be seen from the foregoing that so far little can be observed of lion-human
interactions from the above sources. We must turn to literary sources to get a
glimpse of what was happening at the cusp of the common era.

The earliest "lay" report on India was given by Megasthenes, in his *Indica*. As
Seleucus Nikator's ambassador to Chandragupta Maurya's court (322–298 BCE) at

Pataliputra, he described the country, its geography and climate which he observed in the course of his travels and recorded with remarkable accuracy in some instances and with equal fantasy in some others. It is unfortunate that his writings are fragmentary and have survived in classical literature only through other chroniclers. His observations of the animals he saw (and did not see) are illuminating. He accurately states that there were no hippopotamus in India. On the other hand, he has described some fantastic beasts such as winged scorpions and enormous flying snakes as well, which are difficult to explain. Megasthenes surely knew of both lions and tigers, indeed both these felines were found in substantial tracts of land between Anatolia and the Indus in his time. In fact, Iran and the Indus had both these animals up to the early part of the 20th century when they became extinct. His description of the size of the tiger is curious. Strabo states on the authority of Megasthenes that

> the largest tigers are found among the Prasii (easterners), being nearly twice the
> size of the lion, and [they are] so strong that a tame tiger led by four men having
> seized a mule by the hinder leg overpowered it and dragged it to him.[32]

Killing a mule is no difficult task for a normal sized tiger. However, the lion and the tiger, two of the largest felines, would be of near equal size, and Megasthenes is way off fact in this comparison. He has also recorded an interaction between dogs and a lion which is of particular interest to us. Strabo states on the authority of Megasthenes that

> There are also dogs of great strength and courage, which will not let go their hold
> till water is poured into their nostrils: they bite so eagerly that the eyes of some
> become distorted and the eyes of others fall out. Both a lion and a bull were held
> fast by a dog. The bull was seized by the muzzle and died before the dog could be
> taken out.[33]

We need to examine the dog and the lion episode further. Quintus Curtius Rufus is one of the chroniclers of Alexander's later campaigns leading to the invasion of India in 327 BCE. Not much is known of him though he is believed to have been a contemporary of Emperor Augustus (63 BCE to 14 CE) by some, while others believe that he was a contemporary of Emperor Vespasian (69–79 CE). His narrative is based on Ptolemy who accompanied Alexander to India, from Kleitarchos their contemporary, and from Timagenes who lived during the reign of Augustus. Another chronicler Diodorus the Sicilian was a contemporary of Julius Caesar and Augustus. His narrative of Alexander's invasion appears to have been based on the same sources as those of Quintus Curtius Rufus.[34] Both have described an incident which occurred when Alexander was met by King Sophites (Sobutha or Saubh?) whose kingdom lay to the west of the river Hyphasis (Beas). After initial suspicion Alexander and Sophites came to establish friendly relations with each other. The latter wishing to impress Alexander, gave a demonstration of the ferocity of his dogs and Quintus Curtius Rufus records:

> His country possesses a noble breed of dogs, used for hunting and said to refrain
> from barking when they sight their game which is chiefly the lion. Sophites wishing
> to show Alexander the strength and mettle of these dogs, caused a very large lion
> to be placed within an enclosure where four dogs in all were let loose upon him.
> The dogs at once fastened upon the wild beast, when one of the huntsmen who was
> accustomed to work of this kind tried to pull away by the leg one of the dogs which
> with the others had seized the lion, and when the limb would not come away, cut it

off with a knife. The dog could not even by this means be forced to let go his hold, and so the man proceeded to cut him in another place and finding him still clutching the lion as tenaciously as before, he continued cutting away with his knife one part of him after another. The brave dog however, even in dying kept his fangs fixed in the lion's flesh; so great is the eagerness for hunting which nature has implanted in these animals, as testified by the accounts transmitted to us.

I must observe, however, that I copy from preceding writers more than I myself believe, for I neither wish to guarantee statements of truth of which I am doubtful, nor yet to suppress what I find recorded. [35]

While Quintus Curtius Rufus claims to repeat faithfully what he has received and is not entirely convinced of the veracity of the episode, Diodorus the Sicilian records the same event with a few differences:

Among the many valuable presents which he (King Sophites) bestowed on Alexander were 150 dogs remarkable for their size and strength, and superior also in other points, and said to have been bred from tigresses. Being desirous that Alexander should have proof of their mettle by seeing them at work, he placed a full grown lion within an enclosure, and selecting two of the least valuable of the dogs included in the present, cast them to the lion. When these were likely to be vanquished by the wild beast he let loose two other dogs. Then when the four dogs together proved more than a match for the lion, a man who was sent into the ring with a knife cut away the right leg of one of the dogs. When the king (Alexander) loudly remonstrated, and his bodyguards rushed forward and arrested the hand of the Indian, Sophites announced that he would give three dogs instead of the one which was mutilated. Then the huntsman, taking hold of the leg, cut it away quietly bit by bit. The dog without uttering so much as a yell or a moan of pain, kept his fangs fixed in the bite, until all his blood being drained he drew his last breath on the body of the lion.[36]

A pack of hunting dogs can hold a large prey at bay. Indian wild dogs or dholes are known to hold the tiger at bay and even kill it, though some members of the pack are accounted for by the tiger in the process. Sindhi hounds of today are also fierce, large, and capable of such feats. Such breeds may have been known in Alexander's time, though to dispatch a lion, a large pack would have to attack it and surely several of them would meet their end before the cat was subdued. The accounts we have seen here are exaggerated, but pursuing a large carnivore with a pack of hunting dogs is distinctly possible and the Indians of the time appear to have done so. Actually, A.L. Basham points out that a large hill breed of dog perhaps resembling today's Tibetan mastiff, was famous beyond India, for Herodotus records that the Persian Emperor Artaxerxes I (465–425 BCE) exempted four Babylonian villages from taxation in return for their breeding Indian dogs for war and hunting. These dogs were also known in Egypt of the Ptolemies (304–30 BCE).[37]

Hunting with dogs was a common practice in India which continued up to the first half of the 20th century among the princes. For example, in Kolhapur state (in present-day Maharashtra) they were used for hunting wild boar and deer.[38] Till about the early 1950s some thirty to forty dogs were kept in a bastion of the fort in Karauli state (Rajasthan). Their keepers were the sweepers of the town who bred pigs to clean up municipal areas and they would also handle the unclean pig meat which was fed to the dogs. Tigers and leopards were run down with these packs. Often the prey was finished off by the royal hunter with a rifle shot

Coin of Nahapana
■ Western Kshatrapa ruler, circa 2nd century CE.
The coin is based on a Satavahana prototype. The obverse shows a lion with a prominent mane, standard (*yupa*), inscription above, and three-arched hill below; the reverse has a thunderbolt (*vajra*) and arrow.
Courtesy the Indian Institute of Research in Numismatic Studies, Anjaneri, Nashik.

towards the end of a chase.[39] Thus, the ancient Greek accounts were by no means far-fetched.

Let us now turn to Strabo the famous geographer of Ancient Roman times who was a contemporary of Emperor Augustus. He is believed to have lived long enough to see Tiberius succeed him and is believed to have died in the year 24 CE. He was a keen traveller who had voyaged to Egypt and as far east as Armenia. His knowledge of India is derived from contemporary and earlier sources and his *Geography* is a careful compilation of the history and commerce of the region. He described India's animals too, but what concerns us here is his description of a royal procession.

> When the king washes his hair, they celebrate a great festival and [his subjects] send him great presents.... In the processions at their festivals many elephants adorned with gold and silver are in the train, as well as four horse chariots and yokes of oxen. There comes a great host of attendants in their holiday attire, ... garments embroidered and interwoven with gold, wild beasts such as buffaloes, leopards (*pardalis*), tame lions (*leontes*) and a multitude of birds of variegated plumage and fine song.[40]

Strabo's *Geography* was written in the 1st century CE. But if the passage is based on a description by Kleitarchos who accompanied Alexander on his campaigns and to whom Strabo refers in the passage, he may be describing a royal procession of Poros or the Nandas of Magadha on the basis of what he may have heard or seen. On the other hand if he was describing a procession on the basis of information available to him in his own time, then of course, he could be describing the procession of a Maurya, Kushana, or Satavahana king. Such royal processions were a regular annual feature at Dussehra in Indian principalities large and small until 1947. Only one procession, at Mysore, continues today on a much reduced scale. Those who have seen such processions or read of them, would immediately feel the ring of veracity of Strabo's description. It may be noted that such processions were an annual feature in India unlike the coronation pageants in the tradition of European monarchies which took place but once on the accession of the king to the throne. Strabo records tame lions in a royal procession. Lions can be tamed and indeed they can withstand crowds. Emperor Haile Selassie's court at Addis Ababa is a recent example. In Kolhapur state lions and tigers were tamed to walk with their keepers in the early part of the 20th century[41] and Maharaja Kishen Singh of Bharatpur (Rajasthan) had a tame lion which was displayed on a special cart on occasions of state as was done for the visit to India of the Prince of Wales (later Edward VIII) in 1921.[42] Even the free-ranging wild lions of the Gir are extremely trusting of humans. As for *pardalis* mentioned in the text, the reference is probably to cheetahs rather than leopards which are the least tolerant of humans among the large cats.

This brings us to yet another authority somewhat later than Strabo. Claudius Aelianus who lived in Rome in the 2nd century CE, compiled a work called "On Peculiarities of Animals". His information as far as India is concerned was based on what he had heard or read. Two passages from his text are relevant to us here.

> The Indians bring to their king tigers made tame, domesticated panthers (*pantheras*), and oryxes with four horns.[43]

There is no doubt about the four-horned antelope, and cheetahs were more likely than leopards to be "domesticated". Coming to the tiger, it has to be said that they can be tamed, but to move around with them freely in a crowd would be more difficult than with a tame lion. It is possible that Aelianus could have mixed up the two but no definite conclusion is possible from this short sentence. In another passage he observes:

> I have no reasons whatsoever to doubt that the lions of the largest size are found in India, and what convinces me is that this country is such an excellent mother of other animals. But of all the beasts one can encounter these are the most savage and ferocious. The skins of these lions look black – the bristly hair of their mane stands erect, their very aspect strikes the soul with terror and dismay. If they can be captured before they are fully grown and not otherwise, they can be tamed, and they become so tractable and domestic that they are led by the leash, and with huntsmen and their hounds take part in hunting young deer and stags, and boars and buffaloes and wild asses, for, as I am told, they have a very keen scent.[44]

Some lions in India do have black manes. But there is no record of these animals being used for hunting by man except for the painting from Iran mentioned earlier.[45] Cheetahs and caracals were used for the purpose, but the caracal would find boars, buffaloes, and wild asses difficult to subdue, whereas the cheetah could possibly tackle their young. In all probability Aelianus has mixed up the cheetah with the lion. The point nonetheless is, that the Indians tamed lions by the 1st century CE.

As we shall see in the next chapter, the vedic people knew the lion. Over the centuries, environmental changes caused by prolonged drought as well as the impact of human settlement, had made tracts of Baluchistan, Sind, Punjab, and the Gangetic plain hospitable enough for the lion. Around the 3rd century BCE, about the time a strong monarchical power was evolving in eastern India, the lion assumed centrestage to symbolize royalty. Though large swathes of eastern India were tiger country, the lion became a symbol for the region's dynasties. It being the most visible of large cats it lent itself easily to such symbolism rather than the secretive tiger. In any case it had not represented any earlier cult and was available for its new role.

Unlike in ancient Egypt the lion was not worshipped, but it was tamed enough to be a part of royal processions. There are no signs of its being hunted or becoming royal game in the sources we have seen so far. For these we must look elsewhere.

CHAPTER 4

Mrigaraja: King of the Beasts

THE EARLIEST RELIGIOUS LITERATURE in India is the *Rigveda* which is a collection of 1,028 hymns. The traditional view is that they were composed by a people called the "Aryans" who arrived from Central Asia. These hymns were composed prior to 1000 BCE[1] though they were committed to writing several centuries later. They thus give us glimpses of the lion in India from approximately 1000 BCE onwards. The word *simha* for lion is the oldest and is attested since the *Rigveda*,[2] though its etymology is disputed. Dr M.A. Mehendale informs us that its connection with Armenian *inc* or *inj* meaning "leopard" is not certain and hence the word cannot be traced back definitely to Indo-European times. *Simha* does not have a cognate in Old Iranian (Avesta) either. But Dr Mehendale adds that suggestions have been put forward to connect it with words from middle Iranian dialects, and if this is the case, then it is possible that the word has roots in a third source.

Dr Mehendale feels that the phonetic resemblance between *simha* and the Swahili *simba* "lion" may be accidental or that Swahili may have borrowed it from an Indian source. He goes on to point out that the traditional derivation of *simha* is found in Yaska's *Nirukta* (dated to circa 5th century BCE, this work attempts to give the etymologies of vedic and non-vedic words) as being either from the root *sah* – "to overpower", *hims* – "to injure", or *sam-han* – "to kill". Professor Paul Thieme, the German Indologist, considers the derivation from *hims* more likely and suggests that the transposition of the letters *h* and *s* was for tabooistic reasons.[3] Professor Romila Thapar on the other hand points out that the transposition of *h* and *s* goes back to the *Avesta* and the *Rigveda*.[4]

Thus, it may be asserted that the word *simha* for lion has ancient roots in India. That apart it is pertinent to note that it continues to be in common usage in various Indian languages to this day, some 3,000 years later, denoting unmistakably the same animal even in the languages of the areas of southern India which are beyond the range of the lion in historical times.

The vedic people were sufficiently impressed with the lion to compare it with a God, for He is sometimes described as "frightful like a lion" (*simho na bhimah*) in the *Rigveda*.[5] The lion's roar was regarded with awe. The verb used since the *Rigveda* for the roar is *nad* or *stan* – "to thunder, to roar". Thus the Maruts (the winds) are recorded as "roaring like lions" (*simha iva nanadati*),[6] or a "lion's roars" are heard from the clouds in the sky (*simhasya stanathah*).[7] The compound word *simhanada* "lion's roar" is found in later literature.

Apart from acquiring an exalted position, it appears that the lion was also hunted, for the *Rigveda* alludes to hunting a lion by cornering it from all sides. The enclosing sticks placed round a sacrificial fire are compared to men who corner and stand around an angry lion because "If the sticks are not placed around the newly generated fire, he might jump over them".[8] There is also a reference to catching a lion in a snare.[9] It is not clear from the text as to why lions had to be hunted or caught. There is however, a reference in the *Shatapatha Brahmana* (a compendium of explanations of vedic rituals, ascribed tentatively to circa 800 BCE or later) that when "spirituous liquor" is prepared for the Sautramani sacrifice, the hair of lion, tiger, and wolf are put into it.[10]

Further, lion's flesh was eaten in ancient times. *Sushrutasamhita* (one of the three principal treatises of classical medicine in India which attained its present form early in the common era) has a catalogue of meats which can be consumed. Of these are a class of meats which fall into the *jangala* category i.e. meats of animals that live on dry lands. Within this class there is a sub-class called *guhasya* to which belong animals which have a lair. This category of animals includes lions and tigers whose meats are "sweet, heavy, unctuous, fortifying, they calm wind, (they are of) of hot energy, (and are) good for those who suffer (constantly) from (afflictions of the) eyes and private parts".[11]

Apollonius, the occult from Tyana in Capadosia in Asia Minor, who was a contemporary of Jesus Christ, travelled to India. He confirms the practice of consumption of lion's flesh. According to his biographer Philostratus of Lemos who wrote his work circa 214, Apollonius came to the region between the Caucasus (in the Indian context the "Kaukosos" are identified with the Hindu Kush mountains) and the Kophen river (identified as the Kabul river by Strabo),[12] which is probably the region around Taxila as the Kabul joins the Indus west of Taxila. In this region

***Gold coin of Chandra Gupta II
(376–415)***

■ A lion slayer type coin on the obverse of which the king slays a lion with an arrow, he has a foot on the animal as if to hold it in an advantageous position. On the reverse, the goddess Durga rides her proper mount, the lion. These coins were struck to commemorate the victory over Gujarat.

Courtesy Bharat Kala Bhavan, Varanasi.

Apollonius came across nomads who offered him wine made from dates and honey together with slices of lion and leopard meats which had been freshly skinned. Lions were also "served up whole". The biographer goes on to record a king's banquet:

> The king reclines on a couch and near him recline not more than five of his
> kindred, but all the other guests sit during the meal. A circular table is set in the
> midst, which is about knee high.... On [it] are scattered laurel leaves and another
> leaf like myrtle, which the Indians use as perfume. Fish and fowl are set on it, with
> lions, antelopes and swine, served up whole: but only the hind quarters of tigers,
> for they are unwilling to eat the rest of the animal, because they say that as soon as
> it is born, it lifts its forepaws to the rising sun.[13]

Both these sources are about 1,000 years after the *Rigveda* and therefore by themselves cannot be an indication of practices in earlier times. It would be difficult to conclude from these references when the practices noted by Sushruta and Apollonius started. But tribal peoples do eat meats of carnivores even today and Waghri tribals "relished" lion meat according to a British period source of the 19th century. Lion fat was also used as a cure for rheumatism.[14]

Shatapatha Brahmana has two stories of the origin of the lion. According to one, Indra emitted the *soma* he had forcibly drunk at a ritual Tvashtra sacrifice to which he was not invited. A part of it came out of his nose and that became a lion.[15] According to the other story, when Indra drank the *soma* at the sacrifice,

> his vital power flowed out of every limb. Along with his urine his vigour flowed
> forth and became a wolf. A wolf is the impetuous rush of wild animals; with the
> undigested contents of his bowels, fury flowed forth, that became a tiger. A tiger is
> a kind of wild animal; with his blood his power flowed, that became a lion. A lion
> is a ruler of all wild beasts....[16]

These two stories are a traditional interpretation of the origin of three major carnivores though it is not possible to trace the tradition to its source. It is significant that in the Rigvedic Sautramani sacrifice, the hair of the same three animals is used. The other interesting point is that both the tiger and the lion feature in this creation process and both are seen as paramount over other beasts.

Coming to the various names of the lion, the foremost are *hari*, *haryaksha*, and *kesarin*. All three are attested to since the time of the *Mahabharata*, the great epic said to have been composed between the 4th century BCE and 4th century CE. Hari is a descriptive word meaning brown, tawny, pale yellow, etc. and incidentally, it is also the word for a horse. *Haryaksha* stands for the one with *hari* coloured eyes and *kesarin* means the one who has a mane. The word *mrigendra*, king of "animals" or "beasts" (the word *mriga* is used in its generic sense to denote all animals) has been used in the *Harivamsha*. Similar words such as *mrigapati*, *mrigaraja*, *mrigadhipa*, etc. are used primarily for the lion though occasionally these names are used for a tiger.[17] This signifies a greater familiarity with the lion which as already mentioned is an animal more likely to be seen and observed by humans. There is however one word – *panchasya* and its synonyms *panchanana*, *panchamukha*, and *pancha-vaktra* – meaning "one who has five mouths". How this came about is quite unclear. Some ingenious explanations have been given by commentators,[18] but they are more imaginative than logical.

This brings us to the throne of rulers in ancient times. The vedic word for it is *asandi* and it occurs in connection with the ritual of royal coronation, the *rajasuya* ceremony.[19] The seat on which the ceremony is performed is the *asandi* and it is covered with a tigerskin (*vyaghracharma*).[20] According to the *Shatapatha Brahmana* the *asandi* is made of the wood of the *udumbara* tree (*gular* in Hindi, *umber* in Marathi and Gujarati) or *khadira* tree (*khair* in Hindi, Marathi, and Gujarati).[21] The *asandi*, according to this authority, is to be covered by a blackbuck skin (*krishnajina*).[22]

In the *Mahabharata* and the *Ramayana* (the second great epic believed to date between the 2nd century BCE and 2nd century CE) and later literature, the word *bhadrasana* or *bhadrapitha* is used for the seat on which the king is crowned. The word *simhasana* on the other hand is also current from the *Mahabharata* onwards. The *Shabdakalpadruma* of Radhakanta, the Sanskrit lexicon of the 19th century, explains the word as deriving from *simhachintam asanam* "a seat marked by a lion". This explanation is based on the fact that the throne has lion heads on the arm rests and clawed feet for its legs. But this obviously is a very late explanation as it represents the thrones of Indian princes in use in the 19th to mid-20th century. Dr Mehendale's view is that the *simhasana*, lion's seat, is derived from the words *simhasya asanam*. "Since the lion is looked upon as the chief among animals, and the king is considered chief among men, the seat of the king could be thought of as a seat of the lion among men or, in short, the seat of the lion."[23] This is a plausible explanation, as the roots of such equations go far back in time. In the *Mahabharata* the animals were divided into two categories: *gramya*, "domestic" and *aranya*, "wild". Man topped the former list; the lion, the latter.[24]

Simhavalokana means "viewing, observing like a lion". In the *Raghuvamsha* of Kalidasa, 5th century, there is a description of Raghu's conquest of the four cardinal directions. After defeating the Kambojas, Raghu mounted the Himalaya. It is said that the lions sat unperturbed in their den and viewed the panorama, turning their heads to survey the tumult of battle caused by Raghu's lion-like victorious army. Raghu marvelled at their calm demeanour. The actual words used are *simhanams parivritya avalokitam*, from which is derived *simhavalokita*.[25]

A king's appearance is also compared to that of a lion. Thus the kings who entered the gaming room for the famous dice game in the *Mahabharata* are described as "having necks (possibly manes?) like that of a lion (*simhagrivah*)".[26] Krishna with his awe-inspiring swagger is described as *simhakhelagati*, "one who has the stately walk of a lion".[27] The gait of other great figures of the epic such as Balarama, Duryodhana, and Karna is similarly described, whereas Bhimasena's walk is described as *simhakhela*, "lion's gait".[28]

Kautilya, the minister of Chandragupta Maurya who ruled from 324 to 300 BCE, is traditionally known as the author of the great work on statecraft, the *Arthashastra*, though it is now clear that while the work's earliest portions may be that old, there are several later interpolations. The treatise gives a detailed description of, among other things, the organization of the state, how the land must be put to use, what the king must do, and so on. Among the departments of state enumerated in it, is that of forest produce. It requires the superintendent of the department to prepare

> ... an animal park for the king's recreation ... containing shrubs and bushes bearing sweet fruits, having trees without thorns, with shallow pools of water, and stocked with tamed deer and (other) animals, containing wild animals with their claws and teeth removed (and) having male and female elephants and cubs useful for hunting. And he should establish on its borders or in conformity with the (suitability of the)

Gold coin of Kumara Gupta I (415–455)
■ A lion slayer type coin on the obverse of which the king slays a lion with an arrow though he does not have his foot on the animal. On the reverse, the goddess Durga rides a lion.
Courtesy Bharat Kala Bhavan, Varanasi.

land, another animal park where all animals are (welcomed) as guests (and given full protection).[29]

From the foregoing two important points emerge. Firstly, the park to be set aside for the king's amusement should be such that it poses no danger to his person: the passage goes to the extent of saying that the wild animals' teeth and claws must be removed. This probably applied to large carnivores, most likely tigers, as the jungles in the Maurya kingdom of Magadha with their tall grasses and thick forest cover were more suitable for tigers than for lions. The second part mentions the creation of certain areas exclusively for the protection of wild animals, and this is the earliest record of sanctuaries for flora and fauna.

The Kandahar inscription of Emperor Ashoka informs us:

Ten years being completed king Piyadassi showed piety (i.e. *dhamma*) to men. And from that time (onwards) he made men more pious. And all things prosper throughout the whole world. And the king refrains from (eating) living beings, and indeed other men and whosoever (were) the king's huntsmen and fishermen have ceased from hunting....[30]

The Rampurva pillar edict V of Ashoka declares:

Thus speaks the beloved of the Gods, the king Piyadassi: when I had been consecrated twenty-six years I forbade the killing of the following species of animals namely: parrots, mainas, red-headed ducks, *chakravaka* geese, ... *nandi-mukha*s (birds encountered in rice fields?), pigeons, bats, ants, tortoises, boneless fish, *vedaveyaka*s (?), *puputaka*s of the Ganges (skate fish?), porcupine, squirrel, deer, lizards, domesticated animals, rhinoceroses, white pigeons, domestic pigeons, and all quadrupeds of no utility and are not eaten.... Forests must not be burned in order to kill living things or without any good reason....[31]

Such a change of heart is unique in the annals of history but hunting of wild animals continued after Ashoka and the Mauryas as we shall see below. Here we need to take a leap forward in time to make comparison with a 13th-century source. *Abhilashitarthachintamani* or *Manasollasa* (1129–30) is a treatise of encyclopaedic nature concerning among other things a king's sport and pastime at court. The work is from south India, attributed to the Chalukya king Someshvara III. Among the various types of hunting the work describes are *sarmeyavinoda*, hunting with dogs; *syenavinoda*, falconry; *matsyavinoda*, fishing; and *mrigyavinoda*, deer hunting. The treatise goes on to state that there are thirty different methods of hunting deer of which it describes twenty including *vyaghrajamrigya*, that is coursing *krishnasara*, blackbuck with *chitraka*, cheetahs.[32]

The *Manasollasa* is far more contemporaneous than the *Arthashastra* which anticipates several latter-day hunting practices, particularly those of the Mughals. Though the two works are possibly more than 1,000 years apart, they are at one insofar as neither specifically mentions the hunting of large carnivores. The *Arthashastra* says that the park for the king's recreation must have such animals minus their teeth and claws. It points out the benefits of hunting:

there is exercise, getting rid of phlegm, bile, fat, and (a tendency to) perspiration, practice in hitting the targets of moving and stationary bodies, knowledge of the minds of animals in anger, fear, and condition of ease, and (only) occasional marching.[33]

In other words, the *Arthashastra* recommends hunting to keep the king and courtiers fit for battle and yet does not want them exposed to unnecessary danger.

Leogryph with rider
■ Panel from exterior of a temple, Chaukhandi near Sarnath, Gupta period, 5th century CE.
This is a good example of the lion taking variable forms in art. It acquired importance in regions way beyond its natural range.
Courtesy National Museum, New Delhi.

Lion sculpture in the Five Rathas complex at Mamallapuram
▪ Pallava period, 7th century CE.
Photograph: V. Muthuraman.

As far as the *Manasollasa* is concerned, the treatise concentrates on pleasures, *vinoda*, and pastimes at the court of the king. Hunting large carnivores is not recommended by either text; yet it is known that Indian kings did pursue this sport with vigour, and celebrated their feats.

We have noted that a goddess riding a lion had already appeared on Kushana coins in the 1st century.[34] A similar device of a "goddess seated on lion, and holding a fillet or noose and a cornucopia" appears on the gold coins of Chandra Gupta I (320–)[35] the first king of the Gupta dynasty which restored the magnificence of the Mauryas in Magadha and beyond. However his son Samudra Gupta (335–376), the architect of the new empire, struck gold coins with six different devices, one of them being the tiger-slayer device[36] with the legend *vyaghraparakramah*, "bearing the strength of the tiger". The coin commemorates Samudra Gupta's consolidation of his hold over the Ganga valley,[37] and shows the tiger, the dominant carnivore of eastern India, being shot by the king with an arrow.[38]

Chandra Gupta II (376–415) who succeeded his father Samudra Gupta (or, according to some accounts, followed his brother Rama Gupta) continued the expansion of his empire westwards. His father is supposed to have received tributes from the Shakas who controlled Malwa and Kathiawar and they were finally defeated by him. To celebrate his victory over Kathiawar,[39] gold coins were struck with the lion-slayer device bearing the legend *simhavikramah*, "valorous like the lion".[40] While his father was depicted with the tiger, the animal Chandra Gupta II slays with an arrow is the lion, probably the dominant carnivore of Kathiawar even at the time.

The legend on the coin explains the significance of the portrayal.

Kumara Gupta I (415–455) who succeeded his father, struck fourteen known types of gold coins which included peacock, rhinoceros-slayer, tiger-slayer, elephant-rider-cum-lion-slayer and lion-slayer. The rhinoceros is shown being slain from horseback with a sword or short lance, whereas the lion and the tiger are being slain by bow and arrow and the king is on foot as in the earlier Chandra Gupta II coins. The depiction of the elephant-rider-cum-lion-slayer coin shows the elephant trampling the lion.[41]

The question arises as to whether these depictions are symbolic or an illustration of the royal hunting practice of the time. The coins depict three different modes of hunting. In the first, the lion or tiger is shot by an arrow, a perfectly feasible feat. Of course, it is probable that the king would be accompanied by courtiers who would follow suit with their arrows once the king let fly the first shaft from his bowstring. The second type of scene, with an elephant (with rider) trampling a lion or tiger, has been recorded in several sources. It was common practice to go after large carnivores on elephantback when hunting in tall grass or in thick forest cover. In the third instance, the rhinoceros is being attacked with a sword or a short lance by a horseback rider. This is likely to have been the preferred mode of hunting in such a case, since the thick hide of the animal would make an arrow less effective. In other words, the depictions are realistic enough to be considered authentic illustrations of various methods of hunting, in addition to being symbolic representations of a king's bravery and victory. These coins are an invaluable record as for the first time we see historical personalities hunting lions and other animals, we get a glimpse of their hunting methods and their sport.

At this point we must again leap forward in time to examine a document on hunting of the 16th century. Raja Rudradeva or Rudra Chand was king of Karmachala or Kumaon and a contemporary of Emperor Akbar. He wrote a treatise on hawking, *Shyainika Shastram*, in Sanskrit. The work discusses the various *vyasana*s, vices of men. According to some opinions, hunting is one of the vices, but this treatise also notes its advantages. It also makes a comprehensive survey of various hunting practices current then, which had probably changed little over the centuries. In fact, until the arrival of gunpowder and its use on the battlefield and hunting grounds, there was a remarkable continuity of hunting practices over the millennia from the time man mastered the elephant and the horse and had the use of the bow and arrow, sword, or lance. The third chapter of the work which surveys the extant practices during Rudradeva's time does not report the arrival of the gun on the hunting grounds.[42] Rudradeva records how rhinoceros and lion are to be hunted. For the latter, he says that expert archers on fleet-footed horses could strike an "infuriated" lion in an open field, or ambush it and kill it like a cat. He goes on to add that archers could hunt lions by lying in wait for them and then shooting them with poisoned darts, such a method being most successful at waterholes and in the vicinity of *Belleric myrobalan* trees or in cornfields. (The significance of this tree, called *bahera* in Hindi and Gujarati or *beheda* in Marathi, is not clear. It is a common enough tree found in deciduous mixed forests throughout India[43] and it does not have any special relationship with cornfields.) Another easy way of hunting ferocious animals was to attract them to the bait of a dead cow in a suitable place.[44]

The first method described by Rudradeva does not bear any resemblance to the depiction on Gupta coins we have seen, but it is curiously similar to an Arab practice

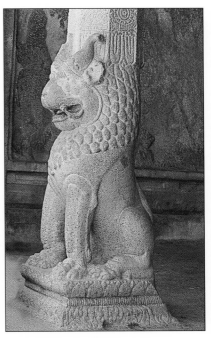

Lion pillar at entrance to temple near the Kiritiarjuniya relief at Mamallapuram
■ Pallava period, 7th century CE.
Photograph: V. Muthuraman.

described earlier in Chapter 2. The second method described by him is similar to the lion-slayer type depictions on coins which show Gupta kings using arrows, not darts which were more likely to be tipped with poison. It is pertinent to note that to this day the Masai warriors of east Africa hunt lions on foot with lances.

Among the earliest Sanskrit lexicons is Amarsimha's *Namalinganushasana* or *Amarakosha* which was possibly compiled between the 4th and 6th centuries. One of its sections, titled "*simhadivarga*", contains words belonging to the class (of animals) starting with the lion. It lists names of several species and it starts by listing six names of the lion: *simha, mrigendra, panchasya, haryaksa, kesarin,* and *hari.* The lexicon goes on to identify the three great cats of India: *shardula,* the lion; *dvipin,* the leopard; and *vyaghra,* the tiger.[45] The lion is so prominent in Sanskrit literature that it has been given over a dozen different names[46] though it shares some of them with the tiger, as we have seen. From the great works of Kalidasa to the compilation of stories with a moral intended for young princes, the *Panchatantra* attributed to Vishnu Sharma, the lion is present in all its splendour. Its courage and strength are sung by poets of old. The poet Vasundhara of whom nothing is known but whose allegorical epigram appears in Vidyakara's *Subhashitaratnakosha* says:

> His body smells of blood, his action runs to slaughter,
> his sense of right and wrong no better than a beast's.
> Thus, there is nothing to admire in a lion
> except his courage;
> but that's enough to make the world seem cheap.[47]

Amarsimha the poet (not the lexicographer), says:

> Be calm oh lion! Leave violence and still your anger.
> The sound that rises is the clouds, not elephants,
> and clouds, insentient, being composed
> of fire and water, wind and smoke,
> do roar by nature. At you
> no creature shows his pride.[48]

An unknown poet gives us a description of an aged lion and his humiliating plight:

> This lion once, the seat of valour and unerring in his wrath,
> did with his roar evaporate
> the rutting ichor of the elephants of heaven;
> who now by fate has grown so weak
> that with his trunk an aged elephant
> can pull his mane.[49]

There was a poetic convention that pearls were to be found from eight sources: elephants, clouds, boars, conches, fish, serpents, mother of pearl, and bamboo. Thus Kalidasa writes in *Kumarasambhava* that Kiratas living in the Himalaya can tell the way the lions have gone by the pearls scattered by their claws although their blood-smeared footprints are washed away by the melting snow,[50] the belief being that when a lion attacks the head of an elephant, pearls from its skull get stuck to the claws.

Lions have not been known in the Himalaya in historical times. Nor are there pearls in an elephant's skull. There are however bony growths recorded at the base of a tusk and in the skull, traditionally considered "pearls". One such "pearl" is on display at the Royal Museum, Kathmandu.[51]

Yet another unknown poet has written:

My friend, oh lord of the herd of elephants

whose eyes are blinded by rut,

Do not stay here in this entangled forest region

even for a moment;

(for) here sleeps in a den a lion

who has split open a number of large and heavy rocks

by his sharp claws mistaking them for elephants.[52]

The Extremist Indian Nationalist leader Bal Gangadhar Tilak (1856–1920) had this stanza printed on the front page of his bi-weekly *Kesari* which was the mouthpiece of his campaign for the independence of India, as a warning to the British to leave the country before they were thrown out by the forces of freedom.[53] The lion at that time was the proclaimed symbol of the British empire whereas the elephant was a great Indian icon. Yet Tilak chose the former to symbolize the dormant Indian strength which would vanquish British power if the latter did not leave India. Tilak used an existing poetic convention of lions triumphing over elephants to make his point.

The lion's position as king of the animal world is acknowledged by a poet in a *Subhashita*. He says:

A lion is neither anointed (as a king) in the forest, nor is any sacrament done on

him;

To him who has acquired magnanimity by his prowess, lordship over animals

comes naturally.[54]

Here is incomparable advice to the king to attain power through his own prowess, for another *Subhashita* says:

Undertakings are accomplished by effort and not by wishes.

The deer do not enter (of their own accord) the mouth of a lion who is asleep.[55]

In sculpture, the lion is found prominently and way beyond its natural range in historical times. It is believed to have been found up to the north of the river Narmada though Shah Jahan hunted the lion just south of it near Burhanpur.[56] Lion representations are so numerous that to even briefly cover a small part of them would be beyond the scope of this enquiry. We shall mention just a few instances. Sejant lions adorn a pillar capital at Sanchi (3rd century) in the heraldic style of Ashoka's pillar at Sarnath along with guardant lions which appear on the high architraves of the Sanchi gateway. Guardant lions also appear at the Mamallapuram Shore Temple built by the Pallavas in the late 7th century and a pride of lions appear at the Krishnamandapam, the rock-cut temple which shows them in their natural habitat at the entrance to their lairs.[57] A sculpture of the Hoysala empire which flourished in Karnataka between the 11th and 14th centuries has King Sala on foot attacking a lion with what appears to be a broad sword[58] which is reminiscent of the "lion-slayer" motif of Chandra Gupta II.

The most well-known aspect of the lion in Indian mythology is Narasimha (half man and half lion), the fourth incarnation of Lord Vishnu who appears for the purpose of destroying demon-king Hiranyakashipu to rid the world of his tyranny. Arguably, the most awe-inspiring sculpture of this incarnation is the product of the Vijayanagara empire centred at Hampi which reached its zenith at the close of the 15th and the beginning of the 16th century.

Curiously, the lion also finds itself depicted as *kirtimukha* "halo-face" or "face of glory". This emblem is rooted in the anger of Lord Shiva when he hears of King

Purushamriga (sphinx type), on a frieze
■ Wall of the Varadaraja Perumal temple, Tribhuvanai, Tamil Nadu. Chola style, early 11th century.
This striding *purushamriga* has the body and mane of a lion, and human face with fangs, crown, and discs in the elongated earlobes (see detail on page 67).
Photograph: Raja Deekshitar.

The incarnation of Narasimha
■ Vijayanagara, 14th century.
This man-lion incarnation of Lord Vishnu rid the world of the tyranny of Hiranyakashipu.
Photograph: Clare Arni.

Jalandhara's desire for his consort Parvati conveyed to him by the messenger Rahul, "the seizer". Shiva opens his third eye, a terrible monster is born whose strength is limitless. In fright, Rahul pleads for divine intervention; Shiva relents and the monster consumes himself until the face is all that remains. This is the *kirtimukha*, a demonic mask or lion's face, which crowns arches, doorways, niches of temples, and sometimes is found on the back of idols. It is meant to terrify unbelievers and demons and protect the devotees.[59] Here the lion acquires a new role as protector of the faithful. A similar role is played by the *yali* or *vyala*, a composite animal, mostly leonine. In south India, we sometimes find sculptures of the *purushamriga*, a sphinx-type composite being, near temple entrances, which devotees believe cleanse them of sins and impurities.[60]

Lions can and do attack elephants in the wild and both did live in the same habitat in India once. Such encounters however are extremely rare and they are usually confined to young or aged or ailing animals. The elephant is too large a target for a lion or a tiger, both of which steer clear of it. Hence the oft-repeated theme of lion-elephant encounters, for example on lintels at Khajuraho, is more imaginative than real.

While the Rigvedic people were aware of the lion and even ate its flesh, the animal's rise as a royal symbol on the gold coins of Chandra Gupta II is no doubt partly a result of the close contact the Magadhan empire had with Persia and further west. The lion's paramount position in the natural world and its "regal" bearing made it an obvious symbol for a king. Observations of lions in the wild led to their being identified with qualities of courage, strength, and fearlessness: the precise attributes a king would cherish. The association continued over the centuries and only ended after the formation of the Indian republic.

The lion did not acquire the status of the tiger or the elephant or the crocodile among the Harappans, as is attested by the seals of the period. It is not possible for the moment to attribute plausible explanations at the current level of our knowledge. The tiger's preference for thick jungle which was always full of unknown dangers, its stealthy behaviour, and possibly almost entirely nocturnal habits were not likely to make it an obvious choice as a royal symbol. But at the same time its stealth, power, and perceived secretiveness made it remarkably suitable as a cult figure even as a god to tribal peoples who inhabit the peripheries of thick jungles.[61] To the royals of India and other kingdoms of Asia, it was better to keep the king of the beasts on an

Gold coin of Krishnaraja Wodeyar of Mysore (1810–68)
■ The lion on the obverse is stylized but basic in execution, its mane depicted clearly enough for identification. The Roman date is below; the reverse has inscriptions in Persian and English.
Courtesy the Indian Institute of Research in Numismatic Studies, Anjaneri, Nashik.

equal footing with themselves rather than elevate it by deification. Thus lion cults, if any, did not acquire the same levels of proliferation in India as did tiger cults. None exists in the Gir or in Kathiawari or Gujarati traditions. There are many lion-headed deities in Buddhism, but the closest the animal has come to being a Hindu godhead is the Narasimha incarnation which remains in the iconography of Hindu gods but is not popularly worshipped per se. The lion of course is the mount of Goddess Durga of the Hindu pantheon, and vigorously continues to be so to the present day in spite of common aberrations where the goddess finds her original maned mount replaced by a striped one!

The lion assumed importance in art and sculpture way beyond its natural range in historical times. This was a result of its perceived qualities identifiable with the desirable qualities of a king and its position as the mount of Durga, but most importantly because of its association with the Buddha. Buddhism under Ashoka acquired the position of the state religion. His empire extended deep into the southern reaches of the peninsula. During Mauryan times and under the Kushanas, notably under Kanishka, the religion became a powerful export to East Asia. With it went the symbolism of the lion.

There is another probable reason. Vedic hymns spread far and wide over much of India as did the Sanskrit language. The latter became the court language of the Hindu kings in India and overseas. Both these sources so familiar with the lion, would have transported it beyond its historical range. Thus today one "Asian Tiger" is a lion city – Singapore, and the island nation of Sri Lanka, *Simhala dvipa*, the island of lions, proudly flies a flag with a passant lion holding a sword.

Over the centuries, the style, shape, size, and accuracy of depiction of the lion changed with the art forms of the styles of various kingdoms and empires. A study of these would be a subject by itself. These depictions do not tell us much of the life of the animal but only reconfirm, over and over again, its importance in the art and culture of India and its inseparable identification with royalty and royal virtues.

CHAPTER 5

Under the Delhi Sultanate

Throughout its history India has been exposed to several foreign influences which manifested themselves in architecture, sculpture, coinage, and language. Simultaneously the traditional cultures and religious callings of the people of India continued to evolve and assimilate new ideas. Besides Hinduism and regional beliefs, two other major faiths, Jainism and Buddhism, were born and prospered on Indian soil. By the middle of the 7th century Islam had been established as a religion. The Arabs had traded with Indian ports for a long time prior to this; however, Islam as a political force was to enter India by way of the conquest of Sind by Muhammad bin Qasim in 712–713 who defeated Dhir, the son of Chach, the usurper brahman ruler of the region, and married the former's wife.[1]

While conquest of a portion of India by a foreign power was nothing new, there was a unique element here. This invasion marked the beginning of the establishment of a religion which had its origins outside India and which came to have a major influence on the subcontinent. Under Islamic rule, the lions of India encountered a new culture born in a foreign land but which had come to stay. To these rulers the lion was no stranger, as it flourished in their homelands. Arabic, Turki, and Persian cultures interacted with local traditions and as we shall discover, lion imagery evolved through synthesis over the centuries.

The period from the 11th century onwards saw the rise and fall of invaders, rulers, and dynasties – from Mahmud of Ghazni and Mohammed Ghori to the Delhi Sultanate founded by Qutb-ud-din Aybak, followed by the Khaljis, Tughluqs, and Lodis. Material relating to the lion from this period is scanty, most of it being from literary sources.

The Islamic invaders continued to hunt as they had done in their own countries, and as their pre-Islamic ancestors had. They even invoked God in their enterprise. 'Isami who wrote his history of India in the middle of the 14th century gives an account of a hunt of Mahmud of Ghazni who attacked India in 1000:

> One day, I am told, the king rode into the desert intending to hunt. In the course of his hunt ranging over a few *parasang*s (administrative units), he stripped mountains and deserts of wild animals. Then a deer sprang before him; and immediately on seeing it he left his troops and guards. In its pursuit he galloped his horse with lion-like boldness. On drawing close to the deer he pulled an arrow from his quiver and shot it.... Thereupon he dismounted from the horse and slaughtered the game citing the name of God. This done, he withdrew and rode back to his own camp.[2]

'Isami records that Qutb-ud-din Aybak who ruled Delhi from 1206 to 1210 rode out of his palace sometimes to go to the race ground or to hunt and

> It looked as if his polo-stick ball had consumed the ball of the earth and the surface of the earth had been stripped of Game.[3]

To the Sultans of Delhi, hunting was a normal royal activity. Iltutmish (1211–36), Balban (1266–87), and Ala-ud-din Khalji (1296–1316) were keen falconers and they went hawking with eagles in winter. They were said to be not fond of big game, while Kayqubad (1287–90) was known to be keen on the chase with his hounds.[4]

A hunt of Mubarak Khalji (1316–20) when he went in the direction of Badaon from Delhi which lasted two to three months is illustrative of the enterprise. He had with him sparrowhawks, kites, falcons, hawks, and "two to three thousand deer-hunting panthers".[5] The reference is obviously to cheetahs though their number is greatly exaggerated. Even the great emperor Akbar, who had far greater resources than the Khalji king, did not have more than a thousand cheetahs at the height of his reign. 'Isami who wrote about the hunt thirty years after the event recorded that the destruction of game was so complete that

> If today anybody visits that meadow where the emperor had hunted in those days, one would find the land, from end to end, to a distance of several *parasangs* full of bones. The royal troops hunted so much game, neither an animal will be born nor will a leaf of grass sprout in that hunting ground till the Day of Judgement.[6]

For elsewhere, in this case in the Deccan, Ala-ud-din Hasan Bahman Shah (1347–58) went on a hunting expedition on his march which continued for a month and which left "the desert and mountains stripped of game and heaven fell into a trance".[7]

Falconry and hunting with hounds were practices equally known in India earlier. However, total destruction of game appears to be the hallmark of this period, a new facet of the royal pastime. At the same time the keen sense of documentation which the Turki, Arabic, and Persian writers had, meant that their records were far clearer than most previous Indian sources. The latter were literary or generic, they were rarely factual or empirical in the strict sense.

From the records it appears that Firoz Shah Tughluq (1351–88) was the keenest hunter of the Sultanate period. He was particularly keen on big game such as tigers, lions, wolves, bears, various species of deer, wild dogs, and antelope.[8] *Tarikh-i Firuz Shahi* of Shams Siraj 'Afif, a contemporary writer, gives the following account:

> Since the monarch, the Elect of the Merciful Lord God, was interested in hunting matters, during his reign he took game of various sorts and devoted much effort to this, taking innumerable game of every kind. He had obtained beasts of prey of every variety. Of the single class of cheetahs and leopards (*yuz u palang*) [in all probability a manuscript error for *yuz palang* i.e. cheetah], he gathered so many that it is beyond computation, and of the class of caracal (*siyah gush*), so many that it cannot be stated in writing, and of the class of dogs so many that it surpassed all comparison. Indeed, during his reign, by the inspiration of the Lord God, Sultan Firoz Shah acquired a number of lions (*shir*).* And of the hawks (*baz*) [in this case the reference is likely to be to goshawks, *Accipiter gentilis* as other birds of prey have been identified separately], peregrine falcons (*bahri*) [*Falco peregrinus calidus*], red headed merlins (*turumtay*) [*Falco chiquera chiquera*], red-capped or barbary falcons (*Shahin*) [barbary falcon, *Falco peregrinus babylonicus* is a rare visitor, whereas *shahin*, *Falco peregrinus peregrinator* is the resident bird commonly used for falconry and is the bird referred to here], *simtans* [?silver-bodied hawks of some kind] and the like there came to be so many that it cannot be brought within the grasp of human comprehension or imagination. All these rending and rapacious animals were entrusted to servants (*bandagan*). Following each animal were two or three servants to take care of them, and all these animal keepers used to go on mounted horses.[9]

Firoz Shah's hunting establishment was large. The foregoing passage testifies to the fact that he was a keen falconer, he coursed blackbuck with cheetahs, and flushed birds of several species with the caracal. The presence of lions in his menagerie is undeniable; however they would have been a symbol of royalty, rather than serving

---

* The Persian word for lion is *shir* whereas the word for tiger is *babr*. In the India of today most people think the other way around. Maharaja Ranjit Singh was called *Sher-e-Punjab*, the lion, not tiger, of Punjab, and even the late Sheikh Abdullah, former Chief Minister of Jammu and Kashmir, was often styled *Sher-e-Kashmir*, the Lion of Kashmir, even though there were no lions in that state!

جنگ آغاز نهادند و خون از جانبین روان سد

The Lion kills Shanzaba
■ Sultanate-Lodi period, 1492. An
illustration from *Kalilah-wa-Dimnah*,
the Arabic translation of the story of the
Lion and the Bull from the *Panchatantra*.
Courtesy National Museum, New Delhi.

Hunting scene
■ Illustration from a *Shahnama*, Parsa, Jaunpur, Sultanate-Lodi period, 1501. Hunting lions from horseback appears to have been a common practice from Persia. The hunter here could well be Bahram Gur who hunted in this fashion. (See Chapter 2.)
Spencer Collection, The New York Public Library, Astor, Lenox, and Tilden Foundations.

any other purpose such as being used for the hunt. Ziya 'ud-Din Barani, the author of another *Tarikh-i Firuz Shahi*, eulogizes the king's prowess in hunting saying that even a lion prostrates himself before the king "curving his back like the horns of a stag" and owing to the desire of "the lion of the earth" (the king) to hunt, "the lion of the sky" (the lion) cries to God for help to rescue him!¹⁰

'Isami uses the lion simile often to describe the valour of generals and kings. Thus in an account of the installation of Raziya as queen in 1236, he writes of how she sat on a golden throne while

> Before her stood the harem like servants attending on kings – inside the seraglio all the women, and outside it the lion-conquering men [generals and officers of the Sultanate]. The chiefs bent their heads, fully resolved to carry out her orders.¹¹

Zafar Khan the general of Ala-ud-din Khalji is described as "slayer of lions and captor of demons".[12] When Ulugh Khan the brother of Ala-ud-din failed to take the fort of Ranthambhore in 1299, "the brave Hindu Rai Hammir" was described by 'Isami as "having resisted like a lion in the forest; and by his wisdom he frustrated all the plans devised by the Turks".[13]

During Ala-ud-din Khalji's reign the Mongols invaded India thrice but were routed. 'Isami somewhat fancifully quotes the Sultan contemplating their defeat and saying to himself:

These people [the Mongols] of impure faith are like dogs in the hour of battle.
A ferocious lion does not pursue a dog particularly where it has taken to flight.
Furthermore, their look is inauspicious; and it behoves not a wise man to cast a
glance at them. As for me, there can be no gains greater than ceasing to look at
them.[14]

Similarly 'Isami describes Ala-ud-din Hasan Bahman Shah who had set up his headquarters at Gulbarga, contemplating some of his intransigent subjects as being not worthy of immediate attention:

Victorious kings do not lay severe hands on the afflicted. Lions who hunt elephants
do not go in for a fight with the fox. The class of people who are scattered about in
my territory are unto me like a prey, sure to fall into my hands, whenever I like.[15]

'Isami also records a dream the king had at Daulatabad in which he chanced upon a lion while on horseback. He cut it in half with a sword given to him by a "good looking man". He ordered that the lion should be cut up into its several body parts which were then to be distributed to all his generals around the country so that they would be reinvigorated by this action in various ways. The chief who received the lion's paw would feel strong enough to crush a lion-like foe. A chieftain to whose share came the breast of the lion or its loins would feel equal to piercing the breast or back of such a foe. Similarly, the chiefs who got in their share the palate, the tongue, or the thigh would be likewise emboldened to attack the corresponding part of the enemy. When the king woke up, he interpreted the dream as a good omen, because to him the fearless lion he had killed represented an enemy who was subdued by his sword.[16] In the event however he was not so lucky!

Under the Delhi Sultanate, the lion was hunted by kings and nobles, and this activity was considered an act of bravery. Equally importantly the lion as a powerful beast was closely associated with a brave king or a general in battle, and as a dignified beast its behaviour was compared to the magnanimity of kings. Even a brave or chivalrous enemy was likened to the lion.

However, one new element in hunting wild animals is recorded for the first time during this period, that is their relentless pursuit and total destruction when encountered. Mahmud Khalji the Sultan of Malwa (1436–69) even went to the extent of ordering his officers to destroy all tigers and leopards in his kingdom as they posed a threat to his human subjects.[17] It is not clear if lions received special protection under the Delhi Sultanate, but the similies freely used by 'Isami would suggest that they were not strictly royal game to be meddled with only by royal permission or sufferance, but that noblemen had freer access to their hunting.

Thus the Sultans of Delhi brought in some new hunting practices while existing ones still carried on and evolved. There was also continuity in the imagery of the lion over the centuries leading up to the period of the Mughal empire which was to follow.

CHAPTER 6

The Great Mughals Go Hunting Lions

THE POLITICAL TURMOIL of Central Asia had many a Timurid prince fighting for his piece of inheritance. Zahiruddin Muhammad Babar of Fargana was no exception, in spite of his illustrious lineage from Timur on the paternal side and Genghis Khan on the maternal. However, there was another unique quality in the man, his inexhaustible energy to conquer and ambition to find himself a permanent place in the sun, which ensured his success in his endeavour for political power.

Born in 1483, Babar's life until 1526 was based in Central Asia and was nomadic in the extreme. Thrice he took Samarkand and thrice he had to leave; consequently his attention turned south, to Kabul and the ever-tempting plains of Hindustan. He made five excursions into Hindustan, the final one in 1526. As the successor of Timur, Babar sent Ibrahim Lodi a goshawk (*qarchigha*) along with a letter demanding his kingdom.[1] The Lodi king did not oblige and the rest, as they say, is history.

Babar lived barely four years after his success at Panipat, but these years and his death while still in India ensured that his son Humayun (1508–56) and later successors would stay and consolidate his conquests. His place in the annals of Asia is assured by his founding the great Mughal dynasty alone, but he is unique also in having maintained a diary and recorded his memoirs, a feat unheard of during his time. Written in his native Chaghatai Turki, it was the forerunner of the imperial accounts commissioned by his grandson Akbar (1542–1605), and the memoirs of his great grandson Jahangir (1569–1627) who chose to write in his own hand in Persian, the court language of his time. Both Babar's and Jahangir's memoirs are remarkable for their candour and for leaving behind a firsthand account of their times. Jahangir referred to the *Babarnama* in his own memoirs and lamented that though his ancestor described what he saw, he left no visuals for the record. The reigns of Shah Jahan (1627–58) and Aurangzeb (1658–1707) were recorded by their courtiers, apart from European travellers who left their own travelogues of the fabulous empire. While this is a firsthand corpus of information of the times, there is yet another, of equal importance, from which one can learn a great deal about the period.

With the return of Humayun from Persia to Kabul, miniature paintings of the Mughal school had their nascent beginning, for he recruited Mir Sayyid Ali, Abd as-Samad, and Dust Muhammad, the principal artists from the court of Shah Tahmasp. The first two came to Hindustan when Humayun returned in 1555. With the continuous and plentiful supply of paper produced at Sialkot, Lahore, and Daulatabad, paintings on a large scale became possible for the first time. Under Akbar who set up an atelier at his court, Mughal painting attained maturity, and under Jahangir it reached its zenith particularly as far as studies of animals and birds were concerned. Though Shah Jahan and Aurangzeb were preoccupied with other concerns, both have left behind visuals of the highest quality and in sufficient numbers to give us a glimpse of their lifestyle including shikar. It is to these sources along with the written records that we must turn to find the lion's position under the Great Mughals.

Issuing forth from the northern fastness of Central Asia and Afghanistan, Babar found Hindustan different from the lands he had known. In his memoirs he describes the country he had conquered and its people. A keen hunter, he was intrigued by the animals and birds that he encountered which he had not known in his own homeland. His descriptions of Indian fauna and avifauna are unique and a worthy forerunner of his eclectic great-grandson Jahangir's descriptions penned over

Akbar on a hunt
■ Mughal 1598–1600.
Akbar slays the lion with an arrow
while it is hunting a wild ass. This
is the only painting in the public
domain showing Akbar hunting
lions.
Courtesy National Museum, New Delhi.

three-quarters of a century later. Babar's descriptions for instance of the peacock, the rhinoceros, and other animals or birds he saw are hard to beat.

Important to our story is the fact that Babar does not mention the lion and says little about the tiger; he was probably familiar with these animals as they were not peculiar to Hindustan. Though he records having killed a tiger,[2] there is no mention of a lion being pursued.

Humayun's intermittent reign was fraught with many a calamity and was finally cut short by an untimely accident. The chronicles of his times were committed to paper years after his death by his daughter and also his ewer-bearer, at the command of Akbar. These throw no light on his interactions with lions. But before we come to Akbar we need to take a look at the size of the Mughal entourage which had grown to immense proportions.

Akbar's consolidation of his domains and his benevolent rule saw the emergence of a fabulously rich empire. The three centres of imperial governance at Agra and Fatehpur Sikri, Delhi, and Lahore came to acquire a grandeur all their own, further embellished by his successors. The Mughal capital or centre of power moved with the emperor – to one of the three cities where the emperor was in residence at any given time, or wherever the imperial cavalcade camped en route, or for that matter anywhere in their far-flung domains. Sir Thomas Roe, Ambassador of King James I of England, records that when Jahangir broke camp to move from Ajmer in 1616 after a stay of three years, his encampment had so acquired the trappings of permanence that "The King gave orders to fire all the *leskar* (camp followers) at Adsmere to compel the people to follow, which was dayly executed...."[3] In 1633 Peter Mundy saw the ruins of many buildings as a result. Sir Thomas Roe estimated that the imperial

camp on the move took twelve hours to pass a spot and when the tents were pitched
– the process took only four hours – "... the circuitt being little less then 20 english
mile, the length some wayes three course, comprehending the skirts...."[4] Jahangir
himself estimated that it would require 100,000 buffaloes of Banjara tribesmen to
keep the large army supplied with grain on its march from Multan to Kandahar since
there was little cultivation in the regions of the army's march.[5]

When the Mughal emperors moved with such large entourage, their pleasure
spots had to be easily accessible from their camps, so it was natural that the imperial
hunting grounds were located in the plains. Irfan Habib lists sixteen such locations[6]
including such celebrated ones as Rupbas and Bari near Agra, Bhatinda and Sunam
in the Punjab, and Jodhpur and Merta in Rajasthan. This meant that the Mughals
were moving about in or near the most preferred habitat of the lion, the vast
grasslands and scrublands of northern India. Francois Bernier who travelled through
the Mughal empire between 1656 and 1668 has left a graphic description of the
Mughal hunting grounds during the time of Aurangzeb:

> I could never conceive how the Great Mughal could hunt with an army of one
> hundred thousand men; but there certainly is a sense in which he may be said to
> hunt with two hundred thousand, or with any number of which his army may
> consist.
>
> In the neighbourhood of Agra and Delhi, along the course of the *Gemna* [Yamuna],
> reaching to the mountains, and even on both sides of the road leading to Lahor,
> there is a large quantity of uncultivated land, covered either with copse wood or
> grasses six feet high. All this land is guarded with the utmost vigilance; and
> excepting partridges, quails, and hares which natives catch with nets, no person, be
> he who he may, is permitted to disturb the game, which is consequently very
> abundant.
>
> Whenever the Monarch is about to take the field, every gamekeeper [*gardes
> chasse*] near whose district the army is to pass is called upon to apprise the Grand
> Master of the Hunt of the various sorts of game under his particular charge, and
> of the places where they are in the greatest plenty. Sentries are then stationed at
> the different roads of that district, to guard the tract of ground selected, which
> extends sometimes four or five leagues; and while the army is on the march on one
> side or the other, so as to avoid that tract, the king enters it with as many *Omrahs*
> [nobles] and other persons as have liberty to do so, and enjoys, leisurely and
> uninterruptedly, the sports of the field, varying them according to the nature of the
> game.[7]

A favourite method of hunting was the Qamargha, the *battue*, an ever-decreasing
circle of men, in this case the army, which would enable the emperor and his chosen
nobles to hunt from horseback to their hearts' content. A variation of this method
was the Shakhbandh which was a stockade. In these methods of hunting the objects
of the pursuit would be usually ungulates and lesser carnivores. In one such, a
stockade at Lahore, Akbar hunted for five days in 1567 and the bag included chital,
nilgai, hare, hyena, jackal, and blackbuck run down by trained cheetahs – as can be
seen from the paintings commemorating the event.[8] Among the other favourite
forms of sport at the time were coursing with trained cheetahs and hawking, both of
these being pursued by the Mughals till the end of the dynasty's rule.

However, neither the Qamargha nor the Shakhbandh was suitable for hunting
large carnivores. It was too dangerous to corner these animals in the chaos and

confusion of other animals and men, for they could attack the hunters at close quarters. Lions were royal game and could be hunted only by the emperor and with his permission by the notables in the empire. Thomas Roe had to take Jahangir's permission to tackle a troublesome lion[9] and Francois Bernier records from Aurangzeb's reign that

> ... of all the diversions of the field the hunting of the lion is not only the most
> perilous but is peculiarly royal; for except by special permission, the king and
> princes are the only persons who engage in the sport.[10]

Thomas Roe reports that the imperial standard sported a couchant lion and the rising sun.[11] A painting by Payag from the *Padshahnama*, the chronicle of Shah Jahan's reign by Abdul Hamid Lahawri preserved in the Royal Library, Windsor Castle, depicts the siege of Qandahar in the Deccan in 1631 by Shah Jahan's army led by Nasiri Khan. The imperial standards are scarlet pennants with green borders with a passant lion and a rising sun behind it in each of them.[12] Another *Padshahnama* painting by the "Kashmiri Painter", of Shah Jahan's royal procession in 1655, clearly shows pennants which have a field of green with a couchant lion and the sun rising behind it in each.[13] This symbolism is ancient and was common in older Persian imagery; it also has echoes of the Hindu sun worship and the lion's association with Hindu royalty and divinity. No doubt the Mughals took these symbols from their own cultural past, but they must have been aware that the lion and the sun held a special place in the tradition of royalty preceding them in India.

Emperor Akbar maintained an account of the game he had shot and even the records of the guns used for the hunt were kept.[14] Jahangir too was equally meticulous. In the eleventh year of his reign he records that in a span of 39 years, as many as 28,532 animals and birds were hunted in his presence of which he himself accounted for 17,167. Lions take pride of place for they appear at the top of the list of the tally and he records that he had shot 86 of them.[15] Not surprisingly, one of the finest studies of an animal in Mughal painting is a painting of the Jahangir period, "Lion drinking water after devouring its kill" attributed to Nanha circa 1618, preserved at the Sawai Man Singh II Museum, Jaipur.[16] The painting is realistic to a high degree in its depiction of the animal, its environment and its prey a bull, or a cow, the remnants of which are being sequestered by a jackal! But in the hunting field the animal was pursued with vigour and its successful shikar was a matter of good omen. Bernier records the following:

> You must know, then, that as it is considered a favourable omen when the king
> kills a lion, so is the escape of that animal portentious of infinite evil to the state.
> Accordingly the termination of the hunt is attended with much grave ceremony.
> The king being seated in the general assembly of the *Omrahs*, the dead lion is
> brought before him, and when the carcass has been accurately measured and
> minutely examined, it is recorded in the royal archives that such a king on such a
> day slew a lion of such a size and of such a skin, whose teeth were of such a length,
> and whose claws were of such dimensions, and so on down to the minutest detail.[17]

Though the weighing and measuring of lions with extreme care was the established Mughal practice, as reported by Bernier, just one record made by Jahangir survives. When the emperor encountered and shot an exceedingly large lion near Rahimabad between Delhi and Agra on December 22, 1623, he took great care to have it weighed and its length measured from the top of its head to the tip of its tail: He noted that in his entire hunting career he had not come across such a large, magnificent, or well proportioned animal. As was his practice he ordered the imperial painters to take its likeness,[18] as he had done several times before when he came across a rare or magnificent bird or animal, such as the turkey, the zebra, or barbary falcon.

It is regrettable that no other such records are available, as much information about these cats could have been extracted from them. The lion shot by Jahangir weighed eight and a half Jahangiri maunds or 255 kilograms (1 Jahangiri maund = 30.10 kilograms[19]). It was three and a half cubits (*zar-i-shari*) and two *tasu* long, i.e. 9 feet 4 inches or about 2.85 metres (1 cubit = 31.7 inches and 1 *tasu* = 1.33 inches[20]). The weight range of a lion is between 145 and 225 kilograms.[21] Jahangir's lion was obviously heavier than usual whereas in length it would be among the larger trophies recorded.[22] From Jahangir's description it is clear that he had the animal measured and not its skin which could have yielded a longer result.

Before we go further it is necessary to examine the words used for the lion and the tiger in the chronicles of the times. The Persian word for the lion is *shir* while it is *babr* for the tiger.[23] The two animals have distinct words, with no hint of confusion in the minds of Mughal emperors or their chroniclers. In India however, by the time the Urdu language got round to recognizing the big cats, the issue got mixed up. By the 19th century therefore the word *babbar* or *babbar sher* came to mean lion in Urdu/Hindustani, and the word *sher* meant tiger – in any case by the second half of the 19th century the latter was largely the only one to survive in the Hindi-speaking belt. (In Sanskritized Hindi the word is *simha* for lion, *bagh* for tiger.) The translators of the Mughal texts who were working in north India in the second half of the 19th century or later paid more attention to the political, social, and other aspects of what the texts contained as far as the accuracy of the translations was concerned. They simply translated *shir* as tiger without much ado.[24] They were also misled by their familiarity with Hindustani in which the word *sher* is used for both lion and tiger, such usage being common even today. In contrast, the Mughal emperors and their chroniclers were closer to nature than their British translators living in presidency towns such as Calcutta or smaller "stations" and they knew what they were seeing and recording.

If we look at the locations where Akbar or Jahangir came across the big cat the picture becomes clear. Akbar encountered it at Mathura and Mewat near Delhi; Jahangir records his encounters with it at Bak Bhal and Nag Thal near Bari, near Dholpur, Palam (the site of the international airport at Delhi), Rupbas near Agra, Ajmer, and Mandu where, as we shall see, Thomas Roe had his problems with a lion. These were all grassland and scrub at the time, which was the preferred habitat of the lion. There may have been stray tigers but they were not likely to have been encountered in groups as described by the Mughals. Of the 33 wild species of the family *Felidae*[25] the lion is the only gregarious cat; the tiger is a solitary creature as a rule except when a female is with cubs.

Another noteworthy fact is that there are no Mughal paintings in the public domain depicting a tiger hunt except one of "Emperor Aurangzeb hunting tigers", a late 18th century version of a Mughal original circa 1780–90, Lucknow, at the National Museum, Karachi; or the study of the tiger as an animal per se. There is one which records the chance encounter of Akbar in 1561 near Narwar in central India when a family of five tigers, two of which were "white", attacked his cavalcade. The event is recorded for all time with a double-page illustration in the *Akbarnama* and Abul Fazl uses the correct Persian word for them, *babri* in the text.[26] Dr Asok Kumar

Jahangir shows his hunting skills

■ Mughal, 1615.
This famous incident took place near Ajmer where Jahangir shot the lioness in the eye as requested by Prince Karan of Mewar. Jahangir uses a matchlock, not a bow and arrow.
Courtesy The Indian Museum, Kolkata.

Das has shown that there are more than thirty paintings of the Mughal period in the public domain depicting a lion, a lion hunt, or a dead lion. It is equally noteworthy that not one illustration in any of the paintings is of a hunt from a machan, unlike the depictions in Kotah paintings where the quarry, either lion or tiger, was hunted in dense jungle rather than grassland or scrub thus necessitating the perch for the safety of the royal sportsman. The open scrub jungles and grasslands were easily accessible from the huge Mughal camps and they usually contained lions, not tigers.

The absence of paintings of tigers does not suggest that the Great Mughals did not hunt them. The *Muraqqa-e-Gulshan* (Gulshan Album) was prepared for Emperor Jahangir between 1605 and 1610 and some folios were added in 1616 and 1617. The album is now dispersed, the bulk of it being preserved at the Gulistan Palace Library, Tehran, with some folios in the Staatsbibliothek, Berlin and the Nelson Atkins Museum of Art, Kansas City. Dr Das who has examined the Tehran folios and studied others, points to the *hashiyas* or margins of the album's folios. They contain monochrome drawings in black and gold which depict hunting scenes. Among them are a tiger behind a hilly outcrop, a tiger killing a spotted deer, a Rajput nobleman shooting a tiger with a gun, a Mughal prince hunting one of a pair of tigers with bow and arrow from horseback. There are also two drawings of a dead tiger being loaded on a saddled elephant.[27] However, barring such exceptions, the absence of paintings per se of tiger hunts and of such descriptions in chronicles testify to the lion's central position in Mughal hunts, while the tiger remained marginal.

A miniature painting has recently been published for the first time, titled "Akbar on a Tiger Hunt" from the *Akbarnama*. A close look at the feline being speared by Akbar's entourage and watched by the emperor from elephantback shows uniform stripes on its body, a leonine mane, a cheetah-like tearline on its face, and a tail which has no feline characteristics.[28] It is obviously a composite animal. Dr Das feels that the painting is of recent origin.[29]

According to his memoirs, Jahangir came across a "*shir babar*" at Giri near "Kaliyadaha" – Kaliyadoh is the current name – in the neighbourhood of Ujjain. Having shot it, he had it opened to find the location of the gall bladder of the animal and it occurred to him that its location within its liver may be a source of its ferocity![30] Both Rogers and Beveridge and Wheeler Thackston translate the Persian word "*shir babr*" as lion but the accurate rendering would be tiger.[31] Wheeler Thackston's translation of Jahangir's memoirs has otherwise consistently and correctly translated the word *shir* as lion. A person with Jahangir's extensive and detailed interest in nature was not likely to make a mistake in the name of the animal he encountered. It may be recalled that he describes at great length other animals and birds that caught his fancy.

There are two instances of Akbar hunting lions which have been recorded in the *Akbarnama*.[32] In 1562 he went lion hunting near Mathura in UP. He chanced upon a pride of seven lions. Abul Fazl records that "five were levelled with the dust by arrow and bullet and one that repository of courage caught alive and so was a subject of a thousand wonderment". The seventh lion he mentions was caught by the combined efforts of Akbar's courtiers. However, he does not describe how the lions were caught. The second incident took place in the Mewat region near Alwar in present-day Rajasthan, in 1568 when Akbar was travelling from Ajmer to Alwar. While out hunting, a lion emerged from the reed bed and was quickly slain by a hail of arrows.

Prince Khurram attacking a lion
■ Painting from the *Padshahnama*,
by Balchand, circa 1640.
The famous incident which took place at
Bari in 1610, where courtier Anup Rai
saved the life of Emperor Jahangir.
Prince Khurram is about to strike the
lion which has pinned down Anup Rai;
the emperor is on the right.
*The Royal Collection ©2002 Her Majesty
Queen Elizabeth II.*

Akbar was most upset and ordered that should another lion come out he would
tackle it himself. At that very moment another lion did come out. Akbar shot it in
the eye with an arrow, but still the animal advanced and sat in such a position that
Akbar could not get a good shot even though he dismounted from his horse. In the
excitement of the moment a courtier shot an arrow which infuriated the lion who
mauled him. The animal had to be finished off by the other courtiers.[33]

In the *Ain-i-Akbari* Abul Fazl records two more instances of Akbar hunting lions.
One incident occurred in Bari where a man-eater attacked Akbar's elephant, and had

Shah Jahan hunting lions near Burhanpur
■ Painting from the _Padshahnama_, attributed to Daulat, circa 1635. Shah Jahan and his entourage hunt from elephantback harnessed with open howdahs which would increase manoeuvrability. The nets are used to confine the quarry, not to prevent them from jumping onto the elephant.
The Royal Collection ©2002 Her Majesty Queen Elizabeth II.

to be killed by his men. In another instance near Mathura, a lion came out to attack when one of Akbar's courtiers, Shujaat Khan, approached too close. But Akbar was able to subdue the lion with just a furious look: "The brute cowered down before that divine glance, and turned right about trembling all over. In a short time it was killed." [34]

There is only one painting of Akbar hunting a lion known to us. Preserved in the National Museum, Delhi, the painting titled "Akbar on a hunt" is by an unknown artist and may be dated circa 1598–1600.[35] The middle of the painting has Akbar on

Aurangzeb hunting lions

■ Mughal, circa 1670–1700.
The emperor sits on an open howdah.
The line of elephants bearing the
imperial party follows a phalanx of
buffaloes which would act as a buffer in
case of a lion attack. Here too the quarry
is confined by nets and a lion attacks an
elephant in the background. The use of
buffaloes to follow up wounded lions or
tigers was practised till the 20th century.
*Reproduced by kind permission of the Trustees
of the Chester Beatty Library, Dublin.*

Dead lioness

■ Mughal, circa 1600.
The quarry is carried home in the time-
tested manner that continued till the end
of shikar in the second half of the 20th
century.
*Reproduced by permission of the Trustees of
the Victoria & Albert Museum, London.*

A lion's court
■ By Miskin, 1596–97.
This painting from the *Anwar-i-Suhaili* shows the lion as the king of the animal world – a position rarely accorded to the tiger.
Courtesy Bharat Kala Bhavan, Varanasi.

Study of a lion
■ This 18th-century Bikaner school painting is in sharp contrast to the painting attributed to Nanha, opposite. The animal is stylized and its mane appears to be in moult!
Courtesy Sudhir Kasliwal, Gem Palace, Jaipur.

a chestnut charger. He has just shot an arrow which has pierced the lion's abdomen and it is bleeding while it is in the act of killing a wild ass. On the lower left of the painting another wild ass is bolting from the scene of action. On the right-hand bottom of the painting are a group of courtiers that include Bairam Khan on a white horse, others carrying mace and gun, and a falconer with a falcon on his gauntlet. In front of Akbar's horse a male and a female blackbuck are leaping away along with other small animals which appear to be foxes and a hare. In the top right-hand corner are a group of men with hawks and a cheetah brought on horseback to the hunting grounds.

Though the painting has been dated circa 1598–1600, it pictures Akbar as a young man. From the foregoing passages we know that Akbar hunted lions with bow and arrow from horseback. The lion being killed while it is on its own kill of a wild ass is reminiscent of the painting of Bahram Gur hunting lions. While this may be a rendering of an actual occurrence, the presence of blackbuck, foxes, and a hare in such proximity to the lion suggests that the painting represents various events of a day's hunting or it is a collage of several hunts depicting Akbar's prowess in the field rather than a single event.

Akbar's bravery and fearlessness in the field have been recorded several times by his chroniclers. It is not at all surprising that he chose to hunt lions from horseback

Lion drinking water after devouring its kill
■ Attributed to Nanha, circa 1618.
The lion is accurately portrayed and the jackal stealing from the remnants of the kill is a fine touch of realism.
Courtesy Maharaja Sawai Man Singh II Museum, Jaipur.

The Shah hunting
■ Late 17th century.
The king, probably Shah Sulaiman of Persia, is out hunting with tame lions. This is the only record in the public domain of such sport.
From the St Petersburg Muraqqa, *after Kostioukovich, 1996.*

with bows and arrows and sometimes even on foot though guns were in common use in his time. His successors who inherited the grand empire, preferred the safer elephant and matchlocks for their lion hunts. (It is however interesting to note here that lions were speared from horseback by the British near Deesa in Gujarat in the 19th century.)

To Jahangir, the hunting grounds were a second home. His passion for the chase and his acute observations of flora and fauna from his memoirs have left us an incomparable record of this facet of his life and times. He could be as considerate as providing warm water for bathing the imperial elephants as they shivered in the cold or building a grand monument to his favourite blackbuck Mansraj at Shaikhupura near Lahore, and yet think nothing of ordering the execution of a servant for inadvertently interrupting his hunt. His records of game bagged show the variety of animals he shot, from the largest to the smallest. The lion hunt to him was special and it always featured at the top of his list. In February and March of 1610 he camped at Mandakar Garden near Rupbas. During his stay there of 56 days he accounted for 7 lions, 70 nilgai, 51 blackbuck, 82 other animals, 129 birds, and 1,023 fish![36] Again he records that over a period of three months at the beginning of 1611 he had accounted for twelve lions.[37] Here we get a clear glimpse of the lion's prey as well. Jahangir was hunting in open scrubland where he accounted for lions as well as their prey, nilgai and to a lesser extent blackbuck. It is interesting to note that he had hunted one lion per week in 1611, an indication of the abundance of these cats in the region. Of the several shikar events concerning lions recorded by him, some may be described here.

In February 1608 Jahangir was informed that lions were making a nuisance of themselves on the road between Panipat and Karnal in present-day Haryana. He went out to the spot, got onto a female elephant, and ordered the rest of the elephants to encircle the lions as in a Qamargha. Here was a quarry-specific variation of the large Qamarghas which used vast resources and in which all and sundry animals were taken. The method was successful and "by God's grace" the emperor was able to "eliminate the evil" of the pair of big cats that had harassed the people.[38] Elephants rather than any other animal were used for encirclement as they provided a perch from which the quarry could be seen, they were large enough to be respected by lions, and finally, they ensured a measure of safety to the imperial person.

Jahangir abstained from hunting with a gun on Sundays and Thursdays; yet when provoked he broke his own rule and it did not take much for him to do so. He records that on Sunday, March 2, 1617 while he was at Mandu, he was informed of the presence of a lion 3 *kos* away from the camp. He promptly rode out on an elephant and when he came to the spot he found the lion sitting under a tree. He fired from elephantback and killed it with one shot. The bullet entered its mouth leaving no external mark of injury. His retinue were baffled when they examined the animal's body, until Jahangir cleared up the mystery by pointing to its mouth.[39]

Jahangir also showed off his hunting skills to the young Mewar prince Karan who was at his court at Ajmer in 1615. On hearing of a lioness in the vicinity of his camp he went out to shoot it. He asked Karan where he should shoot the quarry. Karan indicated its eye. Jahangir obliged successfully, to the astonishment of all present. Jahangir knew that firing from elephantback which is not a steady perch, that too on a windy day and with a smooth bore musket, it was miraculous that the ball should

Ashrafi of Emperor Jahangir
■ One of the gold coins with zodiacal signs showing here the sign of Leo on the reverse, with calligraphy on the obverse.
Courtesy Bharat Kala Bhavan, Varanasi.

find its predetermined minute target. He was honest enough to record in his autobiography, "God almighty did not allow me to be ashamed before the prince, and as I had agreed, I shot her in the eye."[40]

Even for a Mughal emperor and for a keen marksman, things could and did go horribly wrong in a lion shoot. In 1610 when Jahangir was near Bari in Agra *suba*, one of his courtiers Anup Rai came across a half-devoured cow. Suddenly a lion came out of the thicket. It was promptly surrounded and the emperor was informed. Jahangir, Khurram, and others rushed to the spot. Jahangir set his musket on the stand and fired twice but missed as is not uncommon when it comes to judging the "elevation" of a bullet when firing from a height as Jahangir was doing. In the event, the lion charged, Jahangir's retinue bolted, and, according to him, some even trampled him in their flight! Anup Rai saved Jahangir's life by battling the lion almost with his bare hands, while Prince Khurram struck the animal with a sword. At the end of it the lion was dispatched and the emperor was saved. In recognition of his valour Jahangir gave Anup Rai the title of *Ani Rai Singhdalan* meaning commander of troops, lion crusher.[41] This incident shows the personal bonds between the Mughals and Rajputs which held the Mughal domains together until the early 1700s. The fact that Jahangir and Khurram were accompanied by a Rajput courtier in a hunt shows the trust and respect placed in him.

Hunting lions on foot was certainly not a recommended method for Mughal emperors and their family, unless of course the situation arose accidentally. There is an unpublished painting from the personal collection of Maharaja Sawai Bhavani Singh of Jaipur which has been examined by Dr Asok Kumar Das. He dates it circa 1600, it is by an unknown artist and it shows unmistakably a young Jahangir. It depicts a night scene where a remarkably accurately drawn male lion has attacked an attendant of Jahangir in the left hand side of the painting. Though the lion has pinned him down, the attendant is about to plunge a dagger into his tormentor. The night scene is lit by two torch bearers behind the lion while a third holds his torch down near the lion's body as if to illuminate it for Jahangir who stands slightly to the right of the lion. He is about to strike the lion – his arms are raised and he holds a sword. An attendant stands beside him with a mace-like staff in his hand. There is a hill in the background, and a few more torch bearers stand at the top right-hand corner of the painting. The incident is depicted in open country interspersed with tall grass. Hunting antelope, particularly blackbuck, at night with torches was known then. Was Jahangir out hunting antelope that night when his party surprised a lion?

Animals

■ Circa 1610.
An excellent study of the lion in the Jahangir period. On the top left-hand and right-hand corners the lion kills a nilgai and a chital respectively, both being part of the prey base of the lion.

From the St Petersburg Muraqqa, *after Kostioukovich, 1996.*

The painting has the moon partially covered by clouds – did Jahangir purposefully go after the lion on a moonlit night? Or is the painting entirely apocryphal? We do not know. What is certain, according to Dr Das, is that the painting is contemporaneous.[42]

On occasion there was even a romantic twist to a lion hunt. In April 1617 Jahangir went out lion hunting with his harem near Mandu. The party was on elephantback when four lions came out towards the elephants – presumably they were driven towards the hunters. Nurjahan asked permission of the emperor to shoot, which was readily granted. Two lions were dispatched with one shot each and the other two were accounted for by two bullets each, thus four lions were killed with six bullets. Considering that Nurjahan fired from a covered howdah with obviously restricted manoeuvrability, from a mobile, and therefore none too steady, elephant perch, and using a smooth bore musket, it was a truly remarkable feat of marksmanship. Jahangir was so pleased with the empress's hunting skill that he scattered a thousand *ashrafi*s over her head and gifted her a pair of pearls and a diamond worth a lakh of rupees.[43]

In his autobiography Jahangir referred to his father with the utmost reverence and yet if he had scored a point over him, he was quick to document it. For instance, he records that Akbar tried hard to get cheetahs to breed in captivity but failed though he had collected a thousand cheetahs. In the year 1613, however, a pair mated and three cubs were born at Jahangir's court. The emperor states that he has recorded the fact as it was strange.[44] In the same breath he goes on to record that in the benevolent reign of his times wildness had been eliminated, lions had become tame and were roaming in prides among people without the restraint of a chain, not harming them. This is farfetched and if such was indeed the case he would hardly have pursued them so vigorously in the field. However, the fact is that lions can be tamed easily and there is a painting by the artist Padarath depicting a young lion – it has a partially grown mane – being taken for a walk by a keeper, only lightly chained[45] in the manner of a not too aggressive canid. Jahangir notes further that he had heard from physicians that a lioness's milk was very good for the eyes. He tried to have a lioness who had given birth to three cubs milked, but did not succeed. He concluded that the milk could not be obtained owing to the irascible nature of the animal.[46]

As mentioned earlier, Jahangir had ordered a painting of the very large lion he had shot at Rahimabad, but the whereabouts of this painting, if it has survived, are not known. We may however look at another very remarkable work of his period. It is a painting entitled "Animals" in the *St Petersburg Muraqqa*.[47] It is a collage which Stuart Cary Welch calls a surrealistic *omnium gatherum*. The bottom of the painting has goats, sheep, and nilgai; in the lower centre portion a hound suckles one pup while the other two frolic about her. In the upper portion a cat suckles her three kittens. The artist is unknown but the cat with her kittens may have been painted by Abul Hasan according to Welch.[48] The painting has small figures of other animals, including an elephant attacked by a dragon-like creature. Of abiding interest is a couchant lion with the tip of the tail held high. The animal has been accurately rendered, its skin being the exact shade between dark yellow and brown, and its mane in darker brown with lighter hair around its face and sparse over its head as it should be – a characteristic of Indian lions. The tip of the tail is dark and the tuft prominent – another characteristic of the lion from India. Its mouth is slightly open, giving it a truly regal aspect. Of equal interest are the scenes at the top left and right

Maharao Umed Singh I of Kotah hunting lions
■ By Joshi Hathuwa, 1784.
The maharao, in *moongia* coloured shikar dress, accompanied by his courtiers hunts in a stockade in Alnia jungle unlike the classic Mughal hunts of this type which took place in open grasslands.
Courtesy M. Brijraj Singh, Chairman, Board of Trustees and other Trustees, Rao Madho Singh Trust Museum, City Palace, Kotah.

corners of the painting. On the left a lion is in the process of strangulating a nilgai with his hold on its neck. On the right a lion is in the process of bringing down a chital. These are both depictions of a lion's methods of killing its prey and in both cases the animals are its usual prey. The artist was not only a master of his craft but was also familiar with the hunting behaviour of the lion in the wild, which no doubt would have been appreciated by Jahangir's discerning eye.

Though Jahangir's autobiography is replete with instances of lion hunts, only two paintings can be identified with the incidents described there. One is the Anup Rai incident which has been painted several times, the most famous rendering being the one by Balchand circa 1640 in the *Padshahnama*. It shows Anup Rai under the lion, while Prince Khurram is about to strike it. One member of the party strikes the lion on its head with a stick, another has struck it with a sword on its hindquarters, yet another courtier looks on as does Jahangir himself.[49] The other is the incident when Jahangir shot a lioness in the presence of Prince Karan of Mewar.[50]

From these paintings we learn little of the techniques of hunting lions, since one was a chance encounter while another tells us that the shikar took place from elephantback. For this we turn to other sources. Bernier has left a firsthand account of what he saw in Aurangzeb's time (1658–1707). When a lion was located,

As a preliminary step, an ass is tied near the spot where the gamekeepers have ascertained the lion retires. The wretched animal is soon devoured, and after so ample a meal the lion never seeks for other prey, but without molesting either oxen, sheep or shepherds, goes in quest of water, and after quenching his thirst, returns to his former place of retirement. He sleeps until the next morning, when he finds and devours another ass, which the gamekeepers have brought to the same spot. In this way they contrive, during several days, to allure the lion and attach

Maharao Umed Singh I of Kotah hunting tigers
■ By Gumani, 1778.
Accompanied by Jhala Zalim Singh the maharao hunts in the Moti Paj jungle, Darah valley. Tigers and wild boar have been encircled in Qamargha fashion. The jungle here is much thicker than the one in the lion shikar painting.
Courtesy M. Brijraj Singh of Kotah.

him to one place; and when information is received of the King's approach, they fasten at the space an ass where so many have been sacrificed, down whose throat a large quantity of opium has been forced. This last meal is of course intended to produce a soporific effect on the lion.[51]

This time-honoured method, without the opium – Bernier himself states in the narrative that "it is a tale of the vulgar, and the lion is sufficiently disposed to sleep without it when he has eaten to satiety" – has been used in India by maharajas and nawabs for shikar and even in our own times when lions were "anchored" for census operations or for the "lion shows" which were staged until not so long ago for the benefit of tourists in the Gir forest. Bernier continues:

The next operation is to spread by the means of the peasantry of the adjacent villages, large nets, made on purpose, which are gradually drawn closer in the manner practised in hunting the nil-ghaux. Every thing being in this state of preparation, the king appears on an elephant protected in places with thin plates of iron, and attended by the Grand Master of the Hunt, some *Omrahs* mounted on elephants, and great numbers both of *gourze-berdar* on horse back and of gamekeepers on foot, armed with half pikes. He immediately approaches the net on the outside, and fires at the lion with a large musketoon. The wounded animal makes a spring at the elephant, according to the invariable practice of lions, but is arrested by the net; and the king continues to discharge his musketoon until the lion is at length killed.[52]

A painting attributed to Daulat and dated circa 1635 in the *Padshahnama*, "Shah Jahan hunting lions near Burhanpur"[53] illustrates this technique. There are three elephants. Shah Jahan is seated on the middle one, the howdah is designed for the hunt as it is open on all sides to enable the hunter to manoeuvre the gun in all directions. Shah Jahan has rested his musket on the shoulder of the mahout; if he were shooting on the ground, it would have rested on a tripod or a bipod. A lion, a lioness, and two cubs have been encircled by nets though, unlike in Bernier's description, Shah Jahan and the lions are on the same side of the net.

In the incident of Jahangir showing his hunting skills to Prince Karan, there is no sign of the net or for that matter any obstruction between the lioness and the imperial elephant. Colonel Kesri Singh, head of the Shikar Khana of Gwalior state in the 1930s and a renowned tiger hunter of his time, describes a tiger hunt with nets. The occasion was staged for the Columbia Broadcasting Corporation in 1958. In this event the tiger was driven to the nets by a Land Rover whereupon the animal was speared by the people surrounding the net from the outside.[54] Bernier's observation therefore may not have been a common practice, as when the lion was hunted from elephantback with a musket it could be dispatched from a safe distance, whereas keeping the net between the hunter and the hunted would be necessary while using a bow and arrow or using a long spear from elephantback. There are paintings however, of lions being speared without the use of a net by imperial Mughal hunters, as we have noted earlier in the case of a painting of Akbar.

In the hunting field methods of hunting had to be adapted to the circumstances pertaining to the hunting grounds, the quarry, and naturally the wishes of the hunter. In a painting of circa 1660 by an unknown artist, Emperor Shah Jahan and his four sons are depicted. The painting may be titled "Shah Jahan hunting lions with the four princes" and is in the collection of Edmund de Unger. The whole hunting party involving Shah Jahan and all his direct and nearest in the line of succession illustrates the importance of the event. The location of the hunt is unknown but the painting is described by Robert Skelton as follows:

> ... Emperor Shah Jahan ... can be identified [on] the penultimate elephant in a line of five, advancing from the left. The emperor is shown preparing to aim his matchlock at a lion which is attacking the elephant. The howdahs of the three elephants to the right of Shah Jahan contain the figures of his sons Murad Baksh (next to his father), Dara Shikoh, and Shah Shuja. The figure on the elephant to the left of Shah Jahan is evidently one of the leading amirs. On the right hand side of the nullah are three elephants, two taking part in the beat and the central one bearing a prince who can probably be identified as Aurangzeb, about to throw [sic] at a lion which has leaped on to his elephant. On the left bank, three buffaloes ... are advancing on the nullah. A lion springs from a thicket and another lion mauls a fallen shikari. In the background is a line of nets supported by poles enclosing the hunting field. The perimeter is patrolled by elephants and a solitary horseman rides in the distance.[55]

While the net is a feature of the hunt, here the hunters and the hunted are again on the same side of it. Also the presence of buffaloes is not an accident. These animals are used as "stops" to confine the lions in a more or less predetermined area. The use of "stops" in driving game in or towards the desired ground or on the flanks of a beat has been known in India well into our own times. This method was not unique to lion hunts alone, it was used by the Mughals for other game as well such as confining nilgai on the hunting ground, as in the painting of "Dara Shikoh shooting nilgais".[56]

Bernier records that Aurangzeb put his son Sultan Muazzam to a strange test to check out his obedience and courage. He ordered him to attack and kill a lion which

Maharao Durjan Sal of Kotah viewing a lion family
■ By Shevdar Gangeyaji, circa 1750. The maharao with Jhala Sheo Singh and the royal party have come upon a lion family at Joraki Beed. The lions are highly stylized and even the cubs have manes. The manes are much darker coloured than those in Mughal paintings. *Courtesy M. Brijraj Singh, Chairman, Board of Trustees and other Trustees, Rao Madho Singh Trust Museum, City Palace, Kotah.*

had been tracked down without the use of nets – that is without the help of confining the dangerous prey in an area which would give the advantage to the hunter. The prince obeyed, and in the event two or three men lost their lives, some horses were mangled, and the wounded lion jumped on Prince Muazzam's elephant before meeting its end.[57] Here was a peculiar Mughal variant of baptism by fire!

Bernier was also witness to a hunt in which a lion escaped Aurangzeb's gun. The whole army was deployed to locate the escaped beast, it was "subjected to great inconveniencies and thrown into a considerable degree of confusion" as a result and the march had to be halted for three or four days. There were no bazaars pitched at this place and many went hungry.[58] Bernier does not mention what happened to the lion, but its escape was considered a bad omen, just as the king's success in killing it would have been a favourable one. Was this a foreshadow of coming events? Aurangzeb's policies left a fractured legacy and the end of his reign saw the beginning of the decline of the Mughal empire.

Abul Fazl describes another method of hunting lions wherein a hunter rides a male buffalo and makes it attack a lion, the buffalo tossing the lion with its horns

■ Mewar school, 18th century. The animals are somewhat stylized, the lion being the most accurate though its mane is light coloured and artistic in execution rather than real.
Courtesy Bharat Kala Bhavan, Varanasi.

and killing it.[59] This is surely not a method recommended for the emperor or princes, but a variation of it was certainly in vogue. A painting titled "Aurangzeb hunting lions" circa 1670–1700 by an unknown artist, preserved in the Chester Beatty Library,[60] shows Aurangzeb and his entourage on three male elephants on the right-hand side of the painting. The elephants are behind a phalanx of ten buffaloes in front of which are a lion and lioness. Towards the top left is an elephant which has been attacked by a lion from the back; another elephant is crushing a lion with its tusks. The emperor is aiming his gun at the lion while sitting on an open howdah, with the stock of the matchlock resting on its frame. Almost an exact reproduction of the picture is found in a painting from Bikaner by Rashid dated circa 1693. The crucial difference is that the hunters are Maharaja Anup Singh of Bikaner and his three brothers[61] instead of the Mughal party! In both these paintings the hunters and the hunted are both within the nets.

In many ways the Great Mughals were no different from their predecessors. However, unlike the earlier sultans of Delhi, the lion to them was royal game. Though it was not spared in the hunting fields by them, no one else could meddle with it without their permission. It symbolized regal power and it sat proudly on their imperial standards. As was the case with everything they did, their shikar expeditions were larger than life. Their successors in the 18th century continued hunting but the pomp and circumstance progressively waned, until the last of the Mughals, Bahadur Shah Zafar, was exiled to Rangoon, Burma in 1858. The later Mughals were but a shadow of their fabulous predecessors, they could not be expected to add any new dimension to the courtly pursuit of hunting.

Jahangir did not describe a single lion in detail in his memoirs as he did, for example, the turkey, zebra, and barbary falcon. This is not surprising, as lions were plenty in his time, they were commonplace. It is estimated that the Agra *suba* at the heart of the Mughal empire had only 27.5 per cent land under cultivation in about 1600, and other *suba*s in the plains had even less.[62] The rest of the land was either uncultivable or cultivable wasteland. In other words the Mughal empire had large tracts which were suitable habitat for lions. They were numerous enough to be found almost everywhere the Mughal emperors went. They did not have to think of the Gir, the lion's present and only home in India. To them it was a far off corner in their domains and they estimated its area to be no more than 3 x 3 *kuroh*, that is just about 90 square kilometres![63]

But 200 years after Jahangir, lions had almost died out in India. The reasons for this are not far to seek. Unlike their Sultanate predecessors, the Great Mughals restricted the hunting of game animals and birds, and for the smaller creatures which could be snared they set aside large hunting grounds as well. With their eclipse, protection no longer remained effective. The lion was an easy target because of its gregarious nature and diurnal habits. The constant pursuit of this great cat in the field, along with steady encroachment into its habitat, took a heavy toll. The human population within the bounds of India had grown from an extrapolated/ estimated figure of 116 million in 1600 to 159 million in 1800.[64] Just before the last Mughal was to live out the final scene of the great drama, a single British officer is reported to have shot as many as 300 lions. Even if this figure was an exaggeration, which it probably was, we may recall that Emperor Jahangir with all his enthusiasm for the hunt and all the imperial resources at his command, had shot only 86 lions in a span of 39 years! What was left behind by the Mughals was about to be decimated by their successors.

CHAPTER 7

The British Come Calling

WITH THE DEATH OF Emperor Aurangzeb, the last of the Great Mughals in 1707, the fissures in the structure of empire became more than evident, they widened, and ultimately the edifice gave way. European traders had already established bases, and the successive wars among them and those with Indians saw much bloodshed, hardship, and suffering for the people in India. From these chaotic times the British came out winners with the Battle of Plassey in 1757 and the Battle of Buxar in 1764 which made the East India Company the dominant political power in the north. They had come a long way since they had set up their "factory", a trading outpost, at Surat in 1612 – when Emperor Jahangir was on the throne and the Mughal empire was at its zenith.

The British had met the Indian lion very early on. Ralph Fitch who visited Agra and Fatehpur Sikri during Emperor Akbar's reign had reported that the emperor's establishment at the two cities had "as they doe credibly report, one thousand Elephants, thirtie thousand Hourses, one thousand and four hundred tame Deer, eight hundred Concubines: such store of Ounces, Tygres, Buffles, Cockes and Hawkes, that it is very strange to see".[1] "Ounces" are cheetahs, of which there were a thousand at one point in the imperial collection. The word "tygres" was loosely used by European travellers to denote both lions and tigers and sometimes even smaller cats such as cheetahs.

The first "official" contact between India and England was made by Sir Thomas Roe, the ambassador of King James I to the Mughal court. Roe was in India between 1615 and 1619. He was presented to Emperor Jahangir at Ajmer in December 1615. The next year he saw a tame lion at the court and he describes the event thus:

> The King [Jahangir] commanded one of his brothers [Prince Daniyal's] sonnes ... to go strike a lyon on the head, which was brought before the king; but hee beeing afrayd refused yt. Soe the king bad his yongest sonne [Prince Sharyar] to go touch the lyon; who did so without any harme ... wheratt the king tooke occasion to send his nephew away to a prison where hee is never like to see day light![2]

Unlike his first encounter where he was only a spectator, the second one was more troublesome for Roe. The Mughal court with him in tow had moved to Mandu in 1617 where the ambassador had problems with marauders who were after his stocks of food:

> A lion and a woolfe used my house and nightly put us in alarume, fetching away sheeps and goats out of my court, and leaping a high wall with them. I sent to aske leave to kill it, for no man may meddle with lions but the king, and it was granted. I ranne out into the court upon the noyse and the beast, missing his prey, seized on a little Island dogge before me, that I had long kept. But the woolfe one of my servants killed, and I sent it the king.[3]

The lion escaped the English ambassador and thus began an uneasy relationship between the lion and the British, calamitous to the former. By 1947 just 200-odd lions survived.

Fifty years after the Battle of Plassey in 1757, as a result of which the East India Company was established as a temporal power, Captain Thomas Williamson's book on shikar made its appearance.[4] It was the first of its kind, extensively illustrated with forty coloured engravings. From tiger hunting to pig-sticking, the British took to "Oriental Field Sports" with great enthusiasm. Williamson's work being concerned with Bengal, lions do not feature in it. The pride of place among the hunted went to the tiger which came to be called the Royal Bengal tiger though there was nothing

The conquering British lion

■ (opposite) The Seringapatam Medal struck to commemorate the defeat of Tipu Sultan in 1799 has the "British" lion conquering Tipu's tiger.
The Trustees of The National Museums of Scotland.

■ (above) The Burma Medal struck to commemorate the victory of 1826 has the elephant of Ava properly deferential, crouching before the "British" lion.
Courtesy of the Director, National Army Museum, London.

■ (left) The Indian Mutiny Medal struck to commemorate the suppression of the revolt of 1857–58 has Britannia holding a wreath over the "British" lion signalling triumph.
Courtesy of the Director, National Army Museum, London.

Rampant Lions Reguardant
- The Arms of the "United" East India Company 1709.
- The Arms of Rajkumar College, Rajkot with the Sanskrit motto "*yasya buddhirbalam tasya*", "Knowledge is Power", 1870.
Author's collection.

uniquely regal about the animals from Bengal, they being no different from those of the rest of the country apart from regional morphological variations.

But the lion was not far behind. Sir Charles D'Oyly came out to India at the young age of seventeen in 1797. He became Registrar to the Court of Appeal at Calcutta and soon thereafter the Keeper of the Records of the Governor General. He held various other positions in India including Collector of Dacca from 1808–18; he lived in Patna between 1821 and 1831 as Opium Agent and from 1831 to 1833 as Commercial Resident. He was a remarkable artist and his work was much appreciated at the time.[5] Relevant here are his albums of watercolours on shikar.[6]

D'Oyly's two volumes of *Indian Sports* have 30 and 33 watercolours respectively, each of 10.5 x 14.5 centimetres. They depict British persons of means indulging in various types of shikar. The first watercolour is titled "Going Out" (for shikar) while the last, the 63rd, is titled "Coming Home". A quick analysis of the subjects of the paintings is revealing. There are nine paintings of hog hunting or pig-sticking, a sport which the British took to enthusiastically and refined. Tiger shooting is represented in seven paintings, lion shooting follows with six, fishing has six, bear shooting has five, leopard shooting four, elephant shooting three, hunting with hounds, coursing with cheetahs, chital shooting, buffalo shooting, and Bengal florican shooting have two each, black partridge shooting, hare shooting, hog deer shooting, partridge or quail shooting, snipe shooting, rhino shooting, and hunting with caracal all have one painting each. Tame elephants are the standard vehicles of shikar in these paintings and the uniformity of the dress of the hunters and the titles of the first and last paintings suggest that the artist was possibly depicting a series of hunts of the same hunters with whom he may have spent an extended period, observing firsthand the events which he painted. The album depicts almost the entire range of shikar practised at the time, of which hunting lions was a major sport considering the number of paintings in which it finds place.

A cursory look at the game hunted shows that the artist is not depicting the game animals of Bengal alone. For one thing, he has painted lions. Again, though coursing with cheetahs and hunting with caracal were not unknown in Bengal, they were more common and popular elsewhere. The tall grass, the use of elephants and lion as game suggest events in present-day western Bihar, eastern UP, or further northwest. Though D'Oyly got nearest to such areas during his years in Patna from 1831 onwards, the paintings were done circa 1810, the albums being presented to Lady Hastings in that year on the occasion of D'Oyly's marriage to her cousin.[7] But he did travel up north to Kanpur earlier while at Calcutta.[8] He could have seen the events and depicted them, or painted them from memory. In either event his depictions are real enough to be credible and it is important to note that lion and tiger receive equal attention though pig-sticking takes pride of place.

The six lion paintings show the hunters approaching a lion at bay; a lion leaping at a hunter on elephantback while his companions take aim; an Indian horse-rider distracting the lion, the latter giving chase; the lion leaping onto an elephant, dislodging the howdah with the rider; two Indians armed with swords keeping the lion at bay while the hunter aims; and finally the wounded lion glaring defiantly at the hunters approaching on their elephant. Here is depicted a lion shoot conducted with elephants, an essential instrument for shikar in tall grass with horses being used as swift distractions in tight situations.

The last painting however is even more revealing: "Coming Home" shows tents in the background. One tame elephant towards the left of the painting is about to sit down to let her British hunter dismount. The hunter is protected from the sun by an umbrella. A male elephant has sat down and the dead lion strapped on it is being untied. Before it on the ground is, surprisingly, a dead tiger and, even more unexpected, two aquines, one with its throat slit presumably by performing halal to make it permissible meat for consumption. Their long ears make them look like wild asses – a species found at the time only west of Lahore i.e. 75°E longitude.[9] While the contents of this particular painting defy explanation, the other six are realistic enough and provide the earliest depiction of a lion hunt by the British in India. They show the continuation of an Indian hunting practice.

A trained elephant is an indispensable mount in an emergency as recounted by General Godfrey Mundy of a friend's experience about the time of D'Oyly's paintings. His friend was riding elephantback when he wounded a lion. The lion charged him and as he leaned forward to discharge another shot, the front of the howdah gave way and he fell to the ground. The lion though severely wounded attacked the fallen hunter who was saved from certain death by the elephant who, goaded by her mahout, "... grasped in her trunk the top of a young tree, bent it down across the loins of the lion, and thus forced the tortured animal to quit his hold!"[10] Mundy himself made a sketch of the event which took place near Hansi in Haryana. The depiction is accurate enough, though the elephant is shown with tusks which Indian female elephants do not have.

There were more adventurous spirits among the British who found hunting lions and tigers from elephantback a tame affair. In the first half of the 19th century William Fraser hunted lions from horseback or on foot. While he successfully shot the lions, he lost several horses in the process. James Skinner of Skinner's Horse fame and General Lord Lake speared tigers from horseback as well. Both Fraser and Skinner were connoisseurs of matchlocks, preferring and successfully using Indian-made guns for shikar.[11] However, while in the north hunting lions from horseback was a rarity, in Gujarat, particularly around Deesa where the land was flat and arid, the British took to hunting them on horseback as the preferred mode. The reasons for this are simple enough. One was at a more convenient height but could still see long distances; besides horses move swiftly and, the terrain being what it was, safely.[12]

Similarly, in a forest the method had to change again. William Rice who shot in the Gir circa 1850 records that he followed a lion to a "*corindah*" (Karvanda) bush to a distance of a dozen yards. The thick foliage concealed the lion in it and only a growl was heard, he therefore retreated:

> There was a "bastard [stunted] teak" tree close by, so I quietly stepped up its low
> sloping trunk, and there waited concealed by the thick leaves.... After ... a few
> minutes the lion crawled very slowly out and began walking towards [its kill] the
> buffalo, step by step.... At about twenty five paces off he turned slightly sideways,
> when I sent a "shell" into its flank, which shot I distinctly heard burst inside him.
> Instantly with a terrific roar he bounded forward full stretch, and clearing quite
> thirty yards in three long bounds, rolled over under a small bush, when a choking
> "guggle-guggle" noise in his throat, very pleasant to hear, told me it was alright.[13]

Lieutenant Colonel L.L. Fenton found himself sitting on the branch of a fallen tree to shoot a lion in 1880. He used *pagi*s, many of whom were (and indeed are even today) Sidis, of Abyssinian descent, and whose ancestors came to western India in

The gold mohur
■ The currency of The East India Company during Queen Victoria's reign. The reverse has a statant lion in front of a palm tree symbolizing power and longevity.
Courtesy Bharat Kala Bhavan, Varanasi.

The Reserve Bank of India's symbol, 1935

■ (below) The tiger for the Reserve Bank of India's symbol was taken from the gate of the residence of the Governor of Bengal, now the National Library, Kolkata.

■ (right) The "British" lion with its foot on a globe atop the gate of the residence of the Governor General of India, now the residence of the Governor of West Bengal, Kolkata, was not considered for the emblem of the Reserve Bank of India as it was a symbol of imperialism.

Author's collection.

the 16th century according to one source, whereas a recent study states that they have been in Gujarat for many centuries with immigrants arriving from different African origins over the passage of time.[14] He records that these people were the finest trackers he had come across.[15] They had a superb knowledge of the terrain, they knew the territory of each lion, and they were sent out to track and locate the chosen animal to drive it out in a beat to the hunter's perch or machan. Alternatively a bait was tied to attract a lion or leopard so that the hunter could get a shot at it. Fenton enumerates two methods of shooting a tracked lion. One was to drive it in a beat towards the hunter, the other more dangerous one was "walking it up", that is going with trackers on foot to the lion and shooting it. He preferred the latter method as, according to him, it usually gave a good shot.[16]

The Reserve Bank of India's symbol, 1935
■ The tiger in front of a palm tree replaced the lion as the latter was thought to represent imperialism.
Courtesy RBI, Mumbai.

The preferred object of shikar was the male lion. Its mane and larger size made it a good trophy either mounted whole or partly, or as a rug on the floor. C.A. Kincaid, Judicial Assistant at Rajkot went for a shoot to the Gir in 1905. He had permission from Junagadh state to shoot only one lion and he had hoped to shoot a maneater near Talala – a taluka town way out of the jungle today – but only a lioness offered him a shot. On returning to his camp he sent a letter to Nawab Rasulkhanji thanking him for the permission to shoot which he and his wife enjoyed. Quite unexpectedly he received a telegraphic reply stating "Take lioness for Madam Saheb, get lion for yourself". The maneater was tracked down and Kincaid sat in a machan on a tree to shoot it. The lion, he writes:

> ... was a wily old campaigner and had evidently sent out its younger ones [for two cubs came out earlier in the beat] to draw the fire of any lurking enemies. I took rather rashly a snapshot at it, as it galloped past. A lucky shot broke its spine and it collapsed. It was a noble beast but its canine teeth had been broken and it was that misfortune probably that had led it to take exclusively to human diet.[17]

The epitome of shikar for the British in India was a viceregal shoot. Viceroys and Governors of Bombay more often than not went to shoot in the Gir when on a visit to Junagadh state. The final such visitation for the lions was Lord Linlithgow's in 1942. As usual on such occasions the resources of the state were mobilized to the maximum extent possible. For months before the intended visit, baits of male buffalo calves were regularly fed to lions which were large and had good manes, and therefore marked for the event. Thus they were localized and "anchored" to use R.S. Dharmakumarsinhji's phrase, to their respective areas. On the appointed day the Viceroy and his party were installed in secure machans and the beat began. The result was predictable enough. A photograph of this last viceregal shoot shows the Viceroy and the Vicerine with their daughter and a daughter of a former Viceroy, standing in front of a dead lion carefully laid out to record the successful shoot.

Such shoots were a matter of prestige for the state and a failed shikar would be a major embarrassment. An amusing incident took place in 1890 when the Duke of Clarence visited the Gir to shoot a lion. Unfortunately for the administration of the state, the lion did not oblige. In desperation Haridas Viharidas, the Diwan of Junagadh, approached L.L. Fenton who was in charge of the royal party's shoot with a proposal that two lions brought out from the Junagadh zoo the previous night should be set free in the forest and then be driven out to be shot by the royal guest. Fenton notes that he had heard of such goings on in some states of north India – in these cases the quarry would have been the tiger – but he promptly refused. The Duke went home empty-handed[18] as did Prince Philip the Duke of Edinburgh almost a hundred years later in 1983 when he returned from Gir without seeing lions in the wild. Two large males had been "anchored" for him to see and photograph. However, the royal guest could not be taken there as the place had not been "sanitized" by the security personnel in time![19]

One of the perils of shikar is that sometimes things start going horribly wrong for the shikaris. General Godfrey Mundy noted that

> By *crack* sportsmen the lion is reputed to afford better sport than the tiger: his attack is more open and certain; a peculiarity arising either from the noble nature of the jungle king, or from the country which he haunts being less favourable for a retreat than the thick morasses frequented by the tiger.[20]

William Rice strikes a note of caution:

> Following up a wounded lion is considered most awkward work, for they have the credit of making their charge home good, and of not swerving on one side when fired at close enough to singe them almost, as I have known to be the case with tigers on more than one occasion....[21]

He goes on to add though, that he cannot say this from experience as he himself had been lucky enough to find all wounded lions dead.[22] But one British officer, Major H.G. Carnegie, Political Agent of Halar *prant* of Kathiawar at the time, was not so fortunate. He met his end in such circumstances in 1905 when Lord Lamington, Governor of Bombay was shooting in the Gir. Captain Foljambe, ADC to the Governor, fired at a male lion in a beat and missed. J.H. Du Boulay, Private Secretary to the Governor who was accompanying the Governor's party also fired two shots of which the second one struck the lion in the right shoulder. The animal retreated and they caught up with it in a nullah. Suddenly there was "a slight coughing roar", the lion's charge was swift. Carnegie fired a shot and grazed it. The lion went straight for him and struck "a blow on the left shoulder with his right paw, and then seized him and bore him to the ground". Several shots were fired which silenced the lion but Major Carnegie had had his last shoot.[23] Until recently a Carnegie Fountain erected in his memory stood at a major crossroads in Rajkot, a reminder of the sudden end of a popular British officer.

Up to the middle of the 19th century the lion was found all over north India but its frequent encounters with the British had disastrous consequences leading to its near total disappearance from India. This has been recounted by virtually every writer on the subject. A few instances illustrate the widespread devastation. William Fraser shot 84 lions, "being personally responsible for their extinction in the area [Haryana, Punjab]".[24] That was circa 1820. Central India in the 1850s was a stronghold of lions according to one authority. During the upheavals of 1857–58 Colonel George Acland Smith is supposed to have killed more than 300 of them of which fifty were from the Delhi region alone,[25] though this large number appears to be exaggerated. In Kathiawar William Rice shot fourteen lions in Gir in one shoot[26] and a Colonel D. killed as many as eighty lions around 1857.[27] This is only one side of the picture, for Indians were not far behind. Ten lions were shot in Kotah, Rajasthan in 1866.[28] Maharaja Ranjitsingh's lancers bayoneted these cats around Lahore in the 1830s.[29] A decade earlier Raja Bishen Singh of Bundi in Rajasthan

> would *bivouac* for days in the lion's lair, nor quit the scene until he had circumvented the forest king, the only prey he deemed worthy of his kill. He had slain upwards of one hundred lions with his own hand, besides tigers....[30]

In 1842 in Kathiawar peninsula itself "Lions ... [were] to be found in various parts of the country.... Panthers [leopards] cheetahs (or the hunting tigers) are very common" according to Captain George Le Grand Jacob, the Political Agent at Kathiawar.[31] Up to the 1870s rulers in Kathiawar were paying bounties to hunters for killing lions. In three years sixteen lions[32] were killed. From Kutch the lions had disappeared by then and only names such as *sinh khatlo* (lion hillock) and a *sinh jhar* (lion ravine) now remind people of their existence.[33] By 1891 there were only stray reports of lions around Mount Abu,[34] the animal had otherwise disappeared from the rest of India.

By the second half of the 19th century, it required an invitation to Junagadh to be able to shoot a lion. Thus it is not surprising at all that shikar literature of the British period barely mentions lion shikar. Lt. Col. R.W. Burton estimated in 1959 that there were 280 books on shikar and related subjects[35] whereas a more recent bibliography compiled by Kamal Prasad in 1965 lists some 400 books on these very subjects including ornithology and fishing.[36] It is significant to note that throughout the entire British period there were only three authors – William Rice, L.L. Fenton, and C.A. Kincaid – who had a chapter on lion shooting in their books, and all are of experiences in the Gir. Stanley Jepson's collection of *Big Game Encounters* by various hunters includes an encounter T.R. Lively had with three lions in the Gir forest.[37] There is not a single book devoted to lion shikar in the entire period. Two books by R.G. Burton who was the most prolific writer on the subject, have a chapter each on lions, but one has material on the African lion, whereas the other, on the lion in India, summarizes information from earlier sources.[38] In 1904 F.G. Aflalo's book on sporting opportunities in India was published, almost a hundred years after Williamson's work. This book does not mention any lion shooting, as the animal had all but gone from India by then.[39] This is a clear indication of the dramatic decline of the animal in the 19th century. Some of the instances of the number of lions shot by various hunters noted here represent the very last survivors of these animals in India outside of the Gir.

In fact, the game was almost up for the lions outside Kathiawar by the end of the 18th century. The four instances of the 1820s–60s we have noted here, i.e. those of Fraser, Smith, and in Bundi and Kotah, were of large figures and their total comes to 494 lions killed for sport. It is obvious that several hunters hunted in the areas, all details of which are not available. Their shikar bags may not have been so large. Even if one were to assume that 1,000 more lions were destroyed by other sportsmen and military officers during the same period whose records do not exist or are not in the public domain, we arrive at a figure of say 1,500 lions being killed during 1820–70 in India outside Kathiawar. Paul Joslin's compilation of lions shot between 1863 and 1888 outside Kathiawar gives a figure of only 37.[40] Compare this with the figures from a recent study: over 80,000 tigers, more than 150,000 leopards, and 200,000 wolves were slaughtered in the fifty years from 1875 to 1925.[41] Our figure of 1,500 lions and Joslin's 37 are both minuscule by comparison. A total of about 230 cheetahs were seen or shot between 1772 and 1967 on the Indian subcontinent.[42] Lions were probably more abundant during that period than cheetahs, but not as widespread or common as tigers. It is pertinent to note that there were no natural calamities in the 1850s and 1860s of a nature or magnitude that would take a sudden toll of lions during these two decades. Thus it was obviously British and other sportsmen who had delivered the coup de grace to the small pockets of lion populations by the end of the 1860s. The animals that survived

Lion shikar and the British

■ Sir Charles D'Oyly's watercolours vividly illustrate the sport in the field. The last painting shows both a lion and a tiger brought home on elephantback, circa 1810. (See also page 115.)
By permission of The British Library, London, MS WD 4406/F28–34.

Lion and elephant
■ A sketch by General Godfrey Charles Mundy, which records an incident of 1828 when his friend was attacked near Hansi in Haryana. It was the elephant which ultimately killed the lion.
From Mundy 1858.

thereafter were but a few stragglers that were mopped up.

A comparison with the cheetah's disappearance is interesting. The last lion reported outside Kathiawar was in 1891 as noted earlier. The last cheetah seen in India was in 1967–68. Thus seventy years elapsed between the disappearance of the two.[43] The bigger, heavier cat which required bigger prey was the first one to depart from India except for the relict population of the Kathiawar peninsula.

The lion's preferred habitat is grassland and scrub jungle. Yet they were found on the periphery of thick jungles of Kotah and Bundi, and indeed they inhabit today the Gir, parts of which are thick jungle. The cheetah too inhabited the same type of habitat though its range extended further south beyond the Narmada river to the Deccan plateau and beyond. And its last reported sightings and shikar were near the edges of thick jungle in Madhya Pradesh, though jungles were their least preferred habitat. The other big cat, the tiger, also came under severe pressure in the 19th century. According to Valmik Thapar, as many as 20,000 tigers were shot for sport between 1860 and 1960.[44] Mahesh Rangarajan estimates that 80,000 tigers were destroyed between 1875 and 1925 as they were considered dangerous and bounties were paid for their destruction by the government.[45] In spite of such depredations a sizeable population survived, and the preferred habitat of the tiger was the last to be disturbed or substantially destroyed. In 1900 the tiger population was estimated between 25,000 and 40,000.[46]

The pressure on different habitats increased steadily over the centuries as a result of the human population growth between 1600 and 1800 from about 116 million to about 159 million as we have seen earlier,[47] and up to 254.51 million by 1880,[48] during which time most of north India was ruled by the Mughals followed by the British. By 1901 the human population had increased to 283.9 million.[49] The growth in human population implies also growth in cattle, sheep, and goat populations. The hundred years between 1757 and 1858 were a period of uncertainty and turmoil that

Hunting in Gir
■ In this image titled "Lion shooting in the GHEER Kathiawar, Western India", a Britisher is shown hunting a lion with a gun, with "natives" following behind him. This incident is from *The Graphic*, October 4, 1873.
Author's collection.

were part of the consolidation process of the British Indian empire. It would be difficult to assess the loss of grasslands and scrub jungle habitats of the lion as British settlement and other records for most of the region became available primarily in the second half of the 19th century, whereas regional records are beyond the scope of this work. But that their disappearance or reduction accelerated the process of extinction of the lion is a certainty.

Secondly, the depredations of shikar are an even greater certainty. Shikaris and "sportsmen" spared no animal that came their way. The slaughter was merciless and total. It was conducted without any impulse to protect the species. It was only towards the close of the 19th century when an alarmist belief took hold that there were only a dozen lions left in the Gir that the British administration turned its attention to preservation. Lord Curzon's subsequent decision not to go for lion shikar in the Gir during his state visit to Junagadh in 1900 was the high watermark.[50] His subsequent letter to the Burma Game Preservation Association is the first call in modern times for preserving Nature for its own sake from the highest in the empire.[51] The letter's mastery over the broad range of the subject is a delight, and it is a beacon worthy of the lion itself. The issues Lord Curzon addressed are still with us a century later. It is regrettable that his own viceregal successors, other high-ranking British officers, and Indian princes and potentates honoured his call more in its breach.

There was a curious debate during the British period, which continued after independence, about which of the two great cats, the lion or the tiger, was stronger and whether the tiger "drove out" the lion[52] and reduced it to its present minuscule domain. It is not clear how the debate started but it was for decades the subject of many a fireside chat, with even serious shikaris labouring over it.

From the evidence we have it is clear that the tiger was noticed by humans in the Indian subcontinent earlier than the lion. If this is a reflection of the commonness of

Lion shikar from a machan

■ An illustration by William Rice of an incident in the 1850s from the Gir forest which shows the lion bolting after being fired on. The bait used for the shikar is the traditional buffalo.

From Rice, 1884.

Trophy brought home

■ This scene is from the Gir. Before motorized transport and in the absence of elephants an animal the size of the lion could only be brought on a camel through a roadless jungle.

From Leipziger, 1888.

Sasan ness, circa 1880
■ This was a Maldhari outpost in the 19th century – visitors had to "camp" there. A thriving township has sprung up around the nawab's hunting lodge, now the forest resthouse.
From Leipziger, 1888.

a species at a particular period of history, then the inescapable conclusion is that the lion arrived and increased in numbers just before and in the early centuries of the common era. Whether it did so at the cost of tiger habitat and therefore tigers is moot, though such would appear to be the case. Equally importantly there are no records of any natural conflict between the two species. It would be strange if humans failed to record it if it did happen.

The fact is that the two cats lived in different habitats. Even Kotah paintings show lions in thinner jungle than tigers. There is of course a possibility of an overlap in the range of the two species, the most preferred habitat of the one being the least preferred of the other. Skirmishes if any between the two would be rare and peripheral to the issue of one "driving out" the other.

While both cats are of near equal size and weight, lions are gregarious and they live in prides of varying sizes. To expect that a single tiger which is essentially a solitary animal, could succeed in annihilating a pair of lions, leave alone a pride of them, would be in the realm of imagination.

We have seen that one could extrapolate a figure of say 1,500 lions living in India outside of Kathiawar in the early part of the 19th century as against a minimalist figure of 25,000 tigers around 1900. Tigers were reduced to less than 2,000 within the succeeding seventy years, a tiger's fate similar to that of the lion or the cheetah though later in coming. The causes of its decimation, as in the case of the lion or cheetah, were human interference with its life and its habitat. The large swathes of dense jungles where it lived were the last to be attacked by humans.

That having been said, we may turn to the representation of the two cats as symbols of political power. As discussed in earlier chapters, Ashoka propagated *dhamma* in the far-flung Mauryan empire through his edicts on rocks, caves, and pillars – some of the last of which were surmounted by lions. The Mughals had the lion couchant and the rising sun as the symbol on their pennant.[53] The British were no different. They too had their symbols where the lion played a prominent part. Their long journey from trade to empire, though unplanned, had been as bloody as

Lion and buffalo
■ William Daniell records a fight staged in Coorg by the Raja. The buffalo was African, Daniell does not record the provenance of the lion.
From Daniell, 1836.

the foundation of any previous paramount power in India, and with their victory the "British" lion came into its own on military medals and elsewhere.

In European heraldry the lion was by far the most important symbol (one of the exceptions being the Roman empire which adopted and stuck to the eagle throughout its existence). The lion is shown in many positions as heraldry evolved over centuries. When a single lion was to be depicted on a shield, the animal was drawn upright, not a natural position for it. The reason was the shape of the shield and probably also the artists' lack of knowledge of natural history.[54] Thus the armorial bearings granted to the "New" East India Company in 1698 which were then adopted by the "United" Company in 1709[55] were supported by Rampant Lions, Regardant. In the aftermath of the revolt 1857–58, the "Company Bahadur" as the East India Company was called in India, lost complete control of its possessions to the crown, and its arms were replaced by a signet with the lion and the unicorn, made famous by the well known nursery rhyme in which these animals fight for the crown.

While it was natural that the lion with its long history of presence in European heraldry took prominent place in British symbols of power, in India there was a very special reason for its importance, unique to the subcontinent. In the south, the East India Company's march towards supremacy had many hurdles, the most persistent one being the kingdom of Mysore ruled by Haidar Ali and his more famous son Tipu Sultan. Four wars were fought to bring matters to a close. Tipu was a stubborn foe. His name meant tiger and he is reputed to have said that it was better to live two days as a tiger rather than two hundred years as a sheep. His hatred for the British was intense for he saw the end of his own dominance. At his last military conference he is reputed to have said, "Better to die like a soldier than to live a miserable dependence on the infidels' list of their pensioned rajas and nabobs."[56] True to form, he died fighting when his stronghold of Seringapatam fell in 1799.

In the kingdom of Mysore, the dominant carnivore at the apex of the food chain was the tiger and Haidar Ali had given his son a name which signified this cat. Tipu was obsessed by the tiger. His guns had tigers on them, his mortars were in the form of crouching tigers, his infantry wore stripes, his most famous artefact was a tiger killing an Englishman. Tipu's bed chamber was guarded by four tigers "which although tame, would, in case of disturbance, become unruly".[57] Finally and above all he sat on a tiger throne (see Chapter 9).[58] While most kings in the Indian subcontinent, Hindus and Muslims alike, sat on a *simhasana*, he chose a *vyaghrasana* for his regal chair.*

Tipu's throne constructed in 1786 was the ultimate symbol of power. Tiger in form and surmounted by a canopy with a fringe of pearls, it had a large tiger's head and a railing on which there were ten tiger's heads made of gold and inlaid with precious stones.[59] It was dismantled after Tipu's defeat by the conquerors and taken away along with other artefacts as spoils of victory.

With the death of Tipu the British became firmly entrenched in the south. The Battle of Seringapatam had to be marked by a symbol, a medal, and there was no better symbol than a "British" Lion subjugating an "Indian" Tiger. It was engraved by C.H. Kuchler at Mathew Boulton's Soho Manufactory in Birmingham. Medals

---

* Another notable exception is the royalty of Nepal. The king sits on a throne surmounted by the spread hood of a multi-headed *naga*. This is the snake which supports the reclining Lord Vishnu whose incarnation the king is believed to be by his subjects in the Himalayan kingdom.

State lion of Bharatpur
■ Standing in procession to welcome HRH the Prince of Wales (later King Edward VIII) on his visit to the state in 1921.
Author's collection.

were struck in England and Calcutta. The event was considered important enough for the medal to be given to all ranks. In all 113 gold medals were struck (one going to General Sir David Bayrd who commanded the assault), 185 were silvergilt, 3,636 were silver, 5,000 bronze, and 45,000 pewter which went to the sepoys of the Company. This was the first medal to be awarded to all ranks by the East India Company and it was only the second time in British history that such distribution including all ranks took place, the first being the Battle of Dunbar won by Oliver Cromwell in 1650.[60]

The reverse of the medal shows a scene of the attack on the fortress of Seringapatam while the obverse has "a fine picture of a fight between the British Lion and Tipoo Sahib's Tiger, a penon above bears the Union Flag and an Arabic inscription ... Victorious lion of God...."[61]

A similar symbolic use of animals is encountered in another medal. The war with Burma came to an end in 1826 with the Treaty of Yandaboo as a result of which Burma had to yield its recently acquired conquests of Assam, Manipur, the long coastal strip of Arakan, and Tenasserim. The defeat of the kingdom of Ava was another landmark in the advancement of British power. The event was commemorated with a "Burma Medal" the reverse of which showed the storming of the Pagoda. The obverse of the medal shows the Elephant of Ava properly deferential and crouching before the British Lion. Behind the elephant the Burmese standard is submissively lowered while the union flag flutters behind the lion. In the exergue is a Persian inscription: "The Elephant of Ava is obedient to the Lion of England, year 1826."[62]

The unrest with British rule brought the upheavals of 1857–58 at the end of

The last viceregal shikar, 1942
■ Lord Linlithgow, Viceroy and Governor General of India 1936–43, is accompanied by Nawab Mahbatkhanji III, seen in front of the hunting lodge at Sasan.
Author's collection.

which British expansion on the subcontinent became complete. The East India Company lost its possessions totally in the process, the crown took over the government, and Queen Victoria was proclaimed Queen Empress of India in 1877. The Indian Mutiny Medal was struck to commemorate the British victory. Its obverse had the diademed head of Queen Victoria with the legend "Victoria Regina" while the reverse of the medal had a standing helmeted figure of Britannia holding a wreath in her outstretched right hand, the Union Shield over her left arm, behind her the British Lion, and above the word "India". In the exergue are the dates 1857–58. The obverse was designed by W. Wyon while the reverse was designed by L.C. Wyon, the two being renowned designers of the time in the UK. This medal was for all who had borne arms against the mutineers, a total of 290,000 of them were awarded and it turned out to be the last medal issued by the East India Company.[63]

The last free-ranging lions in Europe had gone centuries earlier, yet the animal remained important enough to symbolize British paramountcy in India. Enquiries made extensively have revealed no clues regarding which lions or their likenesses were used by the engravers and designers. It would be logical to assume that they were lions from Africa which had been kept in menageries or elsewhere in England from as early as 1235 when Henry III had them in the Tower of London, a practice which continued till William IV (r. 1830–37).[64] Or likenesses could have been taken from drawings or paintings of these animals. The lions of the medals are accurate but symbolic rather than being actual representations of any subspecies. In any case the earliest record of a lion from India reaching the Tower menagerie in London was of 1829; a pair of lions reached England from India in 1854 to be followed by two lions from Mesopotamia in 1856.[65] They were not likely candidates for use as models (it would never do to have an "Indian" or an "Asian" lion becoming a "British" one) though they had reached London before the designing of the Indian Mutiny Medal.

The Kathiawar peninsula came under British control in the 1820s. It was politically unique as it was isolated from the rest of India insofar as it was entirely governed by princes of large and small states. The British themselves had but small enclaves at Rajkot and Viramgam, the entrance to the peninsula. The princes were cut off from almost all "modern" influences of the time. It was necessary from the British point of view to instil in them a sense of common purpose and loyalty to the empire. With these ideas in mind and with donations from the princes themselves, the British government started the first school for royal students, the Rajkumar College at Rajkot in 1870, which was soon to be followed by other such schools in Ajmer, Lahore, Indore, Raipur, and elsewhere. It was a grand enterprise, an institution which was a symbol of empire in this remote area. Its armorial bearings had to be suitably designed and what better symbol than the lion? The magnificent Arms of the College are supported by two Rampant Lions Reguardant, crowned with Eastern Crowns, and the motto in Sanskrit *yasya budhdhirbalam tasya* (freely translated as "knowledge is power") at its base.[66] This symbol of British empire reigns supreme in the school today, literally carved in stone.

While the 19th century saw the lion ascendant as the symbol of power in India, the 20th saw its decline. The free-ranging Indian lions were now confined only to the Gir, and it was natural that the tiger should make its first major appearance among British symbols. The year 1935 saw the founding of the Reserve Bank of India at Bombay. The authorities were in quest of a symbol and they looked to earlier examples. Gold mohurs with the likenesses of King William IV in 1835 and

The last viceregal shikar, 1942
■ The Viceroy Lord Linlithgow, the Vicereine, their daughter, and the daughter of the former Viceroy Lord Irwin, stand in front of the viceregal lion trophy.
Author's collection.

Queen Victoria in 1841 on the obverse had been struck by the East India Company. The reverse had a statant lion in front of a palm tree,[67] signifying the courage of the lion and longevity of the palm. But in these changed times the lion appeared to be too closely connected with British imperialism, and a decision was taken to replace the lion by the tiger for it was regarded the more characteristic of India.[68] In the process it was forgotten that the lion was the classical symbol of state and that it still held on tenaciously in the Gir after having been hunted out elsewhere. Sir James Taylor, Deputy Governor of the Bank, arranged for a photograph of the tiger atop the entrance to Belvedere, until recently the residence of the Governor of Bengal in Calcutta (Kolkata), to be used as the likeness of the tiger for the new symbol. The monumental gate surmounted by a lion with its front right paw on a globe of the residence of the Viceroy and Governor General of India at Calcutta was simply out of fashion. The tiger and the palm tree thus became the common seal and the symbol of the Reserve Bank of India which flourishes to this day. It was designed by P.W.M. Brindley, artist/engraver, British India Mints. When George VI was crowned king and became Emperor of India in 1937, coins with his likeness were struck, on the reverse of which the same tiger and the palm tree were depicted. The 1947 issue of rupee coins bore on the reverse the "statant tiger" motif similar to that appearing on the Reserve Bank seal.

Thus, towards the end of British rule the lion was unceremoniously replaced by the tiger, as was to happen again in 1973 when Project Tiger was initiated, for reasons somewhat similar to those which caused the tiger to be chosen in 1935.

But Indians of that period had no problems with the lion. In popular art Bharat Mata or Mother India, India's very own version of Marianne of the French Republic, came to ride a chariot drawn by two lions from about 1940.[69] Such motifs with many variations were common in calendar art for several years after India's independence.

CHAPTER 8

Soruth Sarkar Saves Lions

Armorial bearings of Junagadh
■ A banner with these armorial bearings was presented by Queen Victoria to Nawab Mahbatkhanji II. The supporters are naturally lions.
Author's collection.

THE SAURASHTRA OR KATHIAWAR PENINSULA under the British was divided into four sub-cultural and sub-linguistic units – Jhalawar, Halar, Gohilwar, and Sorath or Soruth the central and coastal portion over which the nawabs of Junagadh ruled. The state of Junagadh often used the title Soruth Sarkar for its government. Sorath was of immense historical significance. To the Mauryas the peninsula was important as the Saurashtra *vana* was one of the eight elephant forests, though not the best, that provided them with this indispensable war machine.[1] Emperor Ashoka caused fourteen of his edicts to be engraved on a granite rock at the foot of Girnar mountain on the outskirts of Junagadh, the first edict being an injunction against slaughter of animals and birds for sacrifices and feasts.[2] On the same rock Rudradaman the Western Kshatrapa king of the 2nd century CE engraved his deeds of repairing a dam built by the Mauryas, and Skanda Gupta who once again repaired the same dam added his inscription in the 5th century.[3]

Sorath's fortunes changed with the march of history. It came to be ruled by the Raizada (Chudasama) Rajputs until they were defeated by Sultan Mahmud Begda of Ahmedabad in 1472–73. During Emperor Akbar's consolidation of his empire, the region came under Mughal rule. However by 1735 the Mughal empire had weakened and from its debris arose Sher Khan Babi who threw out the Mughal governor of the region to establish his dynasty around 1735[4] which ruled Junagadh for nine generations until 1947.

The Babis themselves claimed descent from one Abdul Rashid who had been in the service of Paigambar Muhammad himself. Their principality located as it was at such a historically important place, was the premier state of Kathiawar, a fact that was emphasized throughout the dynasty's rule. By the beginning of the 19th century however, the dynasty had to be content under the authority of the new imperial power, the British. The chaos of Kathiawar had to be settled and the British did so with persistence.[5] By 1821 external relations of states of the region were taken over by them under the settlement made by Colonel Walker to the extent that the *zortalbi* tribute collected by Junagadh from 134 states and talukas of Kathiawar would henceforth be collected by the British on the state's behalf,[6] of which naturally the British kept a percentage for themselves by way of a fee. While Junagadh and other large states were more or less free to conduct their own internal affairs, warfare and external relations went out of their hands. Even in the internal affairs of states, the British empire from their paramount position henceforth would ensure restraint.

The first half of the 19th century was a period of considerable turmoil in Kathiawar. There were claims and counter-claims of territories by various states particularly between Junagadh and Baroda[7] and Junagadh and Gondal. The Gir forest itself had become a haven for outlaws – *baharvatia*s who had taken it upon themselves to avenge wrongs done to them by the state.[8] The tract was notorious for being malarious and there were hardly any maps to assist the administration. Matters came to a head when a British officer was taken prisoner by the outlaws. A military expedition by Junagadh and other state forces led by a British colonel had to be mounted to pacify the area. In course of time territorial disputes between states were settled, though Junagadh considered itself the successor to the Mughal empire in the region. Peace was finally attained with a British garrison permanently stationed at Rajkot.

As was to be expected, the relationship with the imperial authority would deepen. During the time of the sixth nawab, Sir Mahbatkhanji II who ruled from 1851 to

1882, a Governor of Bombay Presidency visited the state for the first time. Sir Bartle Frere (who had earlier hunted lions in western India and had killed four lions in a day's shoot)[9] came to Veraval by sea in 1867. He was followed by Sir Seymour Fitzgerald who came to Rajkot to inaugurate Rajkumar College, the princes' college, on December 16, 1870.[10] After this landmark event he proceeded to Junagadh and Gir for shikar. He "bagged" five lions there,[11] thus starting a dubious tradition which was to continue on and off for more than sixty years.

Though stray lions were reported outside Kathiawar up to 1891,[12] in the peninsula itself they were already disappearing, apart from the environs of the Gir forest which spread outside of Junagadh state into Amreli district of Baroda state and the Mytiala area of Bhavnagar state. Good lion habitat extended into the Alech and Barda hills and their environs which came under Porbandar and Navanagar states. Jam Ranmalji who ruled Navanagar from 1820 to 1852[13] is reputed to have hunted one large male lion in 1833, another male in 1842, five lions in 1850, and three more in 1851, in his domains.[14] There is a fresco of Jam Ranmalji hunting lions from horseback with his nobles in the Barda hills in the "Lakhota" bastion in Jamnagar, the capital of Navanagar state. Ranmalji's successor Jam Vibhaji who ruled Jamnagar from 1852 to 1895 had hunted lions in his youth in the same area. According to L.L. Fenton, lions had last been reported in Barda and Alech hills, areas of Chotila and Dhrangadhra, but had all gone by the middle of the 19th century. A lion, a lioness, and a cub were reported circa 1884 in a part of Porbandar state neighbouring Navanagar state, but were killed by Rabaris and Navanagar police stationed there.[15] The upshot of the near total disappearance of lions from the rest of Kathiawar was that Junagadh state which had the largest portion of the Gir forest (though as we have noted some areas of the Gir ecosystem were part of Baroda, Bhavnagar, and other states and talukas where lions were found from time to time) would have to bear the brunt of sportsmen both British and Indian, who were important enough to get a permit from the state. If the imperial government required to obtain a specimen even for its zoological gardens or a museum, it had to ask Junagadh state. Thus in 1867 the political agent in Kathiawar Colonel W.W. Anderson addressed a letter to Junagadh making a request for procurement of a live lion, a lion skin, or a lion's skeleton. Gokulji Sampatram Jhala, Chief Diwan of the state notified the request in the State Gazette and offered rewards as follows:

	Rs
Sawaj (lion) a large live specimen	150/-
A small live cub	50/-
A dead lion's body with skin, bones, and claws intact	50/-
A complete skeleton	35/-
A complete skin	25/-[16]

These rewards were very generous for those times. But it will be noticed that the state did not have the administrative machinery for forest or wildlife management and had to offer a reward to its own subjects to procure lions! It has not been possible to ascertain the outcome of this gazette notification, but a lion reported to be of Asian origin was exhibited at the Alipore Zoo, Calcutta for ten years in the 1870s and a pair was obtained by them though it is not clear from where, in 1884, which was doing fine eight years later.[17]

The first salvo for the protection of lions was fired as early as 1879. Junagadh state had been exercised for some time about the number of lions left. In that year, the sixth nawab, Mahbatkhanji II had ordered strict protection of lions in his domains. He had been encouraged in this endeavour by Lord Sandhurst, Governor of Bombay. The nawab soon asked the Political Agent of Kathiawar Colonel L.C. Barton to help in his effort as a result of which the Agency published the following notification in its gazette:

> At the request of His Highness the Nawab of Junagadh, it is notified for public information that an interdict has been issued by His Highness against the destruction of lions in the Gir forest.
>
> As this order has emanated from a request preferred by His Excellency the Governor of Bombay who fears that this race of free nature [i.e. lions] may become extinct unless means are taken for their preservation, it is hoped by the undersigned that it will be respected by the European sportsmen.[18]

In April 1880, Junagadh state notified rules regarding shikar, which were considered important enough for the notification to be issued over the signature of the Principal Diwan, Khan Bahadur Saleh Hindi himself in the Junagadh state gazette. The notification stated that keeping in mind the Political Agency's notification of February 1880, Junagadh was promulgating the following rules. Firstly, no person within the state boundary would be allowed to do shikar of any type of animal, or trap it, without the permission of the state government. Secondly, the latter would permit such activities solely at its discretion on an application by the interested person. Finally, Junagadh state would allow subjects of neighbouring states to do shikar within its borders only if the state concerned would honour it reciprocally for Junagadh subjects with such permits. The subjects of other states would have to apply to Junagadh for permission on the strength of their state's permit. Anyone violating these rules would be liable to have his weapons confiscated and face other punishment according to the rules.[19] Here is a clear legal expression of monopoly over shikar. It is noteworthy that in British India, while the elephant received protection from 1879 onwards, the 1870s saw a systematic destruction of wild animals. According to one estimate 20,000 animals, including large carnivores, were being killed annually and Kotah state paid Rs 25 for a lion and Rs 10 for a tiger shot.[20] Junagadh state was way ahead of its times in protecting the lion.

These rules were superseded by new rules of the state introduced by a notification issued in 1896 under the signature of the then acting diwan, Behchardas Viharidas. The rules were made more stringent. A person caught poaching would face a jail term of one month and a fine of 200 koris (the Junagadh state currency – 1 imperial rupee = 3½ koris) and anyone found poaching a lion would face a jail term of six months and a fine of 1,000 koris. Permits for shikar would be issued on application to the diwan. A permit would be issued for a specific location, species, and period of time. It would not be granted for the shikar of a peacock or a peahen whereas, for a lion, special permission would have to be sought which would be granted for special reasons and circumstances only. It may be noted though that it was further notified that these rules would not apply for fishing and for snaring of small birds such as parakeets, sparrows, and pigeons.[21]

All these developments meant that henceforth lions were to receive protection and that permits would be granted in rare cases only for special reasons which included naturally raison d'etat. It also meant that permission had to be taken at the highest level. It may be noted as an aside that the nawab was extremely sensitive of his Hindu subjects' religious sentiments and banned the shikar of peafowl throughout his state thus anticipating the Republic of India by 75 years. The Political Agency's notification meant three things. First, Europeans, mainly the British, were to respect Junagadh state's efforts. Secondly, it meant that they could not any longer shoot or spear lions at will even in territories under direct British control, though by this time there were no lions left outside the Gir forest and its environs and in any case there was very little British territory in the Kathiawar peninsula, as it consisted almost entirely of princely states and talukas. However, British officers of stature could and did get permits to shoot in Junagadh state, which it appears were given liberally enough.[22] Finally, it meant that the imperial government fully supported the efforts of Junagadh state. Actually, however, the nawab and his administration were merely giving a "modern" legal form to the age-old custom of shikar where lions were considered royal game and their shikar was permitted only with the nawab's approval. At any rate, these rules and their practices were the basis of lion protection in the state. The dispensation of lion protection that came into being after 1879 remained in force till 1947 with only a few minor modifications.

But there was a major loophole in these arrangements. While Baroda and Bhavnagar states had strong administrations, and lion shikar being the prerogative of the ruler there was a considerable measure of control, there was to be friction between these states and Junagadh from time to time. The more troublesome problem however was of smaller principalities surrounding the Gir forest and Junagadh state, such as those of Jetpur, Mendarda, Bilkha, and other primarily Kathi states, and talukas whose darbars were free to do what they liked in their territories over whose activities neither the nawab nor the British administration had much control. This was the bane of Junagadh and its nawabs.

Junagadh state had an area of 8,499 square kilometres and a human population of 3,95,428 of which 80 per cent were Hindus, according to the 1901 census. The Gir forest extended from the sea coast to Girnar and Datar hills – the latter being a part of the Girnar massif – covering half the area of the state in the middle of the 19th century. When the great trigonometrical survey was done in 1875–76, the Gir was found to be 96 kilometres in length and 48 in width with an area of 3,109 square kilometres. Many parts consisted of thick jungle. Though the state had made some effort at protecting the forest, it was being continuously exploited. In 1879, Colonel Barton, Political Agent of Kathiawar (1878–83), suggested a survey of the jungle to prepare a plan for its protection. This was done by a Mr Bar in 1880, however the effort was found wanting, no action was taken, and almost two-thirds of the jungle was lost in the following twenty years.[23]

In 1892 Nawab Bahadurkhanji III died without leaving a direct heir. His brother Rasulkhanji had no training in statecraft and spoke little English. He was a devout Muslim, and having led the life of an ascetic had no interest in taking over the reins of state. However, he was persuaded by Haridas Viharidas the then diwan to answer the call of duty. He finally agreed to take on the challenge and after various representations to the British authorities he became nawab in 1892 at the age of forty. With the imperial government's acceptance of his accession began his benevolent reign of two decades.

Rasulkhanji had to learn on the job. He was shrewd enough to select able diwans. Haridas having performed his duties retired in 1895, and he was succeeded by several Hindu diwans who were Nagar brahmans, to be followed by Mirza Abbas Ali Beg and Abdullahmian A. Kureishi. During Rasulkhanji's reign, the state had

Nawab Rasulkhanji
■ In robes of state, he stands beside a ceremonial chair with lion armrests. He gave protection to lions which ultimately saved them.
Author's collection.

enlightened administrative policies and it made steady progress on all fronts with religious harmony among its subjects. It went through the disastrous *chappanyo kal* of 1899–1900 (the famine of Vikram Samvat 1956), when 157 relief works were implemented to sustain the poor subjects of the state.[24] Rasulkhanji in his youth was a remarkable marksman, who could toss a coin in the air and take it out with one shot. He had hunted several leopards earlier, but he had never shot a lion and had no desire to do so. With this background the nawab, his state, and the lions entered the 20th century and lived through its first decade. Rasulkhanji died in 1911.[25]

Rasulkhanji's administration had to take steps to protect the Gir which became a priority as the situation had become worrisome. The *Kathiawar Gazetteer* had declared in 1884 that there were only about a dozen lions left.[26] This was alarming enough, and a few years after Rasulkhanji came to the throne, the state as indeed all of Kathiawar, faced unprecedented famine which brought further travails to the lions and the administration of the state. Some measures of protection were taken early in his reign, but by 1906–07 only 883 square kilometres of forest remained with the Forest Department. The nawab decided to add 45,550 acres (18,448 hectares) to this area by transferring land from the revenue department. In the same year F.R. Desai who had been trained in forestry practice at the National Forest School, Nancy, France was appointed the first Conservator of Forests. He toured the entire area of the forest and put up a detailed proposal for its management so that the vandalization of this precious resource would stop and a steady income from its produce would accrue to the state. In 1906–07 the average income of the state on the basis of the previous five years was Rs 34.5 lakhs of which Rs 95,000 was earned from the forest with a net surplus of Rs 69,000.[27] In fact, the state showed a surplus from its forest income right up to 1945.[28] That apart, F.R. Desai had laid down boundaries of the forest, measured the area, divided it into blocks, and produced the first working plan. When Lord Lamington, Governor of Bombay, visited Junagadh in 1906 he publicly acknowledged Nawab Rasulkhanji for agreeing to create a sanctuary for lions in the Gir.[29] The land was earmarked by F.R. Desai and by 1908–09 the area of the Gir forest with the Forest Department had increased to 1,530 square kilometres, which included a sanctuary for lions of 326 square kilometres, a fraction of the area but a beginning nonetheless.[30]

Nawab Mahbatkhanji III
■ The last nawab in full military regalia, a rare picture. He continued the state policy of protecting lions started by his father, taking on the establishment of empire to do so.
Author's collection.

Though the Gir continued to be ravaged by grazing, forest fires, and the like, it came under the systematic control of the administration. It had been terra incognita to most Europeans at the close of the 19th century. In places the jungle was so dense that it was impossible to find a trail or move about without a good guide.[31] To compound the general inhospitable nature of the forest, "a very bad type of malarial fever prevails in the forest and its outskirts especially during the latter end of the rains and cold weather".[32] Which meant that the British would suffer the depredations of mosquitoes the most as they usually travelled in the cool six months between October and March. To top it all, the jungle was still reverberating with the exploits of the outlaws who had made it their home in the 19th century.

C.A. Kincaid, the Judicial Assistant to the Agent to the Governor of Bombay in 1902, sang the praises of the Gir in his poem "Kathiland":

Would you know the joys of waking
ere the earliest dawn is breaking,
Lest the cheetal at the pool should drink his fill?
Would you know the joys of sitting
till the night birds are a flitting,
That the panther may return to his kill?
You shall know them at Tellala
where the Hirun rushes foaming,
As it strives in vain to batter down its weir;
Where the sambhur bells the night through
to the hinds that may be roaming,
And the lions wake the echoes of the Gir.[33]

There were few takers for this sentiment and unfortunately those few were usually after the lion's skin, literally, which led to the alarming drop in lion numbers. Lord Curzon having heard of the lions' plight cancelled his visit to the Gir during his proposed state visit to Junagadh in November 1900. Lieutenant Colonel

H. D. RENDALL ESQR. I. C. S.
ADMINISTRATOR, JUNAGADH STATE

H.D. Rendall
■ He headed the British Administration of Junagadh state from 1911 to 1920, during which period not a single lion was shot by the Viceroy, Governor of Bombay, or any other British officer.
Author's collection.

J.M. Hunter, Political Agent, sent a telegram to Diwan Behchardas Viharidas on October 8, 1900:

> viceroy having heard there are so few lions left thinks it not right to shoot one but does not wish to disappoint Nawab altogether he enquires what other [game] could be shot....

Two days later another telegram from the Political Agent stated:

> viceroy decided to abandon Gir trip at same time wishes me to express to Nawab his sincere regret for disappointment caused. Had his excellency been made acquainted with facts sooner he would not have proposed the shoot.[34]

Just what Lord Curzon heard and from which authority is a matter of speculation. However, Lieutenant Colonel A.H. Mosse, a Political Officer in western India between 1901 and 1936, may well have been right when he wrote:

> During the late Lord Curzon's viceroyalty, a certain amount of pother arose over the announcement that he was about to visit Junagadh for the purpose of shooting one of the few remaining lions. The feeling aroused on the subject found voice in some lines published in the leading Bombay daily. Of these I remember but a word or two contained in a plea that the lions of the Gir should be allowed to remain in their last retreat undisturbed by Viceroy or Vandal.
>
> Great men must of necessity expect to be called hard names – but George Nathaniel Curzon a Vandal!
>
> Whatever the method, the desired result was attained. Curzon went on to shoot no lion. And certainly that was just as well. For if not quite on the verge of extinction, the Indian lion at that date was very near it.[35]

After his visit to Junagadh Lord Curzon wrote to the nawab in response to a letter from him in which he stated:

> Your Highness shewed great amiability in falling in with my views about the Gir Forest and the Lions. I should have been sorry to shoot any of those noble animals, particularly as their numbers are dwindling and I hope Your Highness will refuse permission to other sportsmen.
>
> I also hope Your Highness has remembered your promise to provide better airier cages for the poor lions in confinement at [the Sakkarbag Zoo in] Junagadh![36]

That Lord Curzon took the plight of the lion very seriously there is no doubt. In his celebrated reply to the Burma Game Preservation Association in 1901 he wrote:

> There are some persons who doubt or dispute the progressive diminution of wildlife in India.... Up to the time of the Mutiny lions were shot in Central India. They are now confined to an ever narrowing patch of forest in Kathiawar. I was on the verge of contributing to their still further reduction a year ago myself: but fortunately, I found out my mistake in time, and was able to adopt a restraint which I hope that others will follow.[37]

While the viceroy's wish was honoured mostly in its breach, the nawab lost no time in trying to elicit his support for the preservation of lions.

The famine of 1899–1900 was calamitous for the Gir, too. "Almost all the game died" there and it "undoubtedly seriously affected the already dwindling stock of lions", according to M.A. Wynter-Blyth. He goes on to record that lions were "maddened with hunger at that period".[38] In the year 1901 in Junagadh territory alone 9 men were mauled and 31 were killed; 24 cows, 4 calves, 3 buffaloes, 2 young buffaloes, 25 oxen, and 4 other cattle, 61 goats, 3 camels, 8 mares, 3 fillies, and 10 sheep met a similar end. This could hardly have been the work of a dozen lions – the

page 2
H.H. Jám Raṃmalji hunting lions in the Barda hills. From an old fresco in the "Lakota", Jámnagar.

Last of the lions in Barda hills
■ Jam Ranmalji of Navanagar, 1820–52, hunting lions with his nobles, from a fresco in Lakhota in Jamnagar. Some lions survived a few more years thereafter.
From Fenton, circa 1924.

number put out by some sources at the turn of the 20th century.

On June 19, 1901 Diwan Chunilal Sarabhai Hazrat addressed a detailed letter to Captain R.S. Pottinger, Assistant Political Agent, Sorath Prant, that not enough was being done by the neighbouring states and talukas to protect lions. At one point he stated:

> the late famine and drought were not without their effect on the lions also, for their number small as it was in the beginning has undergone a material diminution, and thus the number of animals required [as prey] for their food is also proportionately less, and the loss cannot therefore be heavy.
>
> ... The [neighbouring] States and Talukedars concerned, aught in compliance with the political agent's advise to make arrangements for driving of the lions from their limits, as our own people do within ours, and you will I trust recommend them to help us in our attempt for the preservation of this race by adopting the usual methods of overawing the lions by loud shouts, beating of drums etc. or by frightening them away by shewing logs of burning wood – methods which are well known....[39]

L.L. Fenton, however, has a less flattering story to tell. He was in Kathiawar in 1899–1900 and saw at first hand the famine conditions. He records:

> At the beginning of the famine of 1900 more cattle than ever were brought into the Gir to graze; so the lions were in fact better off than before, but it was only a matter of time before the wild game, which had all along been mercilessly persecuted by the Darbari police and forest guards, who were supposed to look after their preservation, as well as the cattle, began to die off in hundreds for want of fodder. It was then only that the lions like the panthers, began to feel the pinch, and were gradually compelled to leave their usual haunt in the Gir, and wander in search of food. This, of course, brought them more into evidence, and gave rise to the report that owing to the very strict protection which had been accorded to them by the Darbar they had greatly increased in numbers. This was really not the case. At no time had the preservation of the lions been very strictly carried out. The

Hunting party of Jam Ranmalji in Barda hills

■ Frescos from the Lakhota palace, Jamnagar, depict a noble hunter about to strike a charging lion with a sword, and (opposite) a dead lion about to be carried away.

Courtesy Jaydev Nansy C.E.

Darbar was always very liberal in giving both local officers and others permission to shoot one.[40]

It may be noted that this description of the situation was less than a decade into Nawab Rasulkhanji's reign. The nawab quickly followed with a letter to Lord Curzon the viceroy himself, on August 8, 1901:

Your Excellency's kind and considerate suggestion of preserving the Gir Lion – a noble but a very rare animal – from extinction, is most scrupulously attended to, but the task has become specially hard and difficult because the natural strength and ferocity of the animals has generally been impaired to some extent owing to the scarcity of animals of prey in the Gir Jungle, consequent on the last famine, and one or two have been reported to have died of starvation, some of them have left their lairs in the forest and gone over to the plain country on the borders of the Gir, belonging to my territory, as well as over that under His Highness the Gaekwar and other minor states and Talukas in search of prey.

It is apprehended that their truancy from their ordinary haunts, and falling upon domestic animals such as cattle belonging to the subjects of this state as well as of others in the vicinity and precincts of villages may induce the persons suffering to shoot them.

Orders prohibiting the killing of lions are strictly enforced in the state and as regards other states and Talukas in the neighbourhood, I am trying my best, through the Political Agent, to induce them as to arrange that neither their subjects nor their officers might kill the truants, but drive them back to the jungles by frightening as usual. It is however to be seen how far these endeavours will prove effective.

I have ventured to trouble Your Excellency with this narration as I deem it a pleasant duty to do everything to carry out Your Excellency's suggestion to preserve this rare animal. But in spite of our strenuous efforts in this direction, I am afraid that this noble race will be extinguished by the hands of common people, unless the prohibition of destroying it is strictly enforced in all surrounding places alike.[41]

The problem of Junagadh state is clearly set out here. While protection was enforced within its boundaries, i.e. lions were only allowed to be shot if permission was granted by the state, there was a problem once the lions crossed the state boundary. For the lions of course a state or administrative boundary had no meaning. The British government could only coax, advise, or threaten the neighbouring states and talukas, and there were limits beyond which they could not go. Such actions were not effective enough to preserve the lions, as the rulers of these small principalities were free to do what they chose in their territories. They considered Junagadh's lions "fair game" in their areas.

The silver lining was that, on Junagadh state's prompting, Baroda state amended its law of 1876 to protect lions effectively, though the Gaekwad reserved the right to give permission for killing a lion under certain circumstances.[42] In Bhavnagar state as well, there was a similar ban. But in both states the maharajas kept the right to hunt lions and every once in a while this caused some friction with Junagadh as many a lion was decoyed out of Junagadh to be shot. Fenton records:

> Moreover, although there are no lions in the adjoining district of Amreli under
> Baroda, the country being unsuitable, one of the best jungles on the Junagadh side,
> abuts on the boundary between the two states, and I should be sorry to say how
> many *lions have been decoyed across this line and killed by unscrupulous*
> *sportsmen* [emphasis added].[43]

The end of the famine period also saw what Wynter-Blyth describes as a "profound" change in the behaviour of lions. They were never again heard of as being a menace to humans, which was probably owing to conditions returning to normal in the Gir, the cattle moving out, and the prey base recovering.[44]

Though lion shikar was regulated and controlled by the nawab throughout his reign, he did allow them to be shot off and on. In March 1905 Lord Lamington, Governor of Bombay, went to the Gir. His party shot four lions, Lord Curzon's example notwithstanding. It was in this shoot that Major H.C. Carnegie, Political Agent of Halar, was charged and killed by a wounded lion as we have seen earlier.[45]

In the succeeding year Rasulkhanji permitted Maharana Raj Saheb Amarsinhji of Wankaner to do shikar. He was accompanied by K.S. Ranjitsinhji of Navanagar, better known to the cricketing world as "Ranji", and shot a lion at Talala, then part of the Gir forest.[46]

In order to keep the pressure on, Rasulkhanji issued a notification in 1909:

As lions at present exist only in the Gir Forests in the whole of India, the destruction of lions, lionesses or their cubs is hereby strictly prohibited by the order of His Highness the Nawab Saheb of Junagadh with a view to prevent the extinction of the species.

This notification was also published in the *Kathiawar Agency Gazette* over the signature of C.H.A. Hill, Agent to the Governor. He requested the Political Agent of Sorath to take such steps as necessary to ensure cooperation from the neighbouring states and talukas.[47]

Nawab Rasulkhanji died two years later. During his reign the actions that would be taken in future had been initiated. In brief they were that shikar of lions would be permitted only on permission from the nawab and would be restricted to important persons only and, secondly, continuous pressure would be brought to bear on the neighbouring states and talukas to stop them from shooting lions — no matter how unsuccessful this effort would be.

The ninth and last nawab to rule Junagadh, Mahbatkhanji III, was born in 1900. Like his father he was not born to rule. He succeeded to the throne in 1911 at the age of ten because of the death of his elder brother the heir apparent in 1908. Since he was a minor, the British government took over the administration of the state while the young prince was sent to England in 1913–14 with his English tutor and guardian W.C. Tudor-Owen and his wife. In 1916 he was sent off to Mayo College, Ajmer, another school for princes, with his companion Mahamad Bhai and yet another English tutor and guardian H.A.W. Bladen. He was invested with full powers in 1920 when he became a major.[48]

It will be recalled that Rasulkhanji's accession was orchestrated by the diwan. This time the British were taking no chances. Immediately on the death of Rasulkhanji, Major J.B. Carter assumed charge for a day on January 23, 1911 to be followed by Captain H.H. Strong who held office for fourteen days until H.D. Rendall, Judicial Assistant to the Governor of Bombay, could take charge of the state.[49] His administration lasted till 1920 except for a period of nearly one and a half years from November 1911 to March 1913 when L. Robertson, Political Secretary to the Governor, became administrator as Rendall was away on home leave. A very unexpected change came about for the protection of lions. Whereas Rasulkhanji with all good intentions may have come under local pressure from brother princes and British administration for permission to shoot lions, here was a situation in which a British-led administration backed by the might of the empire would have no such problems. It is significant to note that neither a viceroy nor a governor of Bombay went to the Gir for a lion shoot though one governor, Lord Sydenham Clarke, visited Junagadh in 1913 but did not bag a lion. Sir Patrick Cadell who was to be the diwan of Junagadh from 1932 to 1935 recorded that

During the [British] administration, not even a Governor of Bombay, for whom the shooting of a Kathiawar lion had become almost a hereditary "hukk", was invited to shoot in the forest.[50]

After all it would have been difficult for a British-led administration to explain away

Royal hunters
■ Maharana Raj Saheb Amarsinhji of Wankaner (right) accompanied by Jam Ranjitsinhji of Navanagar – better known to the cricketing world as "Ranji" – stands with his trophy in 1906.
Courtesy Maharana Raj Saheb Pratapsinhji of Wankaner.

shikar trips by top British officials during the minority of the nawab whose father had taken such visible steps to protect lions which were believed to be severely threatened and which were the symbol of Junagadh state.

The year 1911 was also a year of scarcity.[51] It was the first year under British administration and it is significant that both the Gir forest and the nearby Girnar forest were thrown open to grazing by cattle from Kathiawar and Gujarat. The state's administration report for the year blandly states that it was "impossible" to save regenerating "coupes" (copses?) in the forests. Widespread damage was caused to young seedlings and this was particularly in areas earmarked for cattle from Ahmedabad district of British India which were sent under "Government arrangements".[52] The interests of Junagadh state were sacrificed for and subordinated to larger British compulsions.

The same report debunks the earlier reports of Nawab Rasulkhanji's time. It records that F.R. Desai's recommendations for the protection and management of the Gir were not acted upon and his report "appears to have been filed in the Diwan's office"![53] At any rate, the forest administration was tightened up. The services of W.A. Wallinger of the Forest Department of Bombay Presidency were sought in 1913 and his working plan became the basis of resource management and protection of the forest.

On the question of protection of lions, H.D. Rendall took up the matter where the nawab's administration had left it. W.A. Wallinger painted a very gloomy picture of the number of lions left[54] and making that the cause, he dashed off a letter on May 13, 1913 to the Agent to the Governor asking the latter to ensure cooperation from neighbouring states and talukas. In June of the same year, he issued a notification of Junagadh state wherein he referred to the 1909 notification of Nawab Rasulkhanji, stating that the number of lions was now "seriously diminished" and all steps would be taken for the preservation of lions and directed that all "Junagadh subjects should cooperate in this purpose". The same notification was published in the *Kathiawar Gazetteer* under the authority of W.P. Cowie, Personal Assistant to the Agent to the Governor, with the addition that it requested the neighbouring states and talukas to endeavour to cooperate in the effort.[55]

Three princes wanted to shoot lions about this time and approached the administrator L. Robertson. Kumar Shri Vijayrajji of Kutch was informed that two lions had already been promised to other sportsmen and he, therefore, could not be

Protectors of lions

■ Maharaja Sayaji Rao Gaekwad of Baroda shot this lion in Amreli district in 1900, the trophy was among the largest lions recorded in India.
Author's collection.

■ Maharaja Krishnakumarsinhji of Bhavnagar (right) stands beside Yuvraj Pratapsinhji of Wankaner with a lion shot by the latter in Mytiala forest in Bhavnagar state, 1939.
Courtesy Y. Digvijaysinhji of Wankaner.

accommodated. Maharaja Jam Saheb Ranjitsinhji of Navanagar whose depredations
were to exasperate Junagadh was somewhat sternly informed that he could not be
granted permission to shoot in the Gir because, as Robertson put it:

> I say roundly that my jungle [Junagadh's Gir] will be quite enough shot by my own
> friends....
> I hear today that you have gone to shoot at Mendarda, of course the Mendarda
> jungle has nothing to do with me ... and I am sending orders that my men are not
> to prevent animals [leopards] from the Junagadh Gir crossing the boundary should
> they be attracted by your kills [baits].
> I have done so on the understanding that your party will not shoot a lion, should a
> lion appear in any of your beats or at any of your kills.

Navanagar state had extended financial assistance to Jetpur state which had a small
enclave of Gir forest. Ranjitsinhji often camped at Andhaniya in Jetpur territory and
shot lions to the chagrin of Junagadh's nawabs and administrators.

The third applicant Maharaja Ganga Singh of Bikaner was informed through his
private secretary that the request for his visit to the Gir in 1913 could not be
accommodated. Citing Wallinger's findings on how few lions were left in the Gir,
Robertson wrote, surely the Maharaja would take a "sportsman's view and
understand the difficulties of our position", though before Wallinger's report was
received, he had agreed in February to the visit. A few years later in 1917 the Raja of
Poonch, a feudatory of the state of Jammu and Kashmir, was informed that his
request for a lion shoot could not be met as such permissions were given only in
exceptional circumstances and "moreover many applications [were] already upon
our waiting list"![56] After all the ruler of Poonch was not in the same league as the
Maharaja of Bikaner.

Another ticklish problem developed during the British administration of
Junagadh. H.D. Rendall received a letter in 1914 from L. Robertson who by this time
had become Secretary, Political Department of the Government of Bombay
Presidency, that the Secretary of State for India had received a request from the
British Museum, London, for an Indian lion – which meant that a skin and complete
skeleton were required. It may be noted that Nawab Rasulkhanji had sent a live lion
in 1902 to the Alipore Zoo, Calcutta which arrived there much the worse for wear,
and the skin of a lion had been procured for the Bombay Natural History Society.
The administrator was therefore in a delicate position. He replied that the request
should be postponed for at least a year or two because he

> ... had during the last year to refuse requests of several Chiefs for a shoot in the
> Gir. It is extremely difficult to secure cooperation in this direction, and you are
> aware that there have been one or two unpleasant incidents in this connection.
> We might therefore be liable to misconstruction of an undesirable kind if we
> transgressed our own pact, even in the interest of science, and I am particularly
> anxious to avoid any such impression.[57]

In the event, the matter rested there.

It appears that at the turn of the 20th century it was a common practice to send
all captured cubs from the jungle to Junagadh to be kept there in one or another
garden of the town.[58] In 1919 this practice was banned by a state circular addressed
to the officers of the Gir:

> ... a havaldar of a block caught cubs of a vaghan [tigress] and gave them to the
> block officer who in turn sent them to us. In this manner innocent cubs have been

harassed which has not been liked by us at all. Similarly Namdar Hazur Shree [Nawab Saheb] has also not liked it, therefore in future cubs of vaghan [tigress] or singhan [lioness] are not to be caught or harassed....[59]

There were no tigers in the Gir and the cubs could have been those of a leopard. Considering that the circular is signed by K.G. Trivedi, Chief Range Officer of the Gir, it is an inexplicable error.

The British administration also faced other problems of cattle killed by lions in Junagadh and beyond, lions shot in Baroda and elsewhere, and so on. But they remained steadfast in their resolve to enforce protection for these animals. They built on the foundation laid by Nawab Rasulkhanji and his diwans which in itself was supported by the British government.

Many princes had hunting grounds in India and larger states such as Gwalior, Mysore, Cooch Behar, and others had exceptionally good ones. They protected them as state properties, animals were monopolies regulated by the rulers themselves, particularly the large carnivores which were usually tigers. Many of these princes hunted extensively, the epitome of them all being the well known case of the Maharaja Ramanuj Saran Singh Deo of Surguja (r. 1917–48) who accounted for over 1,100 tigers. And yet state monopoly gave breathing space and time to the animals because their habitat was strictly protected and the number of persons hunting them was limited to the maharaja, his family, and perhaps a favoured guest. Two species, the hangul and the sangai, survived because of the protection they received from the administrations of the states of Jammu and Kashmir and Manipur.

While the case of the lion is similar to that of the hangul and sangai it is unique in its own way. Nawab Rasulkhanji had never shot a lion. He was not interested in shooting lions, and their protection he considered to be his responsibility. As he himself has recorded, the lion was to be found only in the Gir in India and its disappearance from there would spell doom for the species.

His bid to give protection to a large carnivore was the earliest anywhere in the world. Though lions were hunted in his state, the numbers of such hunts were very few and permissions were hard to come by. He began the effort that pulled the lion back from the precipice of annihilation.

There is another important fallout from his policy. His demise saw a British administration take charge of Junagadh followed by the effete administration of the last nawab. However, Rasulkhanji had built a tradition which was easy to follow and difficult to ignore. This was his noble legacy.

CHAPTER 9

The Last Nawab Battles On

Tipu Sultan on his throne
■ Unlike other princes and kings in India Tipu was obsessed by tigers, his throne naturally was a "tiger throne".
The Trustees of The National Museums of Scotland.

Honorary Colonel His Highness Sir Mahbatkhanji III, G.C.I.E., K.C.S.I.* Nawab Saheb of Junagadh[1] as he would become by 1947, was invested with full powers in 1920 by the British government on his attaining majority. On ascending the throne he issued a proclamation saying:

> With complete confidence I command my beloved subjects to obey my orders; to be loyal to me as you have been to my dynasty hitherto, to give respect to my duly authorized officers, and to live with each other with understanding, peace and harmony for that is how happiness and development are attained....[2]

With these lofty words began the reign of the ninth and last nawab of the Babi dynasty. In general, in spite of the economic crash of 1929, the second world war of 1939–45, and the turbulent waves of the independence movement beating the shores of princely India, it was a time of peace and progress in the state. The administrative machinery set up over the previous two decades held fast and served the nawab well, with a few hiccups now and then, until everything came apart in the fateful year of 1947. But there were foreshadows of coming events. As early as 1911, the British Administrator had some misgivings about the child who would be nawab, for the state's administration report for that year declares:

> The Minor Chief [Mahbatkhanji] is somewhat backward, but under the care of his tutor and guardian Mr. Turkhad, he has already advanced both in physical and mental attainments....[3]

As mentioned earlier, the teenage prince was sent to England and after that to Mayo College, Ajmer, under the guardianship of English tutors and with his companion Mahamad Bhai. Even after assuming the title of nawab, he remained for the most part, a nominal head of state. It is said that though he took interest in the administration of the state, he preferred to let his diwans have a free hand. Between 1920 and 1924 three Hindu diwans who were Nagar brahmans held office, until his childhood companion Amir Sheikh Mahamad Bhai Saheb, as he was now styled, was elevated to that office in 1924 and held sway till February 1932. He was given the honorific title of vazir in 1931, but came under a cloud soon thereafter and had to suddenly leave his post. The nawab had to fall back on the imperial government's resources and Sir Patrick Cadell took over as diwan. He was followed by J. Monteath in 1935[4] who revamped the entire state machinery. Three Indian Muslim diwans came after this, two of whom served the state faultlessly. The last one presided over the final fateful days of the state.

Today Mahbatkhanji is all but forgotten in India, his one monumental act of political folly having consigned him to oblivion. If remembered at all, it is for his fondness for dogs and his excesses, real or imagined. The redoubtable V.P. Menon, Secretary to the Ministry of States, Government of India, who was one of the architects of the integration of Indian states into the Dominion of India, wrote that the nawab had "hundreds" of dogs and he had organized a wedding for two of his pets on which a huge sum of money was spent, the wedding day being declared a state holiday![5] According to another source, the nawab's favourite golden retriever bitch was "married" to "Bobby" of the Nawab of Mangrol. The groom rode on an elephant and was accompanied by a wedding party of 250 dogs. A three-day holiday was declared in the state to mark the event.[6] While it is true that the nawab was fond

---

* Extra Knight Grand Commander of the Indian Empire and Honorary Knight Commander of the Star of India. The Order of the Star of India was instituted in 1861 and the Order of the Indian Empire was instituted in 1877 by Queen Victoria to honour, among others, Indian princes and British subjects who had served the Indian Empire.

***Junagadh throne and chairs of state
with lion armrest***
■ These are preserved in the Darbar Hall
at Junagadh. The throne is surmounted
by a *chhattra*, the traditional Indian
symbol of royalty. It is like the throne of
any Hindu ruler.
Photograph: Bhushan Pandya.

of dogs and had many of them, enquiries with the late Shambhuprasad Desai, IAS,
who was on the nawab's personal staff, with Jaisukhlal P. Sodha the author of the
only biography of the nawab and others in Kathiawar reveal that such reports were
often exaggerated.[7] All those who knew the nawab talk of his benign and gentle
nature. His love of the Kathi horse (the Kathiawari breed) was legion. He maintained
a fine stud farm and preserved the breed from extinction. These horses, used as
mounts by the Gujarat police today, are a part of his legacy. He was equally fond of
cows and particularly the Gir breed which he protected. Sodha records that the
nawab's two favourite cows were named Kapila and Janaki. The nawab's
administration banned slaughter of draught and milch cattle and forbade selling of
cattle for slaughter in 1944–45.[8] According to Shambhuprasad Desai, the nawab's
favourite cow was called Kaveri and she went wherever the nawab went in his state.
He had to see Kaveri's face first thing in the morning. Once while returning from
Veraval to Junagadh on his special train, he suddenly found that Kaveri had been
left behind. He stopped the train for her to be brought on to it, and when she was,
he went to her, embraced her, and said "Mother, did I forget you? Do forgive me."[9]

   As for the lions, he considered them to be his own. They were royal game and he
shot them as per the custom of his time though he exercised self-imposed limits.
However, his impulse was always to protect rather than shoot. Often the nawab
would go for shikar to the Gir. He would sit on the machan and wait. The Forest
Department staff would have worked tirelessly to produce the largest lion with the
darkest mane for the Master of Junagadh. The beat would begin, the lion would
come through the path in front of the machan but the nawab would not shoot. He
would come down and say *"Mian, kala nahin hai, agle jumme aunga"* (The lion's
mane is not black, I'll come next Friday). He thus made sure that he knew what was
happening in the jungle and generally kept his staff on their toes.[10]

   One way of gauging the number of lions shot by sportsmen is to look at the
records of taxidermists who specialize in making trophies. Of the several
establishments that came up, two stand out – Cuthertson & Harper of Calcutta and

Stamp paper of Junagadh state

■ The older version has the lion with the Junagadh fort and Girnar in the background in a red medallion.

■ (opposite) The last nawab modernized the design but retained the medallion on either side of his own likeness.

Author's collection.

van Ingen & van Ingen of Mysore. The usual practice of Indian princes, as indeed other sportsmen of discerning taste, was to go to one or the other, though some sent their trophies to Rowland Ward in London. Junagadh's trophies went to Mysore. E. Joubert van Ingen, a partner of the firm, sent me copies of what survives of their records.[11] They are complete for the years 1929 to 1932 during which period they received eight lion skins and skulls from Junagadh. In the eight-year period 1940 to 1947 they received six lion skins and skulls from there. Not included in this tally are two lion skins and skulls sent to them by the Mehmandari department of Junagadh state which would mean that these lions were shot by the nawab's guests, though the list would include skins and skulls of lions that may have died in the Sakkarbag Zoo of Junagadh. It is interesting to note that one lion shot by Shahzada Dilawarkhanji, the heir apparent, reached van Ingen on August 23, 1947[12] which means that the shikar may well have taken place a day or two before or after the nawab announced his accession to Pakistan on August 15!

According to van Ingen's record, in the twelve years between 1929–32 and 1940–47 they had received the skins of fifteen lions. How many of these were shot by the nawab and his family is difficult to ascertain; of the fifteen skins sent from Junagadh, eight were from the diwan's office and two were from the chief forest officer's office. These animals may well have been from the zoo, or those that died naturally or were poached. Five skins came from the nawab's office, two in 1938 and one each in 1940, 1944, and 1945.[13] Sir Patrick Cadell, the former diwan of Junagadh records that the nawab was a keen conservationist and that he had shot only *one* lion between 1920 and 1933.[14]

The lion was the largest carnivore in the state and the nawabs took pride in its existence. It was therefore natural that it would occupy a central position as a royal symbol and as symbol of the state. The sixth nawab, Mahbatkhanji II who ruled from 1851 to 1882 is seen in a painting standing by a gilded chair with lion arm rests. Each of his three successors is seen sitting on a similar chair.[15] The nawab held darbar sitting on a *simhasana* like any of his Hindu brother princes of India. On assuming the title Kaiser-i-Hind – Empress of India – on January 1, 1877, Queen Victoria presented Nawab Mahbatkhanji II a banner whose armorial bearings had two argent rampant lions as supporters.[16] Rasulkhanji, the eighth nawab, had adopted a state emblem which had a mountain representing Girnar, a castle representing the fort from which the city and the state took their name of Junagadh meaning "old fort", a rising sun, a lion couchant – the pride of the state and symbol of royalty, and the sea with three masted sailing ships representing the port of Veraval. The oval medallion with this emblem has Junagadh state and Saurashtra written on its border. This symbol was used by the state and the nawabs on their stationery, judicial stamp paper, royal cutlery and crockery. These were discontinued sometime in 1948, the year after the nawab left for Karachi, Pakistan, though I remember using such cutlery and crockery in the nawab's forest lodge in 1958 which by then had passed on to the Forest Department of Bombay state. E.P. Gee records that the Forest Department staff were still wearing the letters "JF" for "Junagadh Forests" on the epaulets of their uniforms in 1956,[17] that is nearly a decade after the last nawab's departure.

Junagadh state even used the lion on postage stamps; in fact it was the first to do so. The modern postal system using postage stamps had started in India in 1852 with the "Scinde District Dak", and about twelve years later Junagadh state set up its

On royal stationery
■ The medallion with the lion in the middle, Girnar mountain and the Junagadh fort with a rising sun forming the backdrop, was used on royal stationery up to 1947.
Author's collection.

own modern postal system. In 1928 a decision was made by the state to issue postage stamps which were to be printed at the Security Press at Nasik. Four symbols were chosen: a likeness of the nawab, Junagadh city, a Kathi horse, and a Gir lion. When the samples of the stamps arrived in Junagadh, the likeness of the lion did not satisfy Diwan Amir Sheikh Mahamad Bhai. He remarked, in a letter to Colonel G.H. Willis, Master of Security Printing, Nasik, India, that it was "... a poor effort, but I think you can perhaps arrange a lion for us. The Gir lion and the African lion are identical as you will see from the picture"![18]

The final result was satisfactory enough and postage stamps were issued with the denomination of ½ anna and 4 annas with the Gir lion and denominations of 2 and 8 annas for the Kathi horse.[19] The mane of the lion and its general aspect are realistic enough to identify it as a specimen from the Gir. This was the first time that any animal had featured on a postage stamp anywhere in the Indian Empire. On an enquiry from one Mr McDonald from Jabalpur, the diwan's office replied on February 28, 1931 explaining the symbolism of the two animals:

> ... "Gir lion" symbolizes the survival of the Indian lion in the Gir forest of this state alone throughout India. The Gir lion, accordingly, is also one of the symbols in the Armorial bearings of this state.
>
> ..."Kathi Horse" signifies *Zortalbi* or tribute formally collected by the Junagadh State Cavalry mounted on Kathi horses (though it is collected since 1821 through the British Government) from no less than 134 out of 193 states and Talukas of Kathiawar.[20]

The lion had to wait another 34 years to again grace a postage stamp in India,[21] while the Kathi horse, once an indispensable war machine, still awaits its turn. It is strange that the lion did not make an appearance on the British period postage stamps as it had done on East India Company gold mohurs very much earlier. Actually, as early as 1853, the East India Company prepared essays (a contemplated design drawn and laid out) for postage stamps with the lion on them. Proofs from steel engraved dies in vermilion, black, and blue were printed. Pulls from copper plates were taken as late as in 1922 as well, but that is where things remained.[22] For whatever reason, these postage stamps were not issued.

The reign of Rasulkhanji and the British administration had set the stage for Mahbatkhanji's battles. He had inherited both the problem and the response to it. It is to his credit that he continued on the path of preservation in spite of all odds. He may have had other faults, but lions for him held a special place as we shall see. Within one year of Mahabatkhanji ascending the throne, he was faced with a full-blown lion crisis. He received a letter from Maharaja Jam Saheb Ranjitsinhji of Navanagar informing him that he and Maharaja Ganga Singh of Bikaner were invited by Darbar Muluwala of Pithadia, Jetpur (a Kathi taluka enclave in Junagadh state) to shoot in the Mendarda portion of the Gir. He was writing to Mahbatkhanji at the request of Maharaja Ganga Singh for permission to shoot a lion. The nawab replied by telegram to say that he could not allow a lion to be shot from Mendarda territory and followed it up with a letter to Jam Saheb Ranjitsinhji to say that twelve lions had been shot that year already and the matter of such depredations in neighbouring territories had already become a subject of correspondence with the British government. He was sure, he added, Maharaja Ganga Singh would not think of shooting "my lions" in the territories of neighbouring principalities. On receiving this letter Jam Saheb Ranjitsinhji sent a letter to Mahbatkhanji asking if he and

Maharaja Ganga Singh could call on him at Junagadh. The same request was made by Maharaja Ganga Singh as well. The nawab sent a polite reply but regretted that he was unable to meet them as he was busy with the approaching Ramazan Id and subsequent engagements in the state![23]

Relations between Jam Saheb Ranjitsinhji and Junagadh state thus reached a nadir. It is interesting to note that in 1907 when Ranjitsinhji had become the Jam Saheb of Navanagar, it was Junagadh state which had been his benefactor. The latter had even provided him with Arab bodyguards, a large retinue of servants and even cooks to accompany him to Jamnagar to ensure his safety when he went there to take charge of his principality.[24] Now in 1920, barely thirteen years later, the son of his benefactor had had enough. Incidentally, Junagadh was not the only state which suffered Jam Saheb Ranjitsinhji's shikar forays; he regularly tied baits for leopards along the Navanagar Porbandar border to lure them into his territory for shikar.[25] Out of exasperation the nawab addressed a letter to E. Maconochie, Agent to the Governor in Kathiawar, along with the correspondence he had had with Jam Saheb Ranjitsinhji and Maharaja Ganga Singh. The letter bears quoting at some length as it hits at the nub of the problem as seen by Mahbatkhanji. He wrote:

> As a matter of fact the real point at issue is the ownership of lions and the political right of inviting distinguished visitors to Kathiawad for lion shikar. The occasional shooting of lions which stray from the forest to surrounding territories is of no particular importance. The race can never be wiped out thereby. But what I complain of is that lions are tempted to stray outside by tying up buffaloes just over my borders ... organized shikar parties go out and shoot lions under cover of the pretext that they are doing damage outside the forest. This is nothing more or less than poaching from which I think I have a right to be protected by [the Imperial] Government. If I were to take the law into my own hands as my forefathers would have done, the result would be a constant series of border affrays which would endanger the peace of this part of Kathiawad.
>
> It is an unquestionable fact that the house of the lion is the Gir forest and equally unquestioned that the forest is my ancestral property. The preservation of the forest which covers about 500 sq. miles [1,295 square kilometres] of my territory is supposed to be of value to the province as a whole, not only as a constant source of grass and fire wood, but also because of its effect on rainfall. But what has undoubtedly weighed with the Nawabs of Junagadh in the past and carries weight also with me is that the forest is the last sanctuary of Indian Lions. If the lion were eliminated, I should certainly adopt a policy of disafforestation which would add to my revenues and simplify the difficulties of administration. The sacrifice which the neighbouring jurisdictional holders are called upon to bear by reason of the existence of the lions is small. The brunt of it is borne by Junagadh and ownership with all that it implies rightly appertains to Junagadh.
>
> I would therefore ask that the [Imperial] Government may fully consider the matter and use their influence to see that my rights are respected and especially the scandal of tying up buffaloes within sight of my borders is stopped.[26]

Apart from the nawab claiming ownership of lions, for the first time he points out that the lion is what we would call today a flagship species for the forest which has wider direct and indirect benefits to humans.

E. Maconochie referred the matter to A. Montgomery, Secretary to the Government, Political Department, Bombay with a covering letter which pointed out:

... lions are a substantial nuisance to Junagadh's neighbours. The latter [small neighbouring states and talukas] are impressed less than in former times by the prestige of the Nawab of Junagadh and are more inclined to stand by their right to shoot wild animals that are found in their own territory, a right which is not easy to question. [Jam Saheb Ranjitsinhji who is not a neighbour but a keen shikari] ... is constantly indulging in vicarious hospitality by promising distinguished personages a lion, if they will pay him a visit. Some of the Kathi Durbars are always anxious to oblige him and his poaching parties are a constant cause of exasperation to His Highness the Nawab ... to the average Englishman the whole question would seem to be one of ordinary gentlemanly feeling between neighbours. I doubt if His Highness the Jamsaheb would in England entice his neighbour's pheasants into his fields and then shoot them. But he apparently sees nothing derogatory in tying up buffaloes all along the Junagadh border with a view to poaching lions.

The question now is what attitude the Imperial and Local governments desire to adopt in the matter. If it is thought that the preservation of the lions is a matter of Imperial interest ... it seems incumbent on the Imperial government to state their views clearly, to support the Nawab's monopoly and to bring such pressure as is possible to bear on Baroda and other states concerned. If they are not prepared to do this the only alternative seems to me to be to inform the Nawab ... that they are not prepared to take any definite action in the matter. Personally I am inclined to regard the lion as a dangerous anachronism, who does a lot of damage and wastes a great deal of my time and I should contemplate his final departure with equanimity.

Here is a bureaucrat at his wits' end only looking for a way out to rid himself of a nuisance. He ends the letter by saying that the nawab's threat of disafforestation need not be taken seriously as it would affect his own state.[27]

The Bombay government sent a reply to E. Maconochie that it would not be possible for the government to intervene though they would regret the complete disappearance of the lion. Further, it was hoped that the nawab would continue to protect lions and give them a sanctuary in his own state, and that his efforts at preservation would be successful. The government also expressed its belief "that His Highness will not seriously contemplate a step so disastrous for his own interests and so opposed to the welfare of the whole province as the disafforestation of the Gir."[28]

The nawab had played his trump card by claiming ownership of all lions, by threatening to take the law into his own hands to protect the lion, and finally to cut the forest for revenue if the lion disappeared. From here he had no fall-back position. The Bombay government sympathized but refused to interfere. Nor did the government react to the nawab's claim to the ownership of lions. It was clear to the nawab that henceforth he would have to battle on alone, with little or no imperial support. It is pertinent to note that this incident took place during the tenure of an Indian diwan, Tribhuvanrai Duleram Rana, and it happened only because the nawab felt so deeply about the protection and ownership of lions. It has been often said that the nawab preserved lions to oblige high ranking British officers and thus seek favours from the imperial government. While there may be some truth in this, it was equally true that such visitations were not an unmixed blessing for the state either. Sir Patrick Cadell who was to be the diwan of the state from 1932 to 1935, noted that not a single officer of Junagadh had shot a lion, the distinction of inviting guests for lion shikar cost the state thousands of rupees, and there was a continuous outflow of expenses to compensate subjects for their animals killed by lions. "When Junagadh hears of people being invited from far to shoot lions which are a charge on the state's exchequer the game sometimes seems hardly worth the candle."[29]

Relations with Baroda state were prickly at best because of the lions crossing over into their territory and being shot there. There was an agreement between Baroda and Junagadh of 1909 which required Baroda state not to shoot lions but drive them back. Only in case of damage done by them in the Gaekwad's territory should they be destroyed, after obtaining permission from Junagadh. In 1922 L.M. Crump, the British Resident at Baroda, proposed to Lieutenant Colonel W.W.P. Wood, the Agent to the Governor in Kathiawar, that while the agreement was in force Baroda state should be allowed to shoot four lions each year. Obviously, this was more for trophy hunting than protecting the cattle and property of the subjects of the Gaekwad. The Junagadh authorities were not taken in by the proposal forwarded to the nawab. In his reply to Colonel Wood, the diwan of Junagadh rejected the idea and pointed out that Junagadh state made no profit out of lions, but their disappearance would be a blow to the prestige of the state as well as "a distinct loss to the zoological world".[30] The lion deserved protection for its own sake as well, and Junagadh lost no time in pressing home this point.

Thus the battle with Baroda carried on with no resolution of the problem. Junagadh would have to use its own resources to protect its lions, usually by scaring or enticing them back from the borders of the state. The method was formalized by a circular with clear instructions from the Chief Forest Officer of the state in 1928.[31]

Junagadh state meticulously maintained detailed records of animals lost to lion and leopard predation and circulated specific instructions to all forest staff on the information that was to be collected from each owner who had lost his cow, buffalo, bullock, etc.[32] On the other hand the state refused to pay compensation to subjects of neighbouring principalities, fearing a plethora of false claims.[33]

Apart from lions, Junagadh was also restricting the shooting of other game animals by neighbouring princes and other shikaris. As early as 1913 H.D. Rendall had turned down a request of Khan Shri Fatehdinkhanji, ruler of the small Babi principality of Manavadar, to shoot leopards in the Gir, on the plea that five of them had been shot recently and that they should not be "exterminated altogether". In any case, he wrote, "the supply of big game does not equal the many demands made upon our resources".[34] Several years later in 1935, Khan Fatehdinkhanji's son Khan Gulammoinuddinkhanji who was to accede to Pakistan in 1947, made a request to shoot wolves. This too met with the same response. Sir Patrick Cadell who had become the diwan of Junagadh informed him that Nawab Mahbatkhanji would not have any objection to his shooting wild boar or chinkara or blackbuck under the permits given earlier, nor did he have any objection to pig sticking, but when it came to wolves it was a different matter because they were so few and they do so little harm "that His Highness does not desire any of them shot".[35] It is noteworthy that this protection came at a time when wolves were being shot as vermin in British India and bounties were paid for leopards elsewhere.[36] Here again Junagadh state was way ahead of its time. Nawab Mahbatkhanji had always been very concerned about depleting wildlife in the state and as early as 1925, the matter was considered serious enough to issue a firman which was the highest form of a declaration, over the signature of the nawab himself, banning all shikar in the state. The firman

explicitly states that the situation was alarming and therefore, all shikar was being
banned until further orders and permission henceforth would be given by the nawab
himself only in exceptional cases.[37] This declaration too was during the tenure of an
Indian diwan, Darbar Viravala Muluvala of Bagasra.

Thus in effect only very limited shikar would take place within the state and more
often than not only Indian princes and British officers were given permission for it.
For example, Maharaja Ganga Singh of Bikaner shot four lions between 1940 and
1941[38] in spite of all the previous problems he had earlier with Mahbatkhanji. Khan
Saheb Gulammoinuddinkhanji of Manavadar sent seven lion skins – three in 1940
alone – to van Ingen & van Ingen.[39] It is likely however, that most of his trophies
were obtained outside Junagadh territory.

While there was a method in the control of shikar within Junagadh, the
neighbouring states and talukas remained a problem. For instance, in 1934 M.K.
Chandrabhanusinhji of Wankaner went to Mendarda for lion shikar on the invitation

of Darbar Mansurwala of Anida, one of the talukadars of the Mendarda enclave within Junagadh state. He shot one lion and three lionesses, though Junagadh had advance information of this shikar and according to Chandrabhanusinhji's diary "The Junagadh people gave us a lot of trouble by firing shots in the air, they used to frighten animals [refers mainly to lions] all day and night."[40]

M.K. Natwarsinhji of Gondal wounded a lion in 1938 near the village of Dadar in the Gondal state enclave within Junagadh. He followed up the animal on foot. According to one source he was carrying his rifle in *dang* (shepherd's staff) fashion across the back of his neck, supporting his hands on it, when he was charged and mauled by the wounded lion. Another source says his shikari who was carrying his rifle ran away on being charged.[41] He was hospitalized in Junagadh but succumbed to his injuries. The internal report of the Forest Officer, Sasan Division which went up to the diwan of Junagadh wryly states that on November 26, 1938 the Gondal prince had wounded a lion or lioness which in turn mauled him and two other men and "it is not clear whether it [the animal] is dead or still alive",[42] but there is no mention of the condition of the prince or any members of his party!

Among the unusual incidents of princely sport was that of Thakore Dharmendra Sinhji of Rajkot who died of a heart attack while drinking coffee after having shot a lion in 1940 at Dalkhania in Baroda Gir.[43] During the early decades of the 20th century one prince took great delight in poaching lions and paying a fine in Baroda territory. When Baroda state wrote to tell him that the next time he wanted to do lion shikar the state would readily make the necessary arrangements, the erring prince lost interest and stopped shooting lions! Another prince is reputed to have brought his son-in-law for a lion shoot. He had an understanding with the Junagadh *pagis* whom he was to pay a truly "princely sum" of Rs 5,000 to drive out a lion from Junagadh into a neighbouring state. Finally, the sum was not paid and the shikar party returned empty-handed. Bilkha, another neighbouring state was ruled by Darbar Rawatvala who was Nawab Mahbatkhanji's contemporary and a close friend. He shot about ten lions between 1937 and 1950. The nawab invited him to Sasan Gir in 1941 and gave him a healthy male lion in the hope that he would stop shooting lions, now that he had his own. It did not have the desired effect.[44]

Among the prominent British personages who went to the Gir for a shoot were Sir George Ambrose Lloyd, Governor of Bombay in 1922, General Lord Rawlinson, Commander-in-Chief of the Indian Army in 1923, and the highest of them all – Lord Linlithgow, Viceroy who shot a lion in 1940.[45] Lord Curzon's plea was conveniently forgotten if his successors were at all aware of it.

It appears that the Junagadh state gave permission to shoot about three lions every year according to one authority, while another mentions a figure of four or five lions per year. Thus about five lions annually were being shot legally within the state.[46] The administration reports of Junagadh started mentioning that steps were being taken to protect lions in the state from 1914–15 onwards right up to 1942–43. The reports for the same years also gave information about lions, which the state had claimed as theirs, that were being shot outside the Junagadh territories without control. The reports give the following figures:

YEAR	NO. OF LIONS SHOT	NO. OF LEOPARDS SHOT
1920–21	12: large and small	
1935–36	12: 5 lions, 2 lionesses, 5 cubs	3: 2 leopards, 1 leopardess
1936–37	4: 1 lion, 3 lionesses	4: 3 leopards, 1 leopardess
1937–38	11: 9 lions, 2 lionesses	
1938–39	6: 4 lions, 2 lionesses	10
1939–40	9: 4 lions, 5 lionesses	4
1940–41	16: 12 lions, 4 lionesses	
1941–42	12: 8 lions, 4 lionesses	
1942–43	7: 2 lions, 5 lionesses[47]	

On an average therefore the neighbouring princes shot 9.6, say ten, lions a year during the eight-year period between 1935–36 and 1942–43 based on the information reaching Junagadh officials. It must be noted however that the information could not have been complete and the actual number may have been higher. Thus, while Junagadh was shooting a maximum of five lions a year, the neighbouring states and talukadars accounted for twice that number in spite of all the efforts of the nawab. Protection of the lion remained the latter's problem till the end. In fact the 1934–35 report mentions that a census had been ordered to see how far poaching from outside the state had diminished the numbers of Gir lions. The next year gives the result of the census and declares that only about 150 lions were left in Junagadh territory.[48]

Effectively, this meant that on an average more than fifteen lions were shot annually. This was after all the efforts the nawab made to protect them and particularly to stop or reduce the number of lions being shot outside Junagadh. What would have happened without his efforts can easily be imagined. It is evident that the nawab's policy was a resounding success, in spite of lions being shot at this level and the chaos of 1947 caused by the nawab's accession to Pakistan, when several more lions were shot. The lion population not only survived but actually increased impressively between 1936 and 1950. M.A. Wynter-Blyth's census figures of 1950 threw up a conservative number of 217 to 227 lions and a maximum number of 243 to 251 lions surviving in that year.

The protection of lions in Junagadh was a result of the traditions and beliefs of the time. Traditionally, the largest predator was reserved for royal game, and in Junagadh this was the lion. The rulers of the state considered the lion their property as indeed were the forests in which it lived. The last nawab of Junagadh laid claim to lions everywhere in Kathiawar on the grounds that his lions were wandering about and the princes of neighbouring states and talukas were poaching his lions when they entered their territories. Though the nawab never propagated a complete ban on shooting lions, he was concerned that the total loss of the lion would be a loss to zoology and though unstated, it would cause the disappearance of a unique source of state pride and patronage as well. Whatever the nawab's other faults, on the matter of protecting lions, he was steadfast in his pursuit. It was the efforts of Junagadh state under the last two nawabs, with some encouragement from the British administration, that we have to thank for the survival of over 200 lions and their habitat, the Gir forest, in 1947.

CHAPTER 10

The Dominion of India Inherits Lions

THE INDIAN EMPIRE WAS a mosaic of British India and what was then called "Princely India". In the latter area the British imperial authority was exercised indirectly with varying degrees of control. In 1947 some 565 princely states were in existence, spread over an area of 1,854,346 out of a total 4,095,858 square kilometres,[1] i.e. a little under a third of the total land mass was princely India. In Kathiawar there were 222 states covering almost the entire peninsula, with an area of 56,955 square kilometres. Junagadh was its premier state which in 1947 covered an area of 8,639 square kilometres with a population of 8,16,344, while the smallest "state" Vejano ness, boasted an area of 0.75 square kilometres with a population of 206 souls![2] No wonder that the nawab of Junagadh warranted a fifteen-gun salute as the premier prince of Kathiawar.

The problem of bringing the states into some kind of a political uniformity and mainstream of governance with the rest of India, had dogged the British for a long time. This problem which had remained on the backburner for years, came to the forefront in the political turmoil of 1947. With the impending departure of the British, the states would technically become sovereign by themselves and theoretically they (through their ruler) had the choice of integrating with India or Pakistan, or even remaining in a state of political void bordering on independence by signing a standstill agreement with the new powers. Junagadh's problem suddenly arose not because of independence, but because of the partition of the empire into India and Pakistan, a fact often not fully appreciated.

The story of the partition of the Indian empire and independence of the two successor states, the horrors of the two-way exodus, and the integration of Indian states has been told several times in the past, but the curious developments in Junagadh await detailed examination more than fifty years after the event. Here it is sufficient to recount the highlights of those tumultuous times in order to explain the effects on the protection of lions and the Gir forest.

Junagadh state had a justly earned reputation of being progressive. It possessed an administration which was fair and even-handed to all its subjects regardless of religion. It had evolved to its 1947 status over the preceding half century or more, which had seen a British-led administration for a decade and two British diwans later on. The last nawab, though now only remembered for his love of dogs, was a popular prince who was respected by his subjects. Yet, he was politically naïve to an unbelievable degree. His reign was a peaceful one and no matters had arisen which could have had any serious impact on the fate of the state or his dynasty, so he had never been called upon to exercise any remarkable political acumen. Nineteen forty-seven was different. Junagadh had a longstanding tradition of having several Hindu diwans, almost all from the small community of Nagar brahmans, most of whom had served the Babi dynasty with distinction. In the 20th century, during the minority of Nawab Mahbatkhanji and later, British administrators and diwans ran the administration of the state. The state also had several Muslim diwans. Sahebzada Sardar Mohmed Khan of Tonk state in Rajasthan was diwan from 1938 for nearly four years. Khan Bahadur Abdul Kadir Mohmed Hussain, Oriental Translator to the Government of Bombay, succeeded him in 1942. Both these diwans administered the state ably. In May 1947 Mohmed Hussain went off to the USA for medical treatment and he was replaced by the Senior Member of the Executive Council of Junagadh state, the highest executive body headed by the nawab himself, Khan Bahadur Sir Shah Nawaz Bhutto[3] who belonged to a renowned landowning family of Sind.

A weak, vacillating prince was more often than not dependent on the diwan who assisted and advised him. At a crucial moment in the history of Junagadh, the diwan was a man whose loyalties lay outside the state, outside the province of Bombay – Sind having become a separate province in 1936, and even outside the Dominion of India to be. It was a combination certain to result in disaster for the nawab and his dynasty. On April 29 Diwan Mohmed Hussain's statement was published in the State Gazette, indicating that Junagadh state would merge with India. On August 14, Pakistan became a Dominion within the British Commonwealth with Qaid-i-Azam Mohammed Ali Jinnah – a Shi'ite Khoja Muslim and like Mahatma Gandhi, himself a Kathiawari – became its Governor-General. Old black and white films of the Films Division of India show his spare figure taking the salute under a flag of a dark field with the word "PAKISTAN" in Latin script in the lower half with a lion couchant above, a crown surmounting the lion. The next day the Dominion of India came into existence, and that very day, Junagadh state announced its decision to join Pakistan. No doubt this was to a substantial extent the work of Shah Nawaz Bhutto, who after joining the Pakistan movement had come to Junagadh with the intention of taking the state into the Pakistani fold particularly because of its wealth, position, and proximity to Gandhi's birthplace.[4]

The nawab was carefully isolated from his old friends. Maharana Raj Saheb Pratapsinhji of Wankaner who was a witness to the events of 1947 in Kathiawar himself informed me that Maharana Natwarsinhji of Porbandar and Maharaja Bahadursinhji of Palitana tried to meet the nawab to persuade him to change his decision. The nawab did not meet them. Gulammoinuddinkhanji, the Khan Saheb of Manavadar, a small principality of 262 square kilometres had also decided to accede to Pakistan. All the efforts of his close and old school friend M. Chandrabhanusinhji of Wankaner bore no result. The nawab told the latter that they were very dear friends and would ever remain so, but his mind was made up: he had given his word to Jinnah.[5] Even when V.P. Menon, Secretary, Ministry of States of the Government of India, tried to make contact with the nawab to persuade him to act otherwise, the nawab did not meet him.

By the end of October, the nawab's position had become untenable. Completely isolated, he had lost touch with reality. Towards the end of September, Arzi Hakumat, a government-in-exile under the presidentship of Shyamaldas Gandhi, a cousin of the Mahatma, had been formed at Rajkot. In the event the nawab fled with his begums by plane to Karachi – though one begum had to stay back to retrieve a forgotten offspring – the heir apparent, along with jewellery, the cash balance of the treasury, and some of the nawab's dogs. It is said that as he left Junagadh he looked for the last time at the majestic Girnar mountain peaks with tears in his eyes. After a thoughtful pause he expressed a memorable lament, sotto voce, to no one in particular: "Who will protect my lions now?"[6]

Shah Nawaz Bhutto finally admitted that "Muslims of Kathiawar seem to have lost all enthusiasm for Pakistan". He asked the Government of India to take over the administration of Junagadh state as law and order had broken down. This was done on November 9 by N.M. Buch, ICS, the Regional Commissioner of Rajkot, Bhutto having left for Karachi before that. Junagadh, with eighty per cent Hindu population, was surrounded by Hindu principalities with pockets of territories meeting in a patchwork quilt-like pattern. It was isolated from Pakistan with only the Arabian Sea in common. Accession to Pakistan was doomed to failure from the start.

Princely shikar in independent India
The control of lion shikar passed on to the Rajpramukh of Saurashtra state, Maharaja Jam Shri Digvijaysinhji of Navanagar, who permitted shikar to favoured princes.

■ Maharaja Sawai Man Singh II of Jaipur, Rajpramukh of Rajasthan, with his lion trophy during this period.

■ Maharaja Hari Singh of Jammu and Kashmir with the Rajpramukh Maharaja Jam Shri Digvijaysinhji of Navanagar and his shikar party.
Author's collection.

The change of guard
■ Dr Rajendra Prasad, the first President of India, on a visit to Gir in 1952. After a decade a head of state had come calling on lions. Unlike his predecessor Linlithgow, he had come only to see them and visit the Somnath temple site nearby.
Author's collection.

The events of 1947 were an unexpected disaster for the Gir and its inhabitants. At the time of independence, 1,720 square kilometres of the forest were under the Forest Department of Junagadh state. Gaekwad's Baroda state had 300, Bhavnagar 37, and Jetpur 51 – that is a total of 2,111 square kilometres.[7] In addition, the jungle extended to smaller principalities in the neighbourhood such as Bilkha and Mendarda. While peripheral areas of the Gir forest became a part of the Dominion of India without a hitch, its heart arrived after much confusion, uncertainty, and vandalization over a period of four months, from August to November 1947. The administration of Junagadh state which had been well organized and strong hitherto, became lame. At its head the nawab, his diwan, and the Executive Council had been engulfed by the larger-than-life events which led to the state itself being snuffed out. The protection of Gir and its inhabitants took a backseat during these tumultuous times. Minor princes from neighbouring principalities and other shikaris who would normally not have a hope of shooting a lion were now emboldened. Most of the principalities surrounding Junagadh had always considered lions fair game if they had strayed out of Junagadh territory. With the central authority of Junagadh weakened and preoccupied, here was a chance not to be missed. It appears that several lions were shot, of which no record exists other than those of fading memories.[8] E.P. Gee recorded that a "wholesale killing of wildlife" took place, "particularly of herbivores".[9] This is not surprising, for venison is a delicacy for a Rajput or Muslim shikari though traditionally minded Kathi shikaris would not kill chinkara or blackbuck. M.A. Wynter-Blyth, Principal of Rajkumar College (the former princes' college at Rajkot which had opened to the public in the early 1940s),

Prime Ministerial visit, 1956
In the early years of independence lions were not used to crowds or colourful clothing.
■ Pandit Jawaharlal Nehru in an overcoat for the jungle.
■ (opposite) Smt. Indira Gandhi having alighted from the Willys Jeep station wagon of the forest department, about to wear an overcoat.
Author's collection.

a renowned lepidopterist whose work is standard reference today half a century after its appearance, and an expert on the Gir and its lions, was far more forthcoming about these goings on. Writing barely 1½ years after these events, he records that "at least 5 lions and 2 lionesses ... [were] shot there [in Jetpur state territory alone, the time honoured recipient of vagrant lions of the Junagadh Gir] in 1947.... The slaughter in this year, however, was exceptional."[10]

Several states provided their police force for security duties in Junagadh state after the administration collapsed. One such state was Lunawada whose ruler Maharana Virbhadrasinhji requested Shyamaldas Gandhi for, and was granted, a lion in recognition of his state's services. He shot a male lion in Savarkundla.[11] I have it on good authority that at least three more lions were shot in the same locality about that time and there were similar reports from other areas on the borders of former Junagadh state territory.

What if anything the nawab thought of this, if he knew about it, is unknown. He had spent his entire reign trying to protect lions, but this destruction was the direct consequence of his own actions, something which he seems to have realized moments after he left his palace for Karachi. But there was yet more to come. Three events took place in quick succession. In January 1948 the princes of Kathiawar signed a covenant "to unite and integrate their respective states to form The United State of Kathiawar". A supplementary covenant appointed Jam Saheb Digvijaysinhji of Navanagar Rajpramukh of this state for his lifetime. And finally, yet another supplementary covenant was signed to integrate the states and principalities of Junagadh, Manavadar, Mangrol, Bantwa, Sardargarh, and Babariawad into the "United State of Saurashtra" as it had now come to be known.[12] Thus, Junagadh's political identity was totally merged into the new dispensation while the nawab was in self-imposed exile in Karachi. It will be recalled that Nawab Mahbatkhanji and his administration had consistently taken exception to Jam Saheb Ranjitsinhji's shikar activities on the borders of Gir in years gone by. Now Ranjitsinhji's successor by adoption, Digvijaysinhji had become the Rajpramukh for life. He was quick to take unto himself the nawab's lost prerogative of protecting and permitting lion shikar! This surely was the unkindest cut of all for the nawab.

It is tempting to speculate about what would have happened if the nawab had acceded to India. As head of the premier state of Kathiawar, he would have ended up being the Rajpramukh. This would have given him direct control over the protection of lions including over his troublesome neighbours for the decade 1947–56, for which he had strived all along. It would also have meant that the virtually free-for-all lion shikar would not have taken place in 1947–48.

However, the administration of the new state quickly recovered and started taking corrective action. Wynter-Blyth observed that the new administration of Junagadh stepped in to enforce protection "even more strictly than before" and the Saurashtra government took steps to "prevent the shooting of lions in its territories adjoining the Gir, they are in no danger of extinction, and, an increase in numbers may well occur. Their only enemy seems to be man, and if left alone by him, I believe them well able to look after themselves."[13] He went on to record that between November 1947 and March 1949 lion shikar was stopped completely and only a "negligible" number of lions was poached. By March the situation was considered stable and encouraging enough to allow trophy shikar of four male lions per year,[14] now the Rajpramukh's prerogative, as had been the practice during the nawab's time, though *his* administration had restricted the numbers usually to three per year. The real achievement would have been to stop the shooting of lions in the territories of the principalities bordering Junagadh, but that would take some time. According to Wynter-Blyth, ten to twelve lions were shot in such encounters annually before the integration and merger of princely states in 1947 and 1948,[15] and this continued for a couple of years more. But there was another downside too. He feared that, with the propensity of lions to multiply fast, if such strict protection was continued the population would increase in a short span of time and lions would wander out far away from Gir, which in turn would increase lion-human conflicts. He therefore saw "no reason to suggest any modification in the quota of permits to shoot lions that are being granted at the moment".[16] It should be noted that he was talking of a time when the administration of the state was far more effective and abuse of the system, particularly for such a visible activity, was hardly possible.

In faraway New Delhi the lion was receiving attention in symbolism of the highest order. The Constituent Assembly had come into being to draft the Constitution of India. It laboured from December 1946 to November 1949 when it completed its task. Its own emblem was an outline of India with a tusker superimposed on it encircled by a double circle with the words "CONSTITUENT

On postage stamps again
■ More than thirty years after its first appearance the lion adorns a postage stamp in 1963. It is the well known "Tilyo".
■ Thirteen years later in 1976 another lion appears on a postage stamp.
■ (opposite) Twenty-three years later another encore, this time four stamps on a first-day cover.
Author's collection.

ASSEMBLY INDIA" in the Latin script. One of its objectives was to decide on the national flag and the national emblem.

At my instance, my son Udaybhanusinh, an advocate of the High Court, Bombay undertook research to ascertain how both the flag and the emblem of the Republic came about (see Appendix 5).

An ad hoc committee chaired by Rajendra Prasad and which included among other luminaries Maulana Abul Kalam Azad, C. Rajagopalachari, K.M. Munshi, and B.R. Ambedkar was constituted to make recommendations to the Constituent Assembly regarding the national flag and the national emblem. The committee met on July 10, 1947 and decided that the flag should be the flag of the Indian National Congress with modifications. The tricolour was to have saffron (kesari) on top, white in the middle, and dark green at the bottom. The emblem on the flag would be the "wheel on the capital of Ashoka's Sarnath pillar" in dark blue colour placed at the centre of the middle white band.

The committee also took a tentative decision regarding the emblem and the seal of the republic-to-be which was that

(1)   The emblem and the seal should be of the same design.
(2)   The design should be an exact reproduction of the whole of the Sarnath Ashoka capital till it joins the stem of the pillar (*sthambha*).
(3)   The words "Republic of India" should be superscribed around the emblem and "seal of the Republic of India" around the seal.

The committee decided to meet again to finalize these decisions. They met on July 18, and decided to go ahead with their decision regarding the national flag, but as far as the state seal and emblem were concerned, the committee felt that the matter "was not of immediate urgency, and [the decision] should be postponed until more designs were prepared"![17]

The Constituent Assembly took up the matter of the national flag on July 22. The resolution for its adoption was moved by Jawaharlal Nehru himself and several prominent members spoke in favour of the proposed flag. The resolution was passed unanimously with the whole Assembly standing.[18] The matter of the emblem and the seal however took a curious turn. The Constituent Assembly never approved it and the deliberations were wound up leaving the matter undecided – Udaybhanusinh's research did not throw up any gazette notification and therefore the reasons for and views about the selection of the Ashokan capital remain a matter of speculation.[19] Upon my request Ashok H. Desai, Senior Advocate, Supreme Court of India and former Attorney-General of India, looked into the matter. He came up with a copy of a Press Communiqué dated December 29, 1947 issued by the Ministry of Home Affairs which records the decision on the state emblem and seal.[20] It reads as follows:

The Government of India have now approved a design of their State Emblem and Seal. It has been decided that the State Emblem and Seal should consist of the Sarnath Lion Capital of Ashoka as it exists at present, looked at from the side which shows the lions standing on an abacus which has a Dharma Chakra in the centre, a bull on the right and a horse on the left, and the outlines of the Dharma Chakras on the extreme right and left. The bell shaped lotus at the bottom of the capital has been omitted as the capital would become too long for effective use as a State Emblem or Seal. The reproduction of the capital should be enclosed in a plain double line (the inner line being thin and the outer thick) rectangular frame.

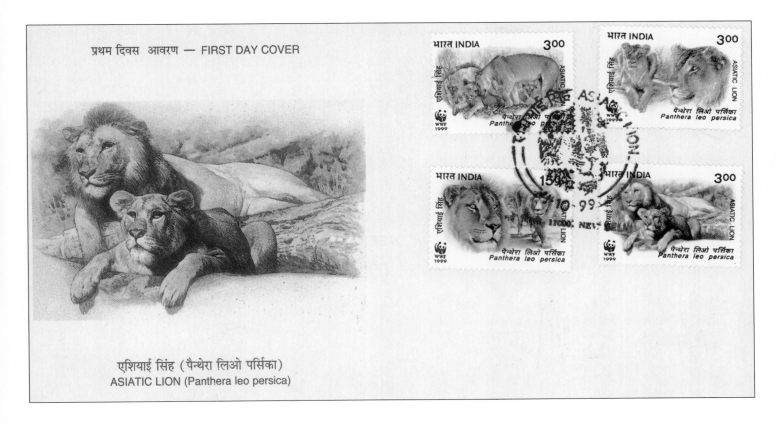

प्रथम दिवस आवरण — FIRST DAY COVER

एशियाई सिंह (पैन्थेरा लिओ पर्सिका)
ASIATIC LION (Panthera leo persica)

A suitable motto will be included in due course as soon as one has been decided upon.[21]

But the emblem had an early critic. M. Krishnan, the conservationist and arguably the most prolific popular writer on nature, was not amused. He wrote:

> Have we no animal more representative of the nation, more nobly rendered in our stone, that could have taken the place of Ashoka's lions, which are not Indian in their art and which are third rate as lions?[22]

He made a plea for the elephant, the "king of our forests" which was "entirely Indian" and was most "brilliantly rendered of all our beasts in our art".[23] Krishnan was from Madras and therefore more familiar with the elephant in art, culture, and in nature. His advocacy of the elephant was natural enough. However, the Constituent Assembly had adjourned, and the elephant was not to be the symbol of the Indian Republic.

Thus, deprived of their lotus base and without the motto of *satyameva jayate* which was to follow, Ashoka's lions replaced the British signet as the emblem of the Dominion of India, its most palpably visible bequest to our republic. That such a momentous decision was taken by an executive fiat and not by the Constituent Assembly is a fact which has passed into history unnoticed. We have inherited the epitome of a monarchical symbol – of Ashoka who was known as *chakravartin*, universal king – for a republican dispensation.

CHAPTER 11

The Great Numbers Game

THE NEED TO PREPARE an inventory of an asset arises because of its perceived value. Such is the case with animals as well. In India the Asian one-horned or Javan rhinoceros barely survived the 19th century while the Asian two-horned or Sumatran rhinoceros was last reported half a century ago – though there was an unconfirmed report of its sighting from Mizoram in 1972.[1] At any rate, both animals became extinct in India without ever having been counted. The Great Indian one-horned rhinoceros on the other hand did get counted or, rather, estimated. It is believed that there were only twelve animals left in the special reserve created for it at Kaziranga in Assam in 1908.[2] The cheetah on the other hand became extinct in India, with its numbers being estimated more than three decades *after* the event.[3] The tiger population was believed to be about 40,000 in India at the turn of the 20th century according to an estimate by E.P. Gee, whereas M.K. Ranjitsinhji and K. Sankhala felt there were between 25,000 and 30,000 of them left at that time.[4] But when the Government of India and various state governments got down to enumerating tigers as a result of the alarming news of their swift decline, they came up with a figure of 1,827 in 1972,[5] which led to a special programme for their protection.

The case of the lion was no different from the general trend though the particulars were unique to itself. The earliest attempt to guess or estimate lion numbers is reported by Major General William Rice of the Indian Army, who knew Bombay Presidency and Kathiawar and had hunted lions in the Gir around the 1850s. According to him "A native Officer, Jemadar J.K., of Joonaghur State, has shot an immense number of lions in the vast 'Gheer Forest', their chief abode." He computed that there were not above 300 lions left in that country.[6] Though lions were encountered and shot outside the Saurashtra peninsula up to 1891,[7] Gir was their last stronghold. Hence the estimate of their numbers would represent almost their entire surviving population at that time. How accurate was this figure is a moot point.

More than thirty years after General Rice's attempt, the *Kathiawar Gazetteer* of 1884 stated that "there are probably no more than ten or a dozen lions and lionesses left in the whole Gir forest".[8] The statement appears to cover the entire jungle in the states of Junagadh, Baroda, and Bhavnagar, including various other principalities which had some part of the jungle in their territory. The basis of this estimate is not known. But in the same year Colonel J.W. Watson's statistical account of Junagadh was published. Under the heading "wild animals", the lion is described as "the most famous of wild animals" and details are given as to its size, habits, the propensity of males to live in pairs, hunting methods, and so on. Watson, however, does not mention any imminent danger of lions becoming extinct or that their numbers were so low. In fact he does not give any numbers at all.[9] Junagadh state appears to have prepared an estimate in 1893, giving a figure of about 31.[10] Colonel L.L. Fenton, who was in Kathiawar during the great famine of 1899 and hunted lions in the Gir, does not express any alarm about the falling lion population, but merely states that these animals are now found only in the Gir. On the contrary, in his opinion, "The Gir [in 1886] was then at its best in the matter of game of all kinds and a terra incognita to all except a few local Europeans" and Junagadh state officials.[11] There is no doubt that the alarming figure of 12 or even 31 was inaccurate. In fact Edwardes and Fraser, the authors of the "authorized" work on Junagadh state, assert that the *Kathiawar Gazetteer*'s reports were "very misleading".[12]

On hearing that very few lions were left in the Gir, Lord Curzon decided not to pursue his earlier goal of shooting one on his forthcoming visit to Junagadh on

November 3, 1900. When the Political Agent, Rajkot, sent a telegram to that effect on October 10, 1900, it evoked an illuminating reply from Nawab Rasulkhan on November 27, after the viceregal visit to Junagadh. In a semi-official letter the nawab wrote:

> I cannot but observe here that though I fully appreciated and admired your noble consideration in abandoning the lion shooting Your Excellency's giving up the idea has greatly disappointed me.
>
> The cry raised on this side of India that the lions were almost extinct in the Gir forest and that the shooting would help in the final extermination of the animal was far from correct. But as Your Excellency's decision had been published, I did not think it proper to request you to alter it immediately.
>
> I propose however to approach Your Excellency later on with the request to favour me with a shooting excursion in the Gir before Your Excellency's departure from India.[13]

Lord Curzon never came back but the numbers game continued unabated. In 1905 Major H.G. Carnegie the then Political Agent at Halar who was soon to meet his end in the Gir, "was at great pains to investigate the matter during his two years' residency in Junagadh...." He said that in one particular week he had so many cases notified to him that he calculated he had heard of 25 separate lions in that week alone. He gave it as his firm opinion, after considering all the information he had collected, that "there were *in 1905 between sixty and seventy* lions in the Gir. The Junagadh authorities basing their belief on the reports of trackers and jungle villagers, hold that the lions at that time numbered *at least one hundred* [emphases added]".[14] It is not out of place to note here that Jam Saheb Digvijaysinhji of Navanagar told E.P. Gee in 1956 that his estimate was that there were a hundred lions in the Gir circa 1900, though Nawab Rasulkhan let it be known that "only a few" were left.[15]

By 1913 there was another scare about a decrease in the number of lions caused ostensibly by the depredations of Junagadh's neighbours who were shooting them beyond the state's control. H.D. Rendall, the Administrator of Junagadh, thought it fit to address a letter to J. Sladen, Agent to the Governor, Kathiawar, asking him for a notification in the *Agency Gazette* for the protection of lions. He stated in the letter that W.A. Wallinger, F.R.Z.S., the temporary Conservator of Forests, Junagadh, had toured the Gir extensively along with Brook Fox the Chief Engineer of the state, who was knowledgeable in his own right. Their estimate was that only six or seven male lions were left![16] In his report on the Gir forest Wallinger goes on to state that during his visit to Gir of two months in 1913, he had heard of four or five kills. He had seen very few pug marks and made his estimation on that basis. He goes on to add:

> I do not feel justified after so short an experience however, to give a very definite opinion on a subject which is of such great importance to India from a Natural History point of view. The total number of lions in the Gir could not be put down, in my opinion, at over 20 with any degree of safety and my advice is to exercise even greater strictness in the matter of granting permits to shoot them than hitherto. Unless this is done, it may be confidently asserted that lions stand in considerable danger of being exterminated altogether, especially in view of the inter breeding that will occur.[17]

Two more estimates were made in 1920, one by P.R. Cadell and another by

M.A. Wynter-Blyth
■ Principal of Rajkumar College, Rajkot (1948–63), he pioneered lion population surveys in independent India, which became the forerunners of tiger censuses in later years.
Photograph courtesy
K.S. Ayazmohmedkhanji of Pajod.

J.M. Ratnagar of the Bombay Forest Service. The numbers that they came up with were "about 50" and "at least 100" respectively![18] This variance alone speaks volumes about the accuracy of these attempts, or the accuracy of any of the numbers made public.

While the lion of the western regions was the first large mammal to be estimated in the Indian empire, at the eastern end an attempt was made to census tigers. In 1934 J.W. Nicholson, Divisional Forest Officer of Palamau Division in the province of Bihar and Orissa, took it upon himself to count tigers in the southern range of the division over an area of 298 square kilometres (115 square miles). The method used was to send staff to every waterhole and river bank in the early hours of the morning of May 1, to measure pug marks of tigers. Eighty-four waterholes and river locations were covered. The count showed 22 tigers and 10 tigresses, a surprising result which was unexpected by Nicholson himself. All this was done at the cost of just 5 rupees and 13 annas (Rs 5.75), being payment for employing 93 persons for the job![19] Two years later Junagadh state made the first, and as it turned out the last, attempt at a systematic enumeration of lions. From the record it is not clear whether the state's Forest Department had access to Nicholson's work, his methods and results, but the chances are that they probably did not.

From a letter dated January 27, 1937, from Major C.W.L. Harvey, Secretary to the Agent to the Governor-General, to J. Monteath, Diwan of Junagadh, we learn that the lion population in Gir was estimated at about 270 as a result of a recent census* conducted by the state, although Monteath believed that the figure was an "over estimate". Below the letter there is a notation dated January 30, 1937, bearing an illegible signature of someone from the Junagadh state's office, stating that a census was taken in Gir forest on April 12, 1936, the results of which were included in the Chief Forest Officer's Report, according to which the total numbers of lions were: males 143, females 91, and cubs 53, making a total of 287. It appears that only 52 big size mature males were encountered. The notation goes on to say: "The method of calculation employed was probably the measurements of various foot prints in the different areas fixed for the purpose, and may require the acceptance of the correctness of the total no., with caution." Another noting dated February 1 under this one, states that: "The exact number is 287 but I should consider this as an over statement. I should personally think there are more than 200 lions in all." The signature is, once again, illegible.

On March 6, 1937, J. Monteath sent a reply to Major C.W.L. Harvey that (emphasis added):

> It is the case that last year an attempt was made roughly to number the lions within the Junagadh limits of the Gir Forest. The total figure recorded cannot be considered reliable, as it was naturally impossible to avoid counting some animals more than once; it may be inferred that *the total is not less than 150*, I think. The males appear to outnumber the females; but I doubt whether this result is also quite reliable.
>
> What appears to be clear is that the females and cubs tend to frequent the outlying parts rather than the more inaccessible jungle; and are therefore more probable victims of poaching.[20]

---

* I have used the word "census" in order to conform to the general usage of the term for the exercise undertaken over the years to estimate lion population. It would be more appropriate to use the term "estimate" which does not imply exact numbers.

Here is a deliberate attempt to underestimate the number of lions as the number decreases progressively from 287 to more than 200 to more than 150. The reasons are obvious enough. The British-led administration was showing a lower figure to exert pressure on Junagadh's neighbours and other eager shikaris who were only waiting to "bag" a lion. Wynter-Blyth, writing about his preparations for the lion census of 1950, mentions that he examined at some length the methodology of the 1936 census. It was based on the counting of fresh pug marks at water sources on the assumption that lions as a rule would drink once in 24 hours. The count was conducted in April, the dry part of the year. To prevent the counting of any lion more than once, pug marks were measured lengthwise and across, and their sex and direction of departure was noted. Wynter-Blyth goes on to write:

> At least this was how it was done in theory, and given a sufficient number of persons competent in jungle craft (and the forest seems well able to furnish these) such a census when undertaken conscientiously should produce a tolerable result. But after making careful enquiries I discovered that certain enumerators, and probably supervisors, added non-existent lions to their totals, on the assumption that the more lions there were recorded, the more lion shikar there would be ... with its attendant opportunities of baksheesh. So that, although I was assured that the census was otherwise very carefully carried out, and that the number of lions so added was very small the result is, to say the least suspect.[21]

J. Monteath's was the conservative official version of a total of about 150 lions in Junagadh Gir. Some latter-day enumerators would have done well to follow this example of caution rather than presume to give exact numbers of lions and tigers in the manner of a drill sergeant counting soldiers on a parade ground by name, rank, and serial number.

That Junagadh state was extremely concerned about the survival of lions throughout the last phase of its existence, there is no doubt. In fact it made seven attempts at estimating their numbers between 1893 and 1936 i.e. on an average in a span of 43 years an attempt was made say every six years. Monitoring of population dynamics was still in its infancy, the methods were very basic and therefore the results were wanting in accuracy, but the attempts were genuine. Except for William Rice's estimate and the figure given in the *Kathiawar Gazetteer* which presumably were for all of Kathiawar, Junagadh state's activities were confined to the Junagadh portion of Gir. In the early part of the 20th century an area of approximately 520 square kilometres[22] of Gir forest was outside Junagadh's domain, being part of Baroda and Bhavnagar states, and several smaller principalities particularly Jetpur's Andhania enclave in the forest, and Mendarda. As such it is fair to conclude that a noteworthy number of lions did not get enumerated at all by the Junagadh state machinery.

It is also obvious that as a result of constant pressure on Nawab Rasulkhanji, on the British administration between 1911 and 1920, and on Nawab Mahbatkhanji thereafter, to allow Indian princes and British officers of high rank to shoot lions, there was a tendency to periodically publicize underestimated figures accompanied by alarmist comments. Between 1884 and 1936, there was only one major calamitous event – the *Chappanyo Kal*, the famine of 1899–1900. That apart, the state suffered no major disasters other than its usual share of scarcity conditions in 1911–12, heavy rains in 1914, the outbreak of influenza in 1918–19, and so on.[23] None of these events except the famine of 1899–1900 could be held responsible for ecological upheavals which could have caused the reported population swings from twelve lions to 150 lions. If the figures were realistic, it is difficult to explain why the population doubled to sixty or seventy animals in 1905 in twelve years and then again reduced to twenty in the next eight years.

On the basis of the data available, it appears that in this entire period, the conservative figure of 150 lions in 1936–37 in Junagadh Gir given out by J. Monteath is by far the closest to reality. If one were to add arbitrarily a figure of another ten to fifteen animals outside Junagadh state territory we get a total of 160-plus lions at that time. Working backwards on an ad hoc basis, it is safe to conclude that the lion population had gone through a severe bottleneck at the turn of the 20th century, but slowly it grew to around 100 in a decade in Junagadh and the neighbouring states combined which continued to increase to the 1936–37 level of 150 in Junagadh plus another ten to fifteen outside of the state territory.

Junagadh state's efforts secured the lions' existence, but by the time the next census came along, momentous events had occurred. The second world war had taken its course, the Indian empire had disappeared, and Junagadh state as a political entity had been consigned to history.

Beyond the boundaries of Junagadh state, the Gir and its lions were of interest primarily to the neighbouring states and some princes. But those apart, the forests and its inhabitants remained largely unknown. The Bombay Natural History Society decided to investigate the status of lions and the task was taken in hand by Wynter-Blyth in 1949. His brief was "to study the present condition of the lions with special reference to the rate of decrease or increase and to consider how continued protection could best be afforded without clashing with human interests". Unlike the usual government attitude today, the Regional Commissioner, the Administrator, and the Chief Forest Officer of Junagadh (it still retained a separate administrative identity) gave Wynter-Blyth their total cooperation, making full arrangements for his visit. Wynter-Blyth made two visits to the Gir, in the summer and winter of 1949, and a decision was taken to conduct a census.

The state of Saurashtra gave full support to the census. Finance Minister Shyamaldas Gandhi who had spearheaded the Arzi Hakumat movement against the nawab, ensured that the funds were made available. Rajpramukh Digvijaysinhji, Jam Saheb of Navanagar, also gave his backing. A test count was conducted in Jamwala division in an area of 285 square kilometres in addition to eight weeks' fieldwork and preparations spread over twenty months. The census was conducted on April 28 and 29, 1950 in an area of "between 700 and 800 sq. miles" (1,812–2,071 square kilometres) of the Gir forest including Girnar hills and Mytiala. Apart from personnel of the Forest Department, two prominent members of the Bombay Natural History Society –R.S. Dharmakumarsinhji of Bhavnagar and Y.S. Pratapsinhji of Wankaner, and Major Dubois – a teacher from Rajkumar College, Rajkot, took charge of various areas to supervise the effort.

The Gir was divided into five divisions and each division was supervised by an expert from outside or a senior forest officer. The methodology of the census was based on the assumption that lions would drink water at least once in 24 hours, that a pug mark was something like a fingerprint and that enumerating them at watering places and roads and paths judiciously selected would yield fairly accurate results. Essentially, the method used was similar to that already tried out in Bihar in 1934 and in the Gir itself in 1936. The crucial difference was that it was conducted

R.S. Dharmakumarsinhji of Bhavnagar (1917–86) with his falcon
■ A keen observer of nature, his contribution to lion population surveys along with M.A. Wynter-Blyth was seminal.
Photograph courtesy John and Frank Craighead.

publicly and supervised by an outside agency and experts who had no bias one way or another, particularly to inflate the figure upwards. Moreover, it must be stressed that the Forest Department was and continued for some time to be manned at the grassroots mostly by persons who were *pagi*s or guards whose families had been in the same profession for generations. They knew the jungle, they usually knew and could recognize individual lions and prides in their respective beats.

At any rate this mammoth exercise yielded a population range of between 217 and 227 lions in the Gir including those of Mytiala, Girnar, and the hill of Sana. These figures Wynter-Blyth regarded as minimum figures. He felt that about twelve per cent of the lions escaped being counted, and thus he estimated a maximum count of between 243 and 251.[24]

Wynter-Blyth was a very exact task-master, a cautious and a thorough naturalist. He preferred to err on the conservative side if at all. He was careful enough not to mention an absolute figure but gave a range of minimum and maximum possible numbers. In the context of the next census of 1955 he gave his guiding principles:

> I possess no form of magic by which I can prove the accuracy of my censuses, nor do I pretend to be able to find exact numbers of lions – only the simple can expect that – but I myself believe that the final figures are not far removed from the truth, and I have been very cautious in my count, I should be very much surprised if there are less lions than the figures I have given.
>
> However what cannot be stressed too strongly, and what it is very difficult to make people realize is that *the main object of the census is to find out the increase and*

***Pagi Bhanabha Kathalbha (above)
and Pagi Abhlabha Jafarbha
(opposite)***
■ Exceptional trackers in the great
tradition of the *pagis* of old, they
communed with the Gir and its lions.
Photographs: Udaybhanusinh.

*decrease in the numbers of lions, since to know this trend is vital to any policy of
protection – much more important than to know the exact number of lions*
[emphasis added].[25]

Though Wynter-Blyth had recommended the next census for 1952, it ultimately
took place three years later. It is notable that U.N. Dhebar, Chief Minister of
Saurashtra, took personal interest in the proceedings and the process went
smoothly, according to Wynter-Blyth, because of "the excellent help I had from my
assistants and the experience gained from the first census, but above all to the fact
that the Chief Minister was especially interested in the matter with the result that I
had every possible facility and cooperation".

The census was conducted between April 11 and 14, 1955. Wynter-Blyth was
assisted by outsiders – this time the renowned wildlife experts and ornithologists
Y.S. Shivrajsinhji of Jasdan and K.S. Lavkumar of Jasdan, the latter also being a
teacher at Rajkumar College, and by Dost Mohmed and Nur Mohmed, both local
persons of substance and ability. The censuses of 1950 and 1955 were carried out in
an "identical manner" hence the findings were of the same level of accuracy or error,
thus comparable. The results showed that the lion population was increasing with
the enforcement of strict protection and had reached a total of between 240 and
314.[26]

With the census of 1955, yet another chapter in the great numbers game ended.
The next census was held in 1963, though it was originally scheduled for 1960. The
exercise had to be postponed as 1960 saw the birth of Gujarat state of which the
state of Saurashtra became a part. Wynter-Blyth went on home leave from the
school in 1963 never to return. He died unexpectedly on a stop-over in Switzerland
en route to London. Gir and its lions lost a true champion who had blazed a trail for
others to follow and set standards for all to emulate.

Regrettably the 1963 effort was not without friction and its echoes were felt in the
census that followed in 1968. While the earlier two efforts had been supervised by
outside experts, this census and subsequent ones were to be Forest Department
enterprises. For the 1963 census, the Forest Department came up with the novel idea
of spraying paint on each lion counted, until all were sprayed! Dharmakumarsinhji
who had been invited by Junagadh's Divisional Forest Officer to join the census was
unable to agree with the method. His objections were obvious. It would take too long
to spray all the lions, the markings might not be conspicuous enough, or could get
rubbed off; further, the sound of the spray guns would either scare off the lions or
make them aggressive. This counting process was to begin at the time of the Holi
festival and Dharmakumarsinhji felt that instead of a riot of colours it "might result
in a blood bath",[27] since no one had informed the lions of this well-intentioned
activity!

Dharmakumarsinhji turned down the offer to participate in the census and
ultimately it was decided to conduct it on traditional lines. Though he was invited
again, he had been treated discourteously by the Forest Department so he declined
once more. The result of the census was given out as 285 lions. In his several visits
to the Gir, Dharmakumarsinhji had noticed that the frequency of lion pug marks
seen had reduced considerably along roads and the Maldharis reported fewer
encounters with lions. He concluded that there was a marked decrease in lion
population since 1956–57 and he had brought his concerns to the attention of the
Indian Board for Wildlife, the highest agency of the Indian government for

conservation, of which he was a member. He was not ready to accept the result of the 1963 census, for he felt that:

> With Government departments there is a sense of prestige, which when queried, will in no way accept defeat. In this case, I was convinced that the Forest Department stood on false prestige and in the 1963 lion census it wanted me, an expert, to be used as a stamp to support their argument, which of course could be contrived, according to their wishes, to accept a certain lion census figure....[28]

For the 1968 census, however, the Forest Department again invited R.S. Dharmakumarsinhji. It is to their credit that in spite of their past differences, the method for the census was what Dharmakumarsinhji himself had propounded in a recent book of his on census methods for large mammals.[29] The method, briefly put, was to locate prides and single out lions in various parts of the forest over the entire area of some 1,800 square kilometres and localize them or "anchor" them with 300–400 baits of male buffalo calves. The forest was divided into five zones, each zone was given up to ten baits per day for five days in the beginning of June. The kills were monitored and figures were compiled. The exercise threw up a figure of 177 lions which is the generally accepted figure, though the earlier pug mark count had thrown up a figure of 166.[30]

With the 1968 census the die was cast for all subsequent censuses right up to the 1995 census as far as the method was concerned i.e. counting lions using baits.[31] In other words, Dharmakumarsinh's pioneering work stood the test of time for thirty years and it was ultimately given up because of unconnected reasons.

Between 1974 and 1995 five censuses were held and the results declared showed a steady increase in the population of lions from 180 to 304 giving the impression that all was well with the Gir, the surrounding areas, and their prized denizens.

In the year 2000, the Forest Department of Gujarat mounted the most ambitious census count till date. The methods to be employed were an amalgam of both pug mark enumeration and ocular lion count at various points where baits were to be tied. M.K. Shivbhadrasinhji and I were invited to observe the process. The Forest Department had mobilized more than 2,000 persons for this exercise. Four hundred and fifty water holes were to be manned for two days on May 17 and 18. The count was to include other large mammals as well. This count was to be followed by observation at baited kills, after a rest of a day. For the purpose 200 male buffalo calves had been bought at the price of Rs 800 each. But before the census could begin, a public interest litigation petitioning to stop the use of live baits was filed in the Gujarat High Court, the plea being that baiting was cruelty. It transpired that the plaint was withdrawn by the party concerned on a technical ground regarding the definition of cruelty, as taking the life of an animal for scientific reasons did not come under the legal definition of the word. A minister of the Central government also objected to live baits. The two outside observers, Shivbhadrasinhji and I, made a public statement through a press release that lions had been killing livestock from time immemorial. Further the baits were male buffalo calves which were of no value to their owners as they were not used as draught animals nor put to any other use in the region. In the event, however, the government decided not to use live baits at all, and to confine the census to waterhole counts. At this point nature intervened. Unexpected unseasonal rains lashed Gir on May 15, waterholes lost all meaning, and so did the census; finally it had to be given up.

Subsequently, the Forest Department did a rapid survey and estimated a lion population of between 310 and 320. Thus ended the millennium numbers game. In 2001 the pug mark method employed in the previous year's rapid survey was refined and a result showing a lion population of between 327 and 332 was declared.

We can identify three distinct stages in the effort at enumeration of lions. The first stage saw efforts stemming from the concern of Junagadh state for the lion's survival and attempts to keep off or reduce pressure on the state from trigger-happy hunters. Thus one sees a marked tendency to underestimate their numbers in this phase. These estimates or censuses were carried out by Junagadh state's Forest Department which jealously guarded its turf.

The second stage was sparked by independence and the consequent annexation of the state by the dominion of India. The Gir and its inhabitants were a largely unknown quantity outside of its immediate environs. The Bombay Natural History Society took the lead to obtain a status report and have the lions counted in 1950. The second census in this phase which took place in 1955 was a continuation of the previous one when it was spearheaded by independent experts and the princes, and actively supported by the government of Saurashtra and its ministers. After all, the lion was a symbol of pride for the people of the peninsular state. Not only were the results published, but also the expert enumerators brought their findings and recommendations into the public domain by extensively publishing their experiences, lessons learnt, and recommendations made.

The third phase was to start with yet another political change. The United State of Saurashtra disappeared in 1956 to form part of Bombay state which came into existence after the linguistic reorganization of states on the loose principle of one-language–one-state. Surprisingly, a bilingual state was created with two contending languages, which took its name from its premier city. The first census in this phase was to take place in 1960 but it was postponed to 1963 as the Bombay state was split into two in 1960 by a process officially called "bifurcation". By this time the nation had gone through two general elections of 1952 and 1957 and was on the verge of a third after the 1962 war with China which had brought it no laurels. But the newly formed Gujarat state was buoyant, the lion was its famous inhabitant and a rare possession. The state thus went ahead with the 1963 census almost a decade before the Government of India and the various state governments woke up to the tragedy of the tigers and held the first all-India census of this other great cat. There was also a qualitative change in the approach of the census. Henceforth "outside experts" were brought in only as observers and their influence varied. The Forest Department was to be the sole authority which published figures – but not findings, recommendations, or conclusions – save for one solitary exception, M.K. Dalvi who published an article on the 1968 census. During this phase the lion population grew steadily while the tiger disappeared from its Gujarat range. There were eight tigers in 1972, nine in 1984 and 1989, but one in 1997,[32] and none by the end of the millennium. It is sad to record that while the government of Gujarat professes to guard lions almost jealously, it allowed the tiger to disappear, thus losing the privilege of having three large cats (including the leopard) within its boundaries, a distinction which was unique in the world for any political entity.

The history of the lion censuses has arrived at yet another crossroads with the new millennium. It is demonstrably possible to argue that it is easier to census lions than say the tiger or the leopard, and therefore more accurate results are possible. Lions are gregarious and they are often found in prides. Most of them do not regard humans as a danger, and even those that do are not afraid of them, having learnt to take their livestock. They are easily approachable and are visible during the day. Except for some parts, most of the Gir forest is not thick jungle. The lions that have chosen to live on the periphery of the protected area and those that have left it are even more visible. In other words, here is a unique animal living in a habitat with great visibility, thus lending itself to far more accurate enumeration than can ever be attained with tigers – though playing Holi with them may be stretching things a bit. Dharmakumarsinhji surely had this in mind when he suggested baiting for census half a century ago. This method has stood the test of time and if one is to question the steady increase of lions according to the censuses between 1963 and 1995 and even 2001, rather than question the method itself, one ought to consider the eagerness of the Forest Department to show increasing figures each time (as was the case in a tiger reserve where some years ago a field director, apart from inflating the figure for tigers, separately enumerated male and female porcupines which are impossible to tell apart unless at close quarters).

The happenings of 2000 have ensured that baiting of lions is no longer practised, and while pug mark censuses may yield satisfactory results, there is need to move with the times. Today's Forest Department staff are not hereditary *pagis* or shikaris whose accuracy of pug mark identification can be safely relied upon. Population densities and dynamics in the case of tigers, can and are being successfully studied in India. Moreover, new techniques of differentiating lions by facial features, primarily of vibrissae (whiskers) pattern, developed by C.J. Pennycuik and J. Rudnai have already been tried out satisfactorily in Serengeti, Tanzania. This method has been refined and tested by Y.V. Jhala and his team from the Wildlife Institute of India, Dehra Dun, for the Gir protected area and its lions. The results of the exercise carried out by them indicate a "population size larger than the official records",[33] an unexpected but welcome compliment no doubt to the government's protection efforts in the Gir forest and the lion's own determination to survive and prosper in an adverse environment. The team has suggested a protocol of continuous monitoring to ensure the evolution of a credible database of population dynamics of lions over an extended period of time.

The Forest Department of the state government must turn to such tested options. The traditional methods of the 20th century have served their purpose admirably and have now run their course.

CHAPTER 12

A Second Home

IF ONE FLIES LOW over the Saurashtra peninsula one sees the over 1,800 square kilometre Gir forest[1] standing out in sharp contrast to fields, barren or green depending on the time of year, surrounding it. It is a fragile ecosystem which is home to the Asiatic lion and to say that it is under constant threat of being overrun, would be to state the obvious. However, among other reasons for finding a second home for the lions, two stand out above all. First, it is now clear that about seventeen per cent of the wild population of lions lives outside the protected area. Second, the total population being so small and concentrated in one large area, it could be exposed to an epidemic of feline disease. One has only to remember that in 1993–94 nearly a thousand lions, one-third of the total population, was lost to canine distemper in Serengeti, Tanzania. The Asiatic lion population is minuscule and it can hardly withstand such an onslaught.

The vulnerability of the lion population has been a matter of concern for a long time. As early as 1952 the Indian Board for Wildlife, the highest advisory body of the Government of India, recommended that a second home be found for the lions.[2] But before we come to the post-independence efforts, two attempts made prior to it in South Asia may be noted.

Maharaja Madho Rao Scindia of Gwalior (1886–1925) was a keen sportsman. Being aware that there were lions in historical times in what was his domain of Gwalior state, Scindia was very keen to bring back lions to his territories. The last lion to be shot in central India was near Guna in 1873 barely 28 years earlier.[3] At Scindia's instance the British Resident of Gwalior wrote to W.P. Kennedy, the Agent to the Governor, Rajkot, requesting help. The latter addressed a letter dated October 24, 1901 to Nawab Rasulkhanji as follows:

> The Resident of Gwalior asks me at the request of His Highness the Maharaja Scindia (who is very anxious to endeavour to breed lions again in part of his territory where they formally were to be found but have been shot out) whether Your Highness could kindly assist His Highness in his venture in letting him have say four lions and four lionesses for His Highness' shooting preserves.
>
> Will Your Highness kindly let me have your reply to the request of His Highness the Maharaja Scindia. I feel sure that Your Highness will do all that is possible to assist in the project giving trial to an experiment which may give the Asiatic lion a fresh lease of life....

However, the request was ill-timed, to say the least. The nawab had taken the reins of government some eight years earlier and in 1901, assisted by his diwan Behchardas Viharidas, had just come out of one calamity: Junagadh was barely recovering from the famine of 1899–1900, and there were persistent reports that very few lions were left in the Gir causing Lord Curzon to cancel his request for a lion trophy. Nawab Rasulkhanji's response was predictable. He wrote on October 31, 1901:

> I ... am much gratified at the laudable desire of His Highness the Maharaja Scindia to give a trial to an experiment of breeding Asiatic lions in part of His Highness' territory.
>
> I am very sorry however, to state that the number of noble animals which was never very large has been so much reduced of late owing to some hunting, fallen victims in the dire calamity of 1900, some having been killed outright by the Gaikwad's subjects and servants of the Kodinar Division [of Baroda State] and some having been otherwise destroyed in the irregular wanderings and savage

freaks [sic] that it is almost impossible ... [to spare these animals for the experiment].[4]

Thus ended the first attempt to translocate lions in India – in fact, Dr Mahesh Rangarajan has pointed out that this was perhaps the first ever plan to reintroduce a locally extinct carnivore to its former habitat.[5] The nawab was trying to preserve his unique position as his greater successor the present state of Gujarat is claiming to do now a hundred years later, giving credence to the saying that coming events cast their shadow.

Just after the first world war, Maharaja Madho Rao Scindia resolved again to introduce lions in Gwalior state. According to one source, lion cubs were received earlier from Lord Kitchener, Commander-in-Chief of the Indian army, and some lions were purchased from Mombasa.[6] The provenance of Lord Kitchener's gift is not clear. Colonel Kesri Singh the famous shikari from Kanota, a *thikana* of Jaipur state, who was then in charge of the Shikarkhana of Gwalior state, recounts a somewhat different tale. According to him a few pairs of lions were imported from Africa and these animals were kept in a special enclosure. He does not mention the location but it was in the jungles of Shivpuri.

One pair of lions was let out of the enclosure in August 1920 and they disappeared in the jungle without a trace. The second pair, on being released, returned to the enclosure and made its environs their home which meant that the movement of men and buffaloes became difficult in the area. The roar of caged lions had attracted tigers which often patrolled the periphery of the enclosure and therefore when the lion of this pair was found dead in a badly mutilated state it was believed to have been killed by a tiger while the lioness, it was felt, escaped the same fate. The third and fourth pair gave no problems initially but soon they took to cattle lifting. When challenged by the villagers they turned to killing villagers, the logical next step. Kesri Singh was informed of these happenings and he had to go and shoot them. He does not say whether he shot all four of them, though that seems to be the case.[7] Three African lions were left at large in central India.

The three animals moved far and wide from their original starting point in Gwalior. A male lion was shot in Panna state by Maharaja Yaduvendrasingh. For this keen shikari it was a rare opportunity to shoot a wild African lion in India and the trophy, mounted whole, reposes in the palace at Panna. One lioness was shot by Maharawal Ranjitsinhji of Baria on the banks of the Kunoo river in Gwalior.[8] According to one source this animal was shot in 1950[9] which seems most unlikely as it would mean that the animal had lived for thirty years or that there was some breeding in the wild. A lion was seen in the Kotah jungles of Shahabad adjoining Gwalior state territory. The shikaris of Kotah who had not seen a lion and were not aware of Kotah's past history, reported to the palace "that a wild animal like a tiger resembling the colour of an ass was seen in the forest" according to Maharao Brijraj Singh of Kotah. The lion was shot by his father the late Maharao Bhim Singh of Kotah on May 17, 1937 at Jaronia,[10] making the animal more than 17 years old. Thus ended this experiment in translocation. Maharaja Madho Rao Scindia passed on in 1925 and the effort was not repeated by his successor at Gwalior. However, a lion which had become a man-eater was reported in Jhansi and it was killed around 1928.[11] There was yet another report of lions found around Jhansi up to 1930.[12] These were reported to be the Gwalior lions, again indicating that there may have been some breeding in the wild.

Kuno, Madhya Pradesh
■ The proposed site of the second home awaits lions from Gujarat state which is in no mood to part with them.
Photograph: Brigadier Ranjit Talwar.

The second attempt at translocation took place in Nepal in 1938–39. An African lion and lioness from the Nepal zoo were released in the terai region of Chitwan. There was however some apprehension about zoo-bred animals being able to fend for themselves and also survive with the tigers which were in abundance in the region. As matters turned out, the pair took to cattle lifting causing an outcry among the local population. A decision was taken to shoot them as it was thought too dangerous to leave them alone. They were both shot in February 1939 and the villagers were compensated for the livestock they had lost. It may be noted that this area was teeming with tigers – six tigers and two leopards were shot in one day. A total bag of 120 tigers, 38 rhinos, 27 leopards, and 15 bears was recorded between December 1938 and March 1939 in the same locality for the shooting party of Maharaja Joodha Shumsher Jung Bahadur Rana, Prime Minister and Supreme Commander-in-Chief of Nepal. There appears to have been no conflict between the lions and tigers, in any case the lions had been in the wild for only a month[13] before they were shot. It is also interesting to note that though these lions were zoo-bred, they took to killing prey, albeit domestic cattle, on release.

In the post-independence era, the Indian Board for Wildlife sponsored the translocation of lions from the Gir to the Chakia forest near Varanasi, UP,[14] in 1957. However, there was a lone voice raised against the proposed translocation. K.S. Lavkumar of Jasdan, a renowned ornithologist and nature educationist, had severe reservations. He observed that lions are essentially animals of the open country and they were found more in the surrounding cultivations than in the forests of Gir except in the eastern part of the reserve. He went on to write:

> That they [lions] are found in the Gir is no doubt owing to the broken nature of the
> terrain which allowed the last of the animals shelter from the shikaris who wiped
> them out over the rest of the country, and possibly also due to the great numbers of
> cattle grazed in the forest, providing them with plentitude of food. In former times
> the lions ranging across the north-west of India must have fed on nilgai and [black]
> buck which were found in plenty in the areas frequented by the lions. Now where is

there a place where these antelopes can be found in the concentrated numbers,
sufficient to support a pride of lions.... Bearing this in mind, would it be fair to
impose economic loss on people living around the proposed new lion sanctuary
[Chandraprabha] and has the danger to these people who are not familiar with the
lion and his ways been considered. Finally, what will prevent the lions from
wandering away as they apparently did when some were introduced by the
Maharaja of Gwalior....

... Lions have existed in the Gir for centuries and even if in the past epidemics
might have reduced the race, they have always managed to multiply again to their
former numbers, so it has never been claimed that the present reduction of the
once widely spread lion to its limited habitat has resulted from causes other than
their destruction by man and by depopulating of the game that comprised their
food. Since the killing of lions has been completely banned, the Gir lions have kept
on increasing most vigorously, and there is every possibility that if the animals are
given continued protection, they will slowly spread out into the country around
their present range. This natural increase will create a need to keep their numbers
down by judicious shooting. It is therefore apparent that there need be no anxiety
about possible extinction of the lion in the Gir and consequently this scheme [of
translocating lions to Chandraprabha] is quite uncalled for, unless of course it is
intended to give another state the pride of being the possessor of Asiatic lions. This
privilege however is fraught with much danger and is not worth the effort.[15]

These words were written nearly half a century ago. In the event however, these
prophetic warnings fell on unheeding ears and the experiment went ahead. Two
possible host sites were initially considered: one was near Tikamgarh in what was
then Vindhya Pradesh and the other was Chakia which was finally chosen. The
question naturally came up regarding the number of lions that should be
translocated for which purpose several authorities were consulted. Keith Caldwell of
the Kenya and Uganda Game Department felt that a whole family of lions i.e. a pride
should be moved so that it would over time split into two and spread. Ideally, he
felt, two families should be moved. C.R.S. Pitman, the Game Warden of Uganda,
suggested two young lions and four lionesses from different family groups. R.A.
Critchley, President of the Game Preservation and Hunting Association of Northern
Rhodesia, agreed with the suggestion. M.H. Cowie, Director of Royal National Parks
of Kenya, also agreed but suggested an alternative of a lion and lioness with female
cubs. Once the cubs grew and moved on, he suggested, a male lion preferably "more
virile" than the first should be introduced who would be willingly accepted by the
cubs which would have grown to become adult lionesses. E.P. Gee concluded from
all this that just one adult male, preferably a good maned specimen, would do the
job with two lionesses and cubs. Once the cubs grew up, a "more virile" lion could be
introduced at a later date.[16] The information was considered by the relevant
government departments – demonstrating a more healthy eclectic approach than
one would expect from the insular park managers commonly met with today.

The executive committee of the Indian Board for Wildlife met at Sasan Gir in
1956 and accepted the offer of the Uttar Pradesh government to introduce lions in
the Chakia forests. An area of 96 square kilometres was set aside as the
Chandraprabha Sanctuary, named after the river which flows through it. The
sanctuary is in the Vindhya Range with similar flora to Gir, and having what was
believed to be an adequate prey base of nilgai, chital, chinkara, sambar, and wild

boar. There were no tigers but only leopards. The sanctuary was fenced with a three-metre-high barbed wire. An inner enclosure of 10 acres was created within the sanctuary where the lions were to be initially released on arrival from the Gir. Here they would be artificially fed to acclimatize them to the new environment before giving them total freedom.

The UP government had requested the Saurashtra government to trap one lion and four lionesses. However only one lion and two lionesses were trapped from the Gir and kept at the Sakkarbag Zoo, Junagadh for nine months. On November 12 the animals began their arduous rail journey which took ten days, causing commotion along the railway line as they chugged along. The Chief Minister of UP, Dr Sampurnanand was at hand to release them from their cages into the inner enclosure. He did, and that is when things started going wrong. It was assumed that the animals would be weakened by their ordeal and eat the live baits provided for them. But the younger lioness crashed through the inner fence and disappeared while the other lioness and lion came out of their cages and took cover where they could find it, ignoring the food. The young lioness reappeared and kept watching the human beings who were perched on the machans. After an anxious wait the lioness moved off, and to everyone's relief the dignitaries were ultimately able to get into their vehicles to be wheeled back safely to urban civilization.

The inner enclosure was broken down on January 8, 1958, the frequency of live baits was gradually reduced to once in four days and on February 28 the older lioness was seen with a cub. The lion population gradually increased to four in 1958, five in 1960, seven in 1962, and to eleven in 1965. They were no longer confined to Chandraprabha Sanctuary, but they roamed about in the forests of Varanasi and Mirzapur. They were reported to be preying on nilgai and sambar. All this was considered by one authority to be the final and successful stage of the reintroduction of lions in UP, and there were even plans to clear the area of tigers, leopards, and wild dogs in addition to creating artificial lakes and salt licks for the ungulates to give lions a free run in their new home.[17]

But as is well known, this was not the happy ending. After 1965, the lions disappeared into thin air. It was presumed that they had migrated to "some unapproachable and remote forests" which was most unlikely, or were simply shot or poisoned which was most likely as these animals would have come in conflict with humans as a result of livestock predation. Be that as it may, the lions were never seen again and that was the unfortunate end of this effort. The reason for this outcome was obvious. The area of Chandraprabha Sanctuary was too small to sustain the lions. Their prey base was obviously insufficient and these large cats which were no strangers to the Maldhari's cattle in their original home, found livestock easy pickings which no doubt must have caused much man-animal conflict. In the early 1970s several stories circulated of people going out to shoot lions in UP. While it was impossible for me to verify them, there was surely more than a grain of truth in them. Lavkumar's frightening prophecy made in 1956 came sadly true a decade later. The Expert Committee of the Indian Board for Wildlife set up to examine "National Parks, Wildlife Sanctuaries and Policy of Wildlife Conservation in India" stated in their report of 1970 that the Indian lion could

> be introduced easily in any tropical dry scrub land in northern India, where its
> food is readily available, and there is no competition with any major contemporary
> predators including man and where total protection can be assured. Unfortunately

at present, there is no such self-contained eco-unit in the country and if another experiment of reintroduction of lions is attempted, it is bound to meet the same unfortunate fate as the lions introduced in Chandraprabha Sanctuary of Uttar Pradesh.[18]

In the early 1970s reports started appearing of housing lions in a 33 square kilometre area of Borivli National Park near Mumbai. Yet another newspaper report on finding another home for lions appeared in October 1972. This prompted G.R. Oza of the Linnean Society of London to voice concern about the proposal. He cited the failure of the Chandraprabha experiment and pointed out that there were no suitable habitat left for lion reintroduction. While he made a plea for conservation of lions in the Gir forest itself, he propounded a total ban on experimenting with reintroduction of these cats, as such an effort was doomed to failure as in the past.[19]

Regardless of the earlier experience, the vulnerability of a lion population confined to one location remains. While all efforts must be made to give maximum in situ protection to the lions and the forest of Gir, the need of the moment is to learn from past experience and try again. The removal of half a dozen lions from the Gir, or better still from the fifty-odd animals that live more or less permanently outside the forest, for reintroduction elsewhere would have no impact on the home population whatsoever.

S.S. Negi, former Chief Wildlife Warden of UP who spearheaded the Chandraprabha experiment, was the first to summarize the lessons learnt from it. He concluded that an area of 96 square kilometres was too small to confine the eleven lions which therefore wandered out of the protected area. Secondly, the forest around the sanctuary was open to heavy grazing which caused continuous disturbance to the animals. Finally, "no scientific methods were adopted to restrict their movement". It was crucial to keep a tab on the movement and behaviour of lions in and around their new home, which was not done.[20] In view of these lessons, Negi recommended that the host site must be not less than 285 square kilometres, it must be closed to grazing by domestic cattle, strong protection should be given against poaching and poisoning of lions (usually resulting from predation of domestic stock). Negi emphasized the need to compensate the owners of livestock for any losses.[21]

The reintroduction at Chandraprabha was a bold experiment, and certainly not a total failure. It succeeded initially insofar as the lion population increased to eleven in a few years. Its subsequent failures were a result of the absence of effective post-reintroduction protection. This can surely be achieved in a future attempt if there is sufficient political will to do so.

One more attempt was made by the Indian Board for Wildlife to find a second home for lions in 1976. A committee of two consisting of R.S. Dharmakumarsinhji and M.K. Ranjitsinhji was set up. Ranjitsinhji inspected Jaisamand in Rajasthan and the committee submitted a report on the steps required to be taken for the purpose. However, nothing came of this effort.

There was one noteworthy proposal for a second home for the Gir lions in Iran. In 1977, during the last years of the monarchy, the administration of Mohammed Reza Shah II Pahlvi mooted the idea of bringing lions from India for release in the plains and reed beds of Arzan, south of Shiraz.[22] In India that fateful year saw the restoration of democracy after a year and a half of "emergency" rule. In spite of the generally unsettled times, there was some talk of sending lions for reintroduction to

Iran in exchange for cheetahs from there which could be reintroduced in India.[23]

In Iran the proposed area was converted into the Arzan National Park. But the project came under severe criticism for it involved buying land from local farmers and resettling them elsewhere. On the other hand, scientists questioned the efficacy of the project on the grounds that the environment of the area may not prove suitable for the lions though it had been their haunt in the past.[24] Two years later the Shah had gone the way of the lion in Iran and the country became an Islamic Republic with a different set of priorities which did not include the restoration of a royal symbol. The idea was soon forgotten in India.

It is heartening to record that the quest for a second home in India for Asiatic lions has never really been given up in spite of all the odds and past experience. A population and habitat viability assessment workshop was held in Baroda in October 1993. The state governments of Rajasthan, Madhya Pradesh, and Gujarat were requested to submit proposals for potential sites. Three sites – Darrah-Jawaharsagar Wildlife Sanctuary and Sitamata Sanctuary both in Rajasthan, and Kuno Wildlife Sanctuary in Madhya Pradesh – were selected for an intensive survey which was done by a team from the Wildlife Institute of India. They recommended the Kuno Wildlife Sanctuary and its environs as the most suitable host site of the three.[25]

This study has made specific recommendations for preparing the host site which briefly include the following: The primary requirement is protection and enhancement of the existing prey base. In the study's model, a biomass of 480,000 kilograms would be required to sustain a growing population of initially eight lions. This chital and nilgai based prey population requirement would take thirteen years to be achieved at the host site. The time period could be shortened to say seven years if 500 chital and 800 nilgai are introduced from elsewhere either from captive or wild populations. This time span is based on the assumption of ideal conditions with a high order of commitment from government agencies and the local human population.

Secondly, the study recommends that an area of 700 square kilometres be declared as a national park. The existing wildlife sanctuary of 344.68 square kilometres which had a human population of 7,400 persons in nineteen villages, would form part of the national park and the villagers and their livestock would have to be resettled outside. The total area of the proposed conservation unit is 3,700 square kilometres – roughly double the total Gir forest area, of which 3,300 square kilometres is forest land.

According to the study, five to eight lions consisting of two or three males and three to five females from a "free-ranging stable social unit" should be captured from Gir and translocated. Since the lions would be from a single pride they would adjust to the new area without internecine aggression. They should be released in a holding pen of 1 square kilometre for a period of ten days to acclimatize them before being freed into their new home. All animals must be radio-collared to check and monitor their activities. Once the initial population has settled down, fresh stock must be brought in to supplement the population by capturing lions from the fringes of the Gir Sanctuary. This is a requirement of population management. The study concludes that it would be possible to establish a population of thirty to fifty free-ranging lions in ten years' time. Though the conclusions of the study are very cautious, e.g. (a) expectations of thirty to fifty lions in ten years and (b) a requirement of forest area twice the size of Gir, it is a viable starting point and a

Kuno river and habitat
■ A second home for the lions of Asia is a necessity to ensure their survival in case of a natural disaster.
Photograph: Brigadier Ranjit Talwar.

guiding beacon for the managers of the effort. With the participation of the Indian government, it is to the credit of the Madhya Pradesh government that it has taken on this difficult but rewarding task.

On the ground, however, the situation has progressed slowly. The work in the last five years has resulted in shifting 23 out of 24 villages from the sanctuary, consisting of 1,650 families with a population of 7,000 persons. Twenty villages have been resettled in Agra on the periphery of the sanctuary. They have been given housing, agricultural land, drinking water, and fair weather roads, while they await electricity and irrigation. Three villages have been shifted to Karahal subdivision and are in an early stage of resettlement. Apart from adding field staff for protection, which has shown results in reduction of illegal grazing, the state government has also notified 1,268 square kilometres as the Kuno Wildlife Division and this area includes the present sanctuary area of 344.68 square kilometres. In addition 923 square kilometres have been transferred from Sheopur division to the new Kuno division thus making unity of management possible and more efficient.[26]

However, there are several problems which need to be addressed urgently. The Wildlife Institute study had recommended that a national park be created with a sanctuary and a buffer zone, as has been noted earlier. So far this has not transpired. The study also envisaged translocation of prey species to shorten the time frame of getting the habitat ready to receive lions. Only three nilgai were translocated in 2001, which is nothing more than symbolic. Further, there is no ecological research in progress to monitor the changes and the health of the fauna and flora of the forest as a result of the various activities.

Besides, the resettlement of the villages though successful so far, can suffer a major setback if facilities such as irrigation and electricity, which were promised earlier, are not expeditiously provided. Some other measures of equal importance awaiting action in the field are extending a public distribution system for grains, a bank, a primary school, and a health centre for the displaced persons. Title deeds are yet to be given to many persons and 310 families are saddled with poor farming lands resulting in very low or zero agricultural output. If these outstanding issues are not tackled urgently by the Madhya Pradesh government, the displaced people may agitate and return to their original abode within the sanctuary.[27]

While there is progress at the host site – albeit slow – there is a spoke in the wheel of translocation from a totally different quarter. Gujarat state which is justifiably proud of having protected lions for nearly half a century in spite of all the pressures it has faced, has suddenly laid claim to exclusive ownership of these cats much in the manner of the nawabs of Junagadh and similar to the instance of the Assam government laying claims to the great Indian one-horned rhinoceros. Gujarat does not want to give lions to Kuno in Madhya Pradesh or anywhere else; it does not want to lose its exclusivity of ownership.

As the news of a second home for lions became public, opposition to removing the lions became vocal. Led by Saurashtra Paryavaran Samrakshan Parishad and other NGOs, people performed a satyagraha in front of the mamlatdar's office at Talala on January 24, 1995 and on February 15 a dharna was performed there.[28] Earlier, in the Lok Sabha, Dilipbhai Sanghavi, MP, had asked Kamal Nath, Union Minister for Environment and Forests, how many lions were required to be translocated. The minister had replied that only two to four lions were required. Sanghavi reminded the minister that he should tread cautiously and warned that there was a strong movement in Gujarat against translocation of lions. On April 19, 1997 the Chief Minister of Gujarat Shankarsinh Waghela, told a gathering of journalists in Junagadh that

> Not a single lion cub, not to mention a lion, shall be permitted to be translocated anywhere. The government of Gujarat was capable of protecting the lions totally [within Gujarat].
>
> Yesterday I was at Sasan [Gir] where I was surprised to read newspaper reports on the subject because the government of Gujarat and its forest department has no knowledge of it. Be that as it may the stand of the state government is clear that lions of Gir shall stay only in the Gir. In this matter we shall take no cognizance of any request from the Central government or the government of Madhya Pradesh.[29]

The opposition to the translocation continues to increase. The Gujarat State Assembly passed a resolution against their translocation. In July 2002, a member of the Gujarat State Wildlife Advisory Board, Amit Jethva made a representation to Chief Minister Narendra Modi and Forest Minister Dolat Desai of Gujarat that under no circumstances should translocation of lions outside Gujarat be allowed. He argued that the Chandraprabha experiment had failed and the Madhya Pradesh government's claim of having made adequate preparations for receiving lions at Kuno was questionable. Keeping in mind the "love" of the people of Gujarat for the lions, they should not be "sent to the jaws of death".[30] Curiouser still was a statement by Dolat Desai that he was totally unaware of any proposal to translocate lions, he had seen no such files, and in any case "people in Gujarat are against the idea and therefore, we will never agree to such a plan". He went on to say that there was no "scientific" necessity for translocation as "The [lions] have been living in Gir, *though lions have died elsewhere in India. They have survived so far. Nature will take care of them. Why should we give our lions to anyone?* [emphasis added]."[31]

We have a curious situation. Though 17 per cent of wild lions live outside the Gir National Park and Sanctuary, the Gujarat government has failed to create any new sanctuaries within the state[32] to protect these lions. Yet it does not want to let go of any of these animals to enable a second population to be built up to secure the future of the Asiatic lion by creating a second home. An oft-repeated argument is that if Gujarat were to lose its exclusivity of lion ownership, it would lose with it the drive and the desire to continue to protect the Gir forest with the same vigour, and this would result in increased vulnerability of the original lion population! In all this, it is forgotten that lions, like any other species, belong to no one but themselves, and should be protected for their own sake. They in turn make no claim that the human beings of Gujarat belong to them. On the contrary, it is the responsibility of human beings since they have appropriated the earth for themselves to ensure the survival and prosperity of other animals and to restore to them their rightful lands regardless of linguistic or other political boundaries.

While various government agencies try to come to grips with the problem, the Asiatic lions have taken the matter into their own paws. They have taken "landscape planning" seriously, and 56 lions out of a total maximum population of 327, have made their home in places outside the Gir National Park and Sanctuary, second homes created by themselves without government help and in spite of the government's efforts in the past to bring the vagrants back into the Gir. How long they can survive or prosper there is another matter.

CHAPTER 13

Life in the Republic: The Lion in Winter

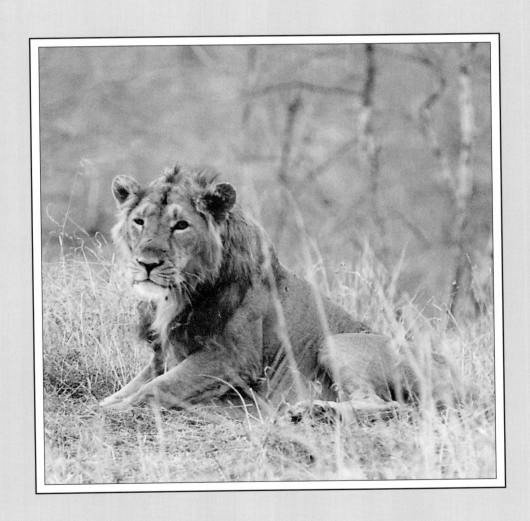

W ITH THE BIRTH OF the Republic of India on January 26, 1950 its Constitution
became its cornerstone. *Forests* and *Protection of Wild Animals and Birds*
found place in its Seventh Schedule as items in the State List.[1] Thus, the
responsibility for the lion rested firmly with the states it found itself in over the
years as a result of the reorganization of the Indian polity. But to the Central
government, its protection became a matter of concern from the very early days.
The Indian Board for Wildlife was formed to advise the Central government on
conservation and the lion itself became the national animal of the country on its
advice in 1952, as it was "more indigenous to India"[2] than the other great cat of
the subcontinent, the tiger. Prime Minister Jawaharlal Nehru took personal interest
in its protection and warned the administration of the new United State of
Saurashtra that it would be a great pity if the lions were to become extinct as a
result of shikar or other reasons. In the peninsula itself, the situation remained
contradictory insofar as the princes of Kathi principalities such as Jetpur,
Waghania, and some others, continued to hunt lions outside the territories of the
former Junagadh state.

It was only in the summer of 1948 that the situation came under control and the
local administration could assert with authority that lion shikar had stopped.[3] This
however, did not include the state privilege hitherto exercised by Junagadh's nawab
and now by Saurashtra's Rajpramukh Jam Saheb Digvijaysinhji of Navanagar and
Uparajpramukh Maharaja Raj Mayurdhwajsinhji of Dhrangadhra. On an average
four lions were permitted to be shot by VIPs which included, over the period 1948–
56, Maharaja Sawai Man Singh II of Jaipur and Maharaja Hari Singh of Jammu and
Kashmir. The Indian states were integrated into the union in 1948–49 but princely
privileges continued until 1956 as far as the lions were concerned. Saurashtra was
merged in the polyglot and short-lived Bombay state in that year, and Bombay state
itself was "bifurcated" in 1960 when the "linguistic" state of Gujarat was born.
Neither Bombay nor Gujarat state issued any permits for lion shikar.

In the field, lions had faced an onslaught in the aftermath of the annexation of
Junagadh state into the Dominion of India and they continued to be hunted
thereafter. As a result the animals turned largely nocturnal in habit and shy of
human beings. When the famous American animal photographer Ylla visited the Gir,
she found herself photographing them from a ground-level hide and also from a
machan, the shikaris having continued the method of the gun for the camera[4]
without realizing that a photograph from a height would be from such a steep angle
that it would not be worth the trouble. E.P. Gee too, found the same practice in
existence in 1956.[5] I photographed the famous Tilyo from the safety of a ground level
hide in the fading light of dusk the following year.

But the situation was changing fast. Jawaharlal Nehru visited the Gir in 1956. The
Prime Minister naturally had limited time, and the lions had to be shown to him.
The shikaris included Haider Ali popularly known as Haidu Jamadar who was
among the last of the famous *pagi*s of Junagadh state. They resorted to the age-old
practice of localizing the lions by regular baiting of male buffalo calves which are
virtually of no use to humans in that area as they are not used as draught animals.
Several reports made the rounds at the time, including one according to which goats
with their legs tied were thrown to lions from jeeps to familiarize them with
vehicles.[6] It appears that hundreds of baits were fed to lions for six months prior to
the prime ministerial visit in several locations of the Gir. Be that as it may, in the

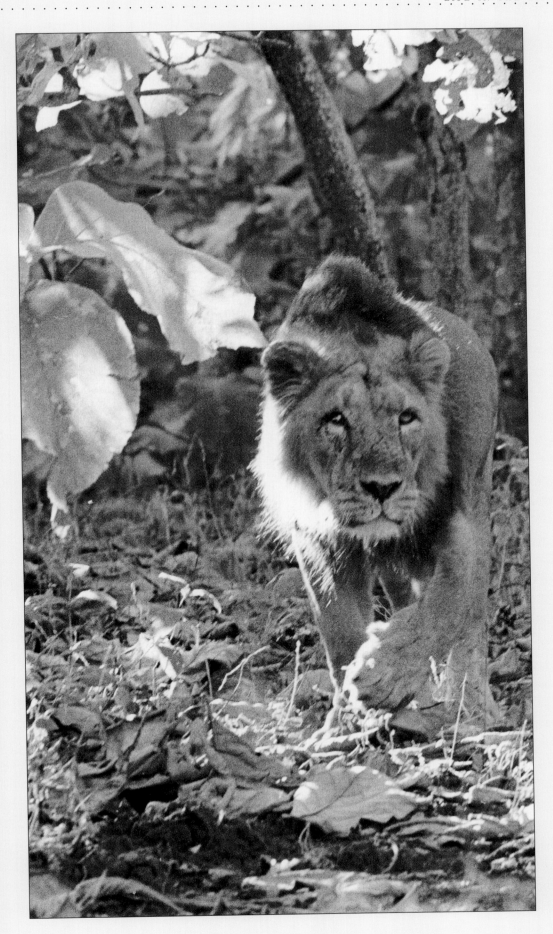

On the prowl
■ A lion moves through thick jungle, passing oversized teak leaves.
Photograph: Divyabhanusinh.

event, Jawaharlal Nehru and Indira Gandhi did meet up with the lions. The Forest Department thought fit to make them wear khaki overcoats before being taking them on foot close to the lions, in order not to alarm the animals. Though the camera had replaced the business end of a rifle, the transition in lion behaviour to familiarity with humans had yet to take place.

All this had a somewhat unfortunate result. The local authorities realized that it would be easy to "anchor" lions to show them to tourists and thus began the infamous "lion shows". Parties of trackers would go out each morning into the jungle, locate a lion or a pride, see where it rested, and then take the tourists in the evening to the site where a goat or a buffalo calf would have preceded them.[7] The bleating of a goat or the yodel of a Maldhari herding his buffaloes imitated by a shikari, became a veritable dinner gong to attract the lions. They would be watched by up to a hundred or more tourists a few yards away, and rewarded with the buffalo calf once the tourists had departed. Over a period of time lions lost their fear of man and pride sizes increased around Sasan, Sandhbeda and elsewhere in the western part of the Gir. In 1958, M.M. Jamkhandikar, Deputy Conservator of Forests records a pride of fourteen animals at Sandhbeda, which he saw at just over 15 metres;[8] M.K. Ranjitsinhji records a pride of eighteen animals waiting for a handout near Vansadhor hill;[9] and I have observed a pride of 21 animals at Sandhbeda with a troublesome male following it at some distance, some years later. The whole process became farcical, visitors thought the lions had become tame and many felt their experience was devalued by this curious spectacle. The Expert Committee of the Indian Board for Wildlife wryly commented in 1970 that there were "... only about 177 lions [left in the Gir] of which the same dozen are seen by more than 90% of the visitors at the lion show".[10]

This was evident, for lions of the rest of the Gir were not used to humans and they reacted very differently to their presence where there were no handouts to be had. At any rate, with the end of lion shikar and policing of the forests, the lions became more visible during the day, though with varying degrees of tolerance to human presence depending on the part of Gir where the animals were encountered. M.Y. Ghorpade recorded with satisfaction that he was able to photograph a male lion on foot from 30 metres and he was even able to "compose" the frame.[11] The spectacle of "lion shows" came to an inglorious end in 1987–88[12] as a result of a general outcry against it. The lions around Sasan, where they are still tracked and located, continue to be more visible and tolerant of human presence as they have seen people and vehicles at close quarters from the time they were cubs.* The big prides have gone, as food is no longer dished out and one sees animals in prides of less than four or five making them more efficient for hunting. Besides, being now more dependent on natural prey than upon livestock, as was the case in Dr Paul Joslin's day 35 years ago, there is neither the need for a large pride as was the case with a Gir buffalo which required a communal effort to pull it down, nor is there as much meat available in a natural prey kill to provide for such a gathering at every meal.

---

* A change in the behaviour of tigers at Ranthambhore National Park is another case in point. In the early 1970s tiger presence was evident from their spoor but one rarely saw them even if one spent several days in the jungle. As protection improved and tigers multiplied in numbers, they became visible to humans in broad daylight and were commonly observed hunting even in mid-afternoon. This was absolutely unthinkable earlier. Such change in the behaviour of tigers is seen in other protected areas as well.

While on the formal level of government regulations and protection efforts the lions had never had it so good, things were going wrong in the field. This was evident from the great numbers game which had thrown up disturbing figures. In spite of the chaos of 1947 there were a maximum of 227 lions in 1950 which number increased to 290 in 1955 and marginally reduced to 285 in 1963. But just five years later in 1968 the population had collapsed by more than a hundred, as the census of that year threw up a figure of 177. The validity or otherwise of absolute figures is not of importance here. Suffice it to say that there was a substantial decline in lion population, which was a cause for alarm. One of the reasons was that the Maldharis had taken to poisoning with insecticides the carcasses of their buffaloes killed by lions. This was a result of the discontinuation of the practice of compensating owners of lost cattle which had been started by Junagadh state. P.D. Stracey emphasized that unless this practice was restored, the lion would not be safe.[13]

As far as the study of the Gir forest and its flora and fauna was concerned, this was a watershed period. Hitherto, sportsmen and princes had observed lions and monitored their condition through numerous and sometimes extended visits to the Gir either for shikar or for conservation. Now on, the flora and fauna would be studied through field research by scientists. First off the block was a combined effort of the School of Forestry of Yale University and the Bombay Natural History Society. A team of scientists came on the scene. Paul Joslin from Edinburgh University studied the lion, Stephen Berwick of Yale University studied ungulates, T. Hodd from the University of Aberdeen studied vegetation, while R. Grubh of the Bombay Natural History Society studied the ecology of vultures. Their theses and reports formed a bedrock of information which could guide the managers of the Gir. Joslin's work reported that lions survived mainly on livestock everywhere and that the Gir sustained 20,000 to 25,000 heads of cattle round the year. About the same number of cattle invaded the forest for a part of the year and even the resident herds outnumbered the six major species of ungulates put together,[14] the natural prey of lions in the Gir forest. While scientists recommended control on number of cattle and wanted twelve to sixteen per cent of the forest freed from livestock, Joslin warned against their sudden removal from the jungle[15] as lions would require to switch over to other prey which in turn needed time to multiply.

On a different plane, things were moving fast. Soon after its formation, Gujarat state had enacted a law – *The Gujarat Wild Animals and Wild Birds Protection Act, 1963* – which replaced the 1951 legislation of Bombay state. Under this act, 1,265 square kilometres of the Gir forest were declared a sanctuary in 1965.[16] However, a simple legislation and ban on hunting for sport and prevention of poaching alone would not suffice in the Gir. The forest was threatened by other factors which needed to be tackled as had become evident by the sudden reduction of the lion population to 177. Such concerns during the collapse of the elected government and the resultant President's Rule in the state presented an opportunity not to be missed. The Gir Lion Sanctuary Project was born in January 1972,[17] thus anticipating the better known project to save the tiger which got off the ground a little over a year later in April 1973. The immediate precursor of the project was the technical session of the International Union for Conservation of Nature (IUCN) held in Delhi in 1969. Paul Joslin's paper on the conservation aspects of the Gir was presented at it. He pointed out that the Gir Sanctuary exhibited overwhelming evidence of progressive and accelerating degradation of the indigenous ecosystem. According to his findings,

A Gir lion in the Berlin Deer Park
■ This Asian lion photographed in 1998 in the zoo in eastern Berlin, came to it from Zurich which had acquired it from India. The lion has over the years developed a luxuriant black mane which covers the lower part of its chest and abdomen similar to the lions found on Assyrian friezes of Ashurnasirpal and Ashurbanipal.
Photograph: Lothar Schlawe.

A crouching lion
■ All attention, it looks past the photographer at a herd of chital.
Photograph: Divyabhanusinh.

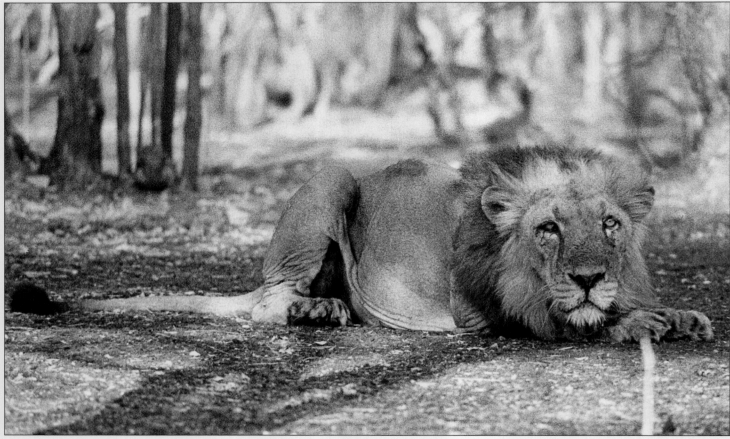

more than 20,000 cattle grazed in it which caused a loss of food for the prey base of the lion. Further, most of the fertile valleys of the sanctuary had come under cultivation. In the absence of their natural prey, lions fed almost exclusively on domestic cattle of which 23 per cent could not be eaten by them as the dead animals were taken away by tanners for removing and curing the skins. In addition, about twenty per cent of the lion population was getting tethered baits. These were warning bells which could not be ignored. Guy Mountfort, International Trustee of the World Wildlife Fund wrote to Prime Minister Indira Gandhi soon thereafter, enclosing a report prepared by experts from India, Britain, and the USA who had visited the sanctuary in December 1970. He pointed out that unless the threats to the lion were tackled swiftly, India's national symbol would become extinct.[18]

The Expert Committee of the Indian Board for Wildlife too had visited the Gir a few months earlier in April 1970 and had expressed its own concerns. Since Gujarat was under President's Rule, Governor Sriman Narayan turned his attention to the establishment of a stable ecosystem wherein lions and other animals could roam freely, as also to the socio-economic upliftment of the Maldharis of Gir. The Council for Ecology was set up in November 1970 by the Government of Gujarat under the chairmanship of Y. Digvijaysinhji of Wankaner, which approved a set of objectives prepared by Amrita H. Patel on behalf of the Ecological Research Centre (a body set up by the Smithsonian Institution, Yale University, Government of Gujarat, and Bombay Natural History Society). These objectives were all-encompassing in their reach. They included, inter alia: to conserve the Gir habitat and if possible improve it; to encourage wildlife for its own sake, especially the lion; to exclude all exotic species; to reverse or minimize human conflict; to protect the habitat from overgrazing and lopping; and to improve the lot of the Maldharis and phase their resettlement outside the sanctuary. Pursuant to these recommendations, the state government issued formal orders on January 17, 1972 to the effect that (a) the sanctuary area was to be permanently closed to grazing by livestock from outside, (b) the area should have a physical barrier to make the closure effective, and (c) Maldharis staying inside the Gir should be shifted along with their cattle in a phased manner and settled in villages around the sanctuary by allotting them land for cultivation as well as common grazing ground for their cattle.[19]

Soon there was a change at Government House. The new Governor, K.T. Satarawala, took a keen interest in the progress of the project. Though the drought of 1972 created problems of grazing as some 70,000 cattle entered the Gir, effective steps were soon taken. A rubble wall over 209 kilometres along the sanctuary's boundary was built by 1975, which was later increased to a length of about 380 kilometres. In 1974, 147 square kilometres of adjoining forest areas of Amreli were added to the Gir Sanctuary. An area of 140 square kilometres of the Jamwala and Chodavdi ranges was constituted as a sanctum sanctorum, which became a National Park under the recently enacted all-India law, *The Wildlife (Protection) Act, 1972*. Its total area was increased to 258 square kilometres in 1978. Further, the government declared its intention to create the entire sanctuary area as a National Park.[20] The relocation of Maldharis was a crucial part of the project. In 1971 there were 129 nesses with 845 families owning about 17,000 domestic cattle according to one government source[21] while another gave a figure of 714 families with a livestock population of about 13,000.[22] The resettlement programme continued till the year 1986–87 and a total of 592 families were relocated.[23] By the year 1995–96, 54 nesses

At a waterhole
■ Lions will avoid getting wet almost at all costs. This lion is about to drink water but has bent his front left leg to avoid getting his paw wet.
Photograph: Divyabhanusinh.

out of the original 129 were left within the protected area, with 361 households, a human population of 2,540 and a livestock population of about 10,000.[24]

Protection yielded visible results. The combined herbivore population of chital, sambar, nilgai, chowsingha, chinkara, and wild boar which was estimated at 5,500 in 1969, went up to 10,000 in 1974, and to 15,000 by 1979. During the same period the lion population went up to 180 in 1974, and 205 in 1979.[25] S.P. Sinha's research on the lion showed that in the years 1982–84 when he collected and analysed lion scats, 48 per cent contained livestock hair as against Paul Joslin's findings of 75 per cent in 1968–71.[26] By 1990, the combined herbivore population had gone up to nearly 33,000 and the lions had increased to 284.[27] Ravi Chellam found remains of cattle and buffalo only in 25 per cent of scats analysed by him in the year 1989.[28]

At the national level the 1970s saw a more widely known wildlife crisis. The realization finally dawned on the powers that were, that they had a near disaster on their hands. A 1972 nationwide census revealed that the total tiger population in the country had collapsed to 1,827 animals which was an indication of the alarming condition of the protection of the forest cover in the country. Project Tiger was quickly put in place and the tiger was "lionized", as R.S. Dharmakumarsinhji put it,[29] as it was anointed the national animal in place of the lion. While Ashoka's lions continued as the national symbol, the wild variety of the species had to be content with becoming the state animal of Gujarat, an indication of its reduced pocket-size range. In the lion's case the state government would have to largely take upon itself the job of protection, unlike the tiger the preservation of which became a national movement of sorts as it caught the attention of the urban middle class as no animal had before.

A battle royal

■ Two free-ranging lions charge an inmate across the fence of the Devalia Safari Park which occupies prime lion habitat in Gir. Here tourists are shown lions at close quarters. This kind of confrontation among lions can lead to injuries.

Photograph: Prerna Kumari Singh.

The mid 1970s were a watershed in Indian politics. The imposition of emergency rule between June 1975 and January 1977 by Indira Gandhi was the dividing line. Subsequent to it, for the first time in India's history, a non-Congress government took office. The Central government was never to exercise the extent of power it had done for the thirty years so far. It is a curious fact that by the Forty-Second Amendment to the Constitution of India which came into effect on January 3, 1977, the two subjects *Forests* and *Protection of Wild Animals and Birds* were taken from the State List and brought to the Concurrent List, giving the Central government the opportunity to legislate concurrently with states on these subjects. This, at a time when the states had become more powerful with local aspirations. It was by the same amendment that a new Directive Principle of State Policy was inserted, by which the state was required to "endeavour to protect and improve the environment and to safeguard the forests and wildlife of the country".[30]

The foregoing narration gives the impression that the lion is more or less secure in its habitat, and the template for strict preservation of the species and its habitat is in place. But the problems both lions and their habitat face are serious and their solutions are in the realm of human action or the lack of it at the local level. The lion population has increased steadily over the years. At the last count in 2001 it stood at 327 and the total of the six herbivores had reached about 55,000, increasing at the rate of 14 per cent annually during the preceding three decades.[31] The forest within the National Park and Sanctuary limits was preserved and the lion had gone back in large measure to predating on its natural prey. Any way one looks at it, here is a success story, and those involved in making it happen deserve the nation's appreciation. Having said that, it must not be forgotten that success brings in its

Marking territory
■ A lion demarcates his territory by spraying. A male can traverse territories of more than one lioness or pride.
Photograph: Divyabhanusinh.

wake a new set of problems which need to be addressed at the earliest, in addition to the existing unfinished agenda.

The Gir forest has never carried more than 300 animals – 267 in 1990, 262 in 1995, and 271 in 2001. The eastern Gir portion of the protected area which had very few lions earlier showed a remarkable change. By 2001 it had 106 lions in an area which was half that of the western portion. Also, the lions had started moving away and establishing themselves outside the protected area.[32]

In 1995 as many as 42 lions lived outside the Gir protected area, whereas by 2001 the number had increased to 59. It was natural that they would move within their earlier haunts. The Girnar mountain, at the foot of which is the city of Junagadh, was originally part of the Gir forest but now it is 22 kilometres away from the nearest boundary of the Gir Sanctuary with an area of 180 square kilometres of deciduous and dry scrub patches. It was always home to lions with a relict population up to 1963. However, dispersal of lions started after the drought year of 1987 and the censuses of 1995 and 2001 recorded 13 of them there. In the Mytiala forest of the old Bhavnagar state, there were three lions in 1995, but their number had increased to sixteen in 2001. It lies due east at a distance of 6 kilometres from the boundary of the sanctuary with an area of just 19 square kilometres. In the Hapavadli zone beyond Mytiala in the eastern part of Bhavnagar district, eleven cubs were reported in the 2001 census. The coastal forests of Una-Rajula-Jafrabad and of the Kodinar-Sutrapada belts had 26 lions in 1995 and the animals were breeding there. In 2001, however, the number had reduced to 20. This forest is dominated by *Prosopis chilensis* and the planted *Casuarina equisetifolia*, and harbours nilgai and wild boar, both of which are a nuisance to the farmers. But they form a part of the lion's diet, though livestock has remained the major food source for them here. Seven lions were also reported from villages near the Gir protected area.[33]

By the roadside
■ Lions often sit on the road or in clearings nearby. Still, they merge beautifully with their surroundings and are often missed from a moving vehicle.
Photographs: Divyabhanusinh.

A lioness and two cubs were found on the island of Diu, having crossed the creek presumably by the bridge, in 1996. A lion and a lioness pair were found near Porbandar, which killed and ate five domestic cattle in February 2003. These lions died in mysterious circumstances after they were captured and brought back to the Gir Sanctuary.[34] A lioness was reported from Kotda Sangani almost on the outskirts of Gondal.[35] All these instances are of lions found several kilometres away from the nearest forest boundary. Lions had lived so close to human populations in ancient Palestine that the Hebrew Bible could record "The slothful saith, a lion is in the street",[36] and one wonders if it is about to happen again, in Saurashtra this time. It is not fanciful to imagine a sizeable stable lion population living near human settlements surviving on wild boar and nilgai, which are also found in increasing numbers outside protected areas, and on cattle.

The immediate action that is required is the upgradation of the forests, thickets, and grasslands now occupied by lions, and their protection by making sanctuaries of these areas. Equally important is the preservation of the "corridors" used by lions to migrate out. In these, particularly between Gir forest and Girnar – the largest forest patch chosen by lions, the distance is large and their passage is of necessity through open and cultivated lands. It is estimated that the home range of the lion was spread over 8,500 square kilometres in the year 2000,[37] whereas its range has increased to about 10,000 square kilometres by 2004.[38] There is relentless and increasing human pressure on such areas which would make it difficult to leave them in the present state of development. A detailed study would advise if acquisition of some of these lands is at all possible. Hitherto land is acquired by government through fixed rates which are way below market rates. A method must be found to make such transactions voluntary which may be done through offering market rates. Here is a role for non-government organizations to bring in funds and expertise. A plan already exists for the "ecorestoration" of Girnar and an overall strategy for regional planning across the lion's home range has been prepared.[39] The Girnar forests have an additional problem as the mountain harbours Hindu and Jain shrines of antiquity which results in large-scale influx of pilgrims several times a year. And there is a large and increasing human population all around. The prey base is very low as there are few sambar and chital. There is even talk of a ropeway to cart pilgrims to the shrines on the mountain, which will bring in its wake its own problems. The task is enormous, but it has to be attempted to make a success of the lions' own survival plan, for it is they who have spread out without help from us. If urgent steps are not taken to secure the habitat, the increase in their population may spark another lion migration elsewhere. There was a recent newspaper report that a lion and a lioness which had made the *Prosopis chilensis* thickets of Savarkundla taluka their home were reduced to drinking water from cattle water troughs in villages and sometimes ended up drinking the water overflow from such troughs.[40] Such occurrences may increase in time which would have their own implications for lion-human conflict.

The one locality which the government of Gujarat has often talked of as a possible area for lion reintroduction is the Barda Wildlife Sanctuary. It is near the coastal city of Porbandar with an area of 192 square kilometres. Its major problem is that today it has 68 nesses with 750 families of Maldharis, a total population of 4,000.[41] The lions themselves have shunned the area so far and, if the matter is left to them to decide, it appears to be out of the running for their reintroduction for the time being.

The mating game
A lion and lioness come together to mate
when the female is in oestrus. Over a
period of four or five days they mate
repeatedly for a few minutes each time,
and then go their own way.
- Ready to mate.
- The lion mounts and licks the lioness.
- The lion bites the lioness and
dismounts.
- Time to rest again.
Photographs: Divyabhanusinh.

While the lion population is definitely on the increase, the question must be asked – just how many lions can their present home range sustain? According to H.S. Singh's estimation, up to 400 lions is a possibility but not the magical figure of 500,[42] unless they spread farther afield along the coast and also occupy outlying forest patches around the hills of Alech, Dalasa, Barda, and Shetrunjay. While absolute numbers need not detain us here, it is evident that the increasing population by itself is reason to remove some lions to a second home large enough to sustain and further increase the population there. None of the areas where the lions have moved within Saurashtra is large enough to sustain a healthy breeding population on a long-term basis. On the other hand, if the lion population goes up in such pockets, they could become potential flashpoints of human-lion conflicts. It is in the interest of the species to have a viable home such as Kuno-Palpur or elsewhere for their long-term survival.

The other Damoclean sword over the lion is the ever-present threat of a natural calamity such as drought, fire, or an epidemic. Serengeti in Tanzania lost over 1,000 lions in 1993 to a canine distemper. This disease is prevalent in India as is *Ehrlichiosis*, the Nairobi bleeding disease, which is fatal if not treated in time. It is endemic in Mumbai's canine and feline populations. The disease has spread to tigers

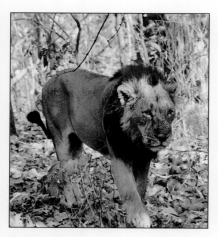

On the prowl
■ A solitary lion walks beside a road, patrolling its territory.
Photograph: Divyabhanusinh.

in the Safari Park at Borivli and recently to leopards in a zoo in Lonavla. Such diseases could assume epidemic form and strike a small felid population in a restricted area such as the Gir. Serengeti could sustain the loss and recover. Such an occurrence would be calamitous to Gir and its lions. This is yet another reason for the government of Gujarat to agree to the transfer of a few lions to Kuno-Palpur to establish a second home, and to support this satellite population on a continuing basis to ensure its health.

With the dense human and cattle population around the Gir protected area, there is constant and relentless pressure on it for fuel, grazing, and other forest produce. There are 79 villages located within a periphery of 6 kilometres all around the Gir Sanctuary with a human population of 1,36,000 and domestic livestock population of 1,00,000. Since 1995–96 the government has embarked on an ambitious Eco-Development Project from the funds made available from the Global Environment Fund and the World Bank. This is a unique experiment insofar as the government is trying to implement the project with local support through village level Eco-Development Councils where their participation is sought in providing liquid propane gas units in villages for cooking, land levelling, barbed-wire fencing, supplying agricultural implements, and so on. While the target of this project includes peripheral villages and the Maldharis' nesses inside the protected area, it also targets improvement of the protected area and its management such as preventing soil erosion, removal of the menace of the "mad babul" – *Prosopis chilensis*, and *Lantana camara*, training of the Forest Department staff, improvement of their living conditions, and other such activities. Between 1995–96 and 1999–2000 a sum of Rs 472 lakhs was spent on the project.[43] It has also initiated ten studies including man-animal conflict, study of satellite lion populations, impact of tourism, studies of lesser known fauna, and so on.[44] The results of these studies are now in the process of becoming available to the managers in the field. The human population in India is likely to keep growing at an average of around 1.5 per cent per annum till 2016.[45] A continuous audit by independent experts is essential, to assess the direct impact of the project on the Gir forest, such as reduction in livestock grazing through increased stall-feeding, reduction in amount of fuel wood being removed from it through greater use of gas for cooking purposes, reduction in damage to fauna and flora, etc. These would be the true indicators of the project's success or otherwise, and would help to identify what mid-course corrections are required. Any project targeted at the human population must therefore continue over a long term with increased resources.

In the final analysis, the success of the project depends on how speedily and honestly it is carried out by the administration of the state government. Delays and leakages have caused the failure of so many schemes of socio-economic benefit that there is a real danger of this project going the same way.

In the meantime threats to the lions from various quarters still exist. Lions on the periphery of the forest continue to predate heavily on livestock. In 1998–99 alone 1,902 cattle were killed by them, of which 1,329 were compensated for at a total cost of approximately Rs 1.15 crores.[46] The government's procedures and false claims denied compensation for 573 claims of cattle kills. This is a source of constant friction.

Lion-human conflicts are another continuous occurrence in the Gir. A study of the problem revealed that there were totally 193 attacks by lions between 1977 and

1991 with 28 human mortalities, i.e. an average of 2.2 per year. The year 1987–88 was witness to the severest drought since 1918, which profoundly altered the conflict ratio: in that year alone, forty attacks were recorded,[47] reminiscent of lion attacks causing 66 people to lose their lives during the years 1901–04 that followed the great Chappanyo Kal of 1899–1900.[48] Between 1991–92 and 1994–95, 54 persons were injured by lions, of whom six lost their lives.[49] There is no simple solution for such conflicts which can only be reduced substantially if humans and lions do not need to interact as much as they do, and this does not seem likely to happen in a hurry, if at all.

The relocation of Maldharis which started under the Gir Lion Project in 1973–74 continued till 1986–87. The impact on the forest was visible for all to see and the lion's food content changed dramatically as we have noted earlier. This in itself is sufficient proof of the benefits of the effort. However, the matter is now at a standstill and 54 nesses with 2,500 people and about 13,000 livestock remain according to the 2004 figures. In 1971 there were 714 Maldhari families and about 13,000 cattle in the Gir protected area, of which 592 families were relocated.[50] In other words around 10,700 livestock moved out of the protected area (if we are to take an average of eighteen heads of livestock per person) leaving behind some 3,000. Given the 2004 figure of about 13,000, the growth in livestock population has negated the process of relocation. This tendency, if not checked, is a potential threat to the sanctuary.

It is a matter of record that the resettlement of Maldharis was fraught with problems. Of the 592 families resettled, only 323 families remained in their new homes by 1992–93,[51] the others having moved on or returned to the Gir to one of the existing nesses. The relocation of Maldharis needs to be done in a phased manner and it can succeed only if the scheme is implemented sensitively, giving them facilities which are attractive enough to persuade them to move. The first effort in the 1970s fell short of success; the next one does not have room for error. If the Maldharis continue to remain within the sanctuary, their numbers and their livestock numbers must be limited. In a study of the impact of management practices on lion and ungulate habitat of Gir, Diwakar Sharma recommends a minimum distance of 8 kilometres between two nesses to leave disturbance-free forest of sufficient size between them for sambar. This would involve relocation of some thirty nesses and their livestock.[52] Popular government and local resistance has ensured the virtual abandonment of any relocation and that is why the conversion of the entire sanctuary into a National Park remains unfulfilled.

Apart from the Maldharis, there are fourteen forest settlement villages in the sanctuary with a human population of about 4,500 and a livestock population of about 4,200[53] which pose a similar problem. In the past, man had a niche in nature. When one propagates traditional rights in protected areas one forgets that human and cattle populations were naturally controlled before the advent of Western medicine and veterinary services. Besides, even fifty years ago the forest cover was larger and the human population far smaller. Today if such populations grow in protected areas – as they will surely do – their existence and prosperity will be at the cost of their immediate environment.

There are three places of worship which are in the Gir, namely Tulsishyam, Banej, and Kankai shrines. The last mentioned is the most frequented of the three. Situated in the heart of the sanctuary, it has expanded into a complex of 24

A solitary lion emerges from thick jungle
■ Lions adapt to different types of habitat easily, though their preference is for scrub jungle or grassland.
Photograph: Divyabhanusinh.

The lion at ease
■ Sitting in the open, it enjoys the evening breeze as can be seen from its wind-blown mane.
Photograph: Divyabhanusinh.

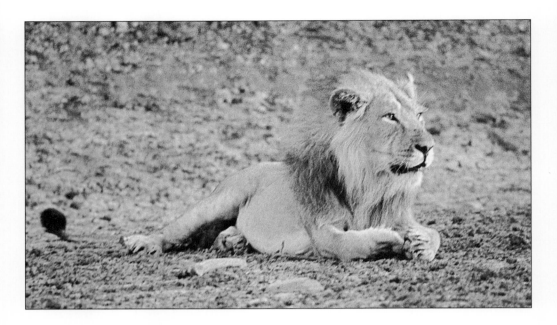

permanent structures covering an area of 9,516 square metres. I remember the shrine as a small, charming, and peaceful spot in the mid-1950s, which is long gone. In 1987–88 it was visited by over 8,000 pilgrims in 1,049 vehicles. In 1997–98, nearly 50,000 pilgrims visited it in 4,700 vehicles! The demands of the temple are manifold and ever-increasing, and it is a source of major problems to the preservation of the sanctuary.

The number of tourists visiting the Gir has increased exponentially. In 1977–78 there were 14,000; this figure increased to over 57,000 in 1994–95 which brought a revenue of nearly Rs 13 lakhs.[54] While the state government has still not found a way to divert such income entirely or substantially to the Gir, there is also a need to monitor and regulate this activity. Many of the tourists visit the Lion Safari Park at Devalia which no doubt brings down the pressure on the rest of the sanctuary. However, this park built over an area of 400 hectares in prime lion habitat, should never have come up in the first place at this location. It should have been built on revenue land abutting the sanctuary, not inside it. It certainly would be worthwhile to consider this option and convert the existing enclosure into a non-invasive research centre for conservation or better still, remove the structures and restore the natural vegetation. The lions within it brought from Sakkarbag Zoo, Junagadh, often attract their wild counterparts from the surrounding sanctuary area, causing them to make futile attacks on the chain-link fence of the Safari Park which could cause them grave physical harm.

The railway line running through the forest and the 89 kilometres of Public Works Department roads (including 29 kilometres of State Highway between Jamwala and Sapnes) are a constant threat to the lions. As many as eleven lions were killed on the railway tracks between 1983–84 and 1995–96.[55] It is a metre gauge line and it should be discontinued. Ideally, the roads too need to be permanently closed, which has not happened because of heavy pressure from the users. In fact there are constant demands for their improvement. The recent decision of the local administration to restrict vehicular movement on the 16-kilometre-long Visavadar to Sasan road has led to strong protest,[56] and it remains to be seen if the government will be able to weather the storm.

Lions are also being poached or killed. In all, fourteen lions were done away with between 1985–86 and 1994–95. Of these, three were killed inside the protected area.[57] The reason for such killings appears to be either accidental or it is sometimes the result of poisoning. As of now there is no reason to believe that any of these animals were killed for "sport" though in May and June of 1996 there were several reports in *Phulchchab*, a popular Gujarati daily published from Rajkot, of the arrest of a gang of poachers who were killing lions to sell body parts. Claws fetched a sum of Rs 500 locally,[58] as these are believed to be "charms" which protect humans from diseases and the evil eye.

The problems of the Gir forest are well known and the more prominent ones have been briefly stated here. The forest and its flora and fauna, including the lion itself, have been subjects of intense study and reports in the last half century by princes, naturalists, and lately by scientists from India and abroad. There is no dearth of technical information or analyses, there are proposed solutions to the issues facing the lion and the Gir forest. The Indian government and particularly the government of Gujarat have managed to preserve a viable ecosystem so far; lions and other animals in the Gir forest have increased under their stewardship for which kudos to them. But the relentless increase in human population with the attendant livestock population reminds one of an increasing number of mice gnawing away at the same small piece of cheese. Our administrative dispensation and conservation efforts are largely continuations of the British imperial and Indian princely traditions. More and more local aspirations are at variance with them and the republican top itself is not as strongly or personally interested in conservation as was the case in days gone by. Preservation of forests and their non-human inhabitants usually goes against the vote-giving estates of our law-makers. Lions and tigers have no votes, so the politicians do not need them to survive in the short term – and they are interested only in the short term. On the other hand, successful local community movements for conservation are few and far between despite all the fanfare that often attends them. They would have an impact only if they can replicate their smaller local successes on a large enough scale and on a continuing basis. Under these circumstances, the efforts of the government of Gujarat to take local communities into their programme of eco-development are a step in the right direction. The success or failure of the programmes will be known only in the years ahead. In the meantime an honest, committed administration backed by a strong political will is the need of the hour.

The crux of the problem of preserving the Gir forest is the same as elsewhere: the exploding human population is likely to negate most efforts. In 1951 still 361 million in strength, by 2001 we are 1,027 million strong[59] and we are growing. We have put ourselves above the environment and we are cutting the very branch of the tree on which we are sitting, like Kalidasa of ancient times. He at least got enlightened in the process of the fall. No such spark has yet become apparent in our case. Surely, Reginald Heber, Lord Bishop of Calcutta (1823–26) was right when he lamented, albeit in a different context:

Though every prospect pleases
And only man is vile:
In vain with lavish kindness
The Gifts of God are strewn....

references

CHAPTER 1

ASIA'S LIONS TODAY

1   Wynter-Blyth, c. 1961. Though dated, this little essay is by far the most instructive on the subject.
2   Singh, 2001, pp. 67–74.
3   Sunquist and Sunquist, 2002, p. 238.
4   Mr Bharat J. Pathak, pers. comm., 2004.
5   Chellam, 1993.
6   O'Brien, 2003, p. 47.
7   See Appendix 2.
8   Dr M.A. Mehendale, pers. comm., 1999.
9   Anon, 1833; Pocock, 1930.
10 Patterson, 1907, frontispiece, pp. 92–93, 103.
11 Caputo, 2002, p. 146.
12 Freer Gallery of Art, Washington D.C., Acc. No. 48.8 in Welch, 1978, pp. 56–57.
13 The British Library, London, Acc. No. 1920, 9.17.05 in Pal, 1991, p. 29.
14 Bharat Kala Bhavan, Varanasi, Acc. No. 9069/6 in Krishnadasa, 1999, p. 70, plate B. See also p. 101.
15 Kostioukovitch, 1996, pp. 97–98, plate 146/folio 72 recto. See p. 106.
16 Falk and Digby, 1983, p. 22, plate 10.
17 Maharaja Sawai Man Singh II Museum, Jaipur, Acc. No. Ag. 863 in Rashid and David, 1992, plate 5. See p. 103.
18 Soustiel, 1973, pp. 20–21.
19 Beach and Koch, 1997, pp. 77–78, plate 30. See p. 98.
20 Ibid., pp. 110–11, plate 46. See p. 99.
21 The Chester Beatty Library, Dublin, Acc. No. In. 11A.28. See p. 100.
22 Falk, Smart, and Skelton, 1978, p. 60, plate 69.
23 Stuart Cary Welch Collection, Arthur M. Sackler Museum, Harvard University Arts Museum, Cambridge, Mass., in Kossak, 1997, pp. 62–63.
24 Rao Madho Singh Trust Museum, in Singh, 1985, p. 26, plate I. See p. 108.
25 Jerdon, 1867, pp. 90–91.

26 Prater, 1948, p. 67.
27 Pocock, 1930.
28 See Appendix 3.
29 Dollman and Burlace, 1935, pp. 365–67.
30 Smith, Mcbee, and Mathews, 1989, pp. 752–58.
31 See Chapter 11.
32 Wynter-Blyth, c. 1961, p. 2.
33 Wildt, et al., 1987.
34 O'Brien, 2003, p. 51.
35 Fenton, c. 1924, p. 6.
36 Rangarajan, 2001.
37 Ranjitsinh, 1997, p. 50.
38 Ibid., p. 51.
39 Watson, 1884, p. 6.
40 Apte, 1965, p. 934.
41 Monier-Williams, 1899, p. 1105.
42 Gida, 1999.
43 Meghani, 1997, pp. 538–40.
44 Meghani, 1997A.
45 Sursinh, 1893, pp. 73–74.
46 Desai, 1983, p. 125.

CHAPTER 2

AN ORIENTAL PATRIMONY

1   Macdonald, 1992, p. 62; Turner, 1997, pp. 72–73.
2   Hemmer, 1974, pp. 229–34, 271–72.
3   Houlihan, 1996, p. 2.
4   Ibid., pp. 94–95.
5   Guggisberg, 1962, pp. 244–45.
6   Houlihan, 1996, p. 93.
7   Ibid., pp. 41, 70–73; Guggisberg, 1962, p. 156.
8   Houlihan, 1996, p. 71.
9   Saunders, 1991, p. 83.
10 Reade, 1983, p. 72.
11 Moscati, 1960, pp. 62–63.
12 Reade, 1983, p. 39.
13 Van Buren, 1939, p. 3.
14 Luckenbill, 1927, p. 363.
15 Weissert, 1997.
16 Reade, 1983, p. 74.
17 Weissert, 1997.

18 Reade, 1983, p. 73.
19 Mukherjee, 1969, pp. 11–12.
20 Ibid., pp. 9–10.
21 Ibid., p. 90.
22 Albenda, 1974.
23 Reade, 1983, pp. 72–79.
24 I am grateful to Dr Julian Reade for pointing out the unsculpted outlines of the tails on the exhibits at the British Museum.
25 Pocock, 1930; Hemmer, 1974.
26 Reade, 1983, p. 72.
27 Layard, 1853, p. 487.
28 Bodenheimer, 1960, p. 134.
29 Toynbee, 1973, p. 19.
30 Judges 14:6; Daniel 6:2.
31 Ezekiel 20: 3–9.
32 See Chapter 6, pp. 109–10.
33 Modi, 1932.
34 Hartner and Ettinghausen, 1964.
35 Godrej and Mistree, 2002, p. 670; Humphreys and Kahrom, 1995, p. 80.
36 Godrej and Mistree, 2002, p. 670.
37 Titley, 1983, pp. 14, 87. See p. 50.
38 Graves and Ali-Shah, 1967, p. 53, verse 18.
39 Hassan, 1937, pp. 4–5.
40 Ibid.
41 Ibid.; Layard, 1853, pp. 556–57.
42 Harting, 1883, pp. 364–65.
43 Rawlinson, 1898, pp. 149–50.
44 Layard, 1853, p. 487.
45 Kostioukovitch, 1996, pp. 95–96, plate 136, folio 100, recto. See p. 103.
46 Dr A.H. Morton, pers. comm., 2002.
47 Ibid.
48 Heptner and Sludskii, 1971, p. 82.
49 Balfour, 1885, pp. 719–20.
50 Pocock, 1936A.
51 Heaney, 1944.
52 M.K. Ranjitsinhji, pers. comm., 2003.
53 Harrington, 1977, pp. 72–73.
54 Ms Daphne M. Hills, pers. comm., 1999; Pocock, 1930. See p. 22.
55 Joslin, 1973; Kinnear, 1920.
56 Guggisberg, 1962, p. 42; Kinnear, 1920.

CHAPTER 3

A SEARCH THROUGH ANTIQUITY

1 Chattopadhyaya, 2002.

2 Thomas and Joglekar, 1994.

3 Ibid.

4 Dutta, 1976, quotes Pilgrim, 1910, 1938.

5 Kinnear, 1920.

6 Sunquist and Sunquist, 2002, p. 286.

7 Mahadevan, 1977, pp. 793–94.

8 Jarrige and Hassan, 1989.

9 See Chapter 2. I am grateful to Dr Julian Reade for specifically drawing my attention to this anatomical aberration while showing me the black obelisk at the British Museum.

10 Jarrige and Hassan, 1989.

11 Schwartzberg 1978, p. 11, plate II-5.

12 Iyer, 1977, p. 14.

13 Possehl, 1999, pp. 198–99.

14 Parpola, 1994, pp. 246–47.

15 Mahadevan, 1977, p. 793.

16 Misra, 2000.

17 Irwin, 1973, 1974, 1975, 1976, 1983, 1985. These articles must be read as one whole. The conclusions which are summarized in this chapter are culled from them.

18 Thapar, 1961, p. 269.

19 Prof. Romila Thapar, pers. comm., 2003.

20 Prof. Helmut Hemmer, pers. comm., 1999. For a description of the "flehmen" expression see Schaller, 1972, p. 95; Allaby, 1985, p. 252.

21 Prof. Helmut Hemmer, pers. comm., 1999.

22 Ibid.

23 Irwin, 1976.

24 Ibid.

25 Thapar, 1961, p. 261.

26 Irwin, 1973.

27 Bopearachhi, 1998, plates 13–14.

28 Zeuner, 1963, p. 419.

29 Allan, 1936, pp. 223–27, plates XXXII–XXXIII.

30 Jha and Rajgor, 1994.

31 Rapson, 1908, pp. 2, 10–13, plates I, III.

32 McCrindle, 1877, Fragm. XII, pp. 56–57.

33 Ibid.

34 Ibid., pp. 10–12.

35 Ibid., pp. 220–21.

36 Ibid., pp. 280–81.

37 Basham, 1954, p. 196.

38 Pathan, 1921, pp. 31, 33, 41, 42.

39 Mr Shantanu Kumar, pers. comm., 2003.

40 McCrindle, 1901, pp. 74–75; Jones, 1966, 122.

41 Pathan, 1921, plates 44–51.

42 Mr Shantanu Kumar, pers. comm., 2003.

43 McCrindle, 1901, p. 144; Scholfield, 1959, p. 235, Vol. III.

44 McCrindle, 1901, p. 149.

45 See pp. 48–49, 103.

CHAPTER 4

MRIGARAJA: KING OF THE BEASTS

1 Thapar, 1966, pp. 29–31.

2 *RV*, I 64.8, 95.5, 174.3; Banerjee, 1980, p. 153.

3 Through exchanges of letters between September 1998 and January 2000, Dr M.A. Mehendale of the Bhandarkar Oriental Research Institute, Pune, very kindly guided me with literary sources. This portion of the chapter is based on the information he so generously gave on the lion in early literature.

4 Prof. Romila Thapar, pers. comm., 2003.

5 *RV*, 9.97.28.

6 Ibid., 1.64.8.

7 Ibid., 5.83.3.

8 Ibid., 5.15.3.

9 Ibid., 10.28.10.

10 *Śat. Br.*, 5.5.4.18.

11 Zimmermann, 1987, pp. 100–05.

12 McCrindle, 1901, pp. 14, 31.

13 *Life and Times of Apollonius*, Book ii, 28, pp. 53–54 quoted in Modi, 1932.

14 Rangarajan, 2001.

15 *Śat. Br.*, 5.5.4.10.

16 Dr M.A. Mehendale, pers. comm., 1998–2000; *Śat. Br.*, 12.7.1.1 and 8.

17 Dr M.A. Mehendale, pers. comm., 1998–2000.

18 Ibid.

19 *Ait. Br.*, 8.2.1; *Śat. Br.* 12.8.3.4.

20 *Ait. Br.*, 8.5.6.

21 *Śat. Br.*, 5.2.1.22–23; 5.4.4.1; Bole and Vaghani, 1986, pp. 49, 33.

22 Dr M.A. Mehendale, pers. comm., 1998–2000.

23 Ibid.

24 Zimmermann, 1987, p. 215.

25 Dr M.A. Mehendale, pers. comm.,

1998–2000; *Raghuvaṁśa*, IV.72.

26 *Mbh.*, 2.53.19.

27 Ibid., 5.135.23.

28 Ibid., 5.154.18; 6.93.22; 12.1.119; 6.22.12.

29 Kangle, 1963, 2.20.3, p. 59.

30 Thapar, 1961, p. 260.

31 Ibid., p. 264.

32 Misra, 1966, pp. 393–404; Shrigondekar, 1939, 1715–24, Vol. II, pp. 303–04.

33 Kangle, 1963, 8.3.46, p. 395.

34 See Chapter 2, p. 42.

35 Mukherjee and Raychaudhuri, 1990, p. 14.

36 Ibid.

37 Iyer, 1977, p. 63.

38 Sivaramamurti, 1974, p. 14, fig. 20b.

39 Iyer, 1977, p. 63.

40 Mukherjee and Raychaudhuri, 1990, p. 15; Sivaramamurti, 1974, p. 14, fig. 20a.

41 Mukherjee and Raychaudhuri, 1990, p. 15, plates IVA, IVB.

42 Shastri, 1910, pp. 79–93.

43 Bole and Vaghani, 1986, p. 15.

44 Shastri, 1910, p. 85, III 41; p. 89, III 58, 59.

45 Dadhimatha, 1915, p. 183.

46 Sharma, c. 1970, p. 105; Monier-Williams, 1851, p. 457.

47 Kosambi and Gokhale, 1957, p. xcvii; Ingalls, 1965, Sec. 33, No. 1091, p. 315.

48 Kosambi and Gokhale, 1957, p. lxx; Ingalls, 1965, Sec. 33, No. 1071, p. 312.

49 Ingalls, 1965, Sec. 33, No. 1034, p. 306.

50 Suryakanta, 1962, 1.6.

51 Sarma, 1991.

52 *Subh.*, 38, p. 623; tr. by Dr M.A. Mehendale, pers. comm., 1998–2000.

53 Dr M.A. Mehendale, pers. comm., 1998–2000.

54 *Subh.*, 7, pp. 621–22; tr. by Dr M.A. Mehendale, pers. comm., 1998–2002.

55 *Subh.*, 5, p. 358; tr. by Dr M.A. Mehendale, pers. comm., 1998–2002.

56 See Chapter 6, p. 99.

57 Iyer, 1977, pp. 62–69.

58 Ibid., pl. 91.

59 Campbell, 1974, Vol. II, pp. 118–27; Liebert, 1976, p. 138.

60 Deekshitar, 2004.

61 Thapar, 2002. This work is a brief but

wide-ranging survey of the various tiger cults in India and elsewhere in Asia. It has surveyed several instances of tiger worship.

CHAPTER 5

UNDER THE DELHI SULTANATE

1 Rizvi, 1987, pp. 8–9.

2 Hussain, 1967, 1017–1025, Vol. I, p. 108.

3 Ibid., 2006–2007, Vol. I., p. 214.

4 Nizami, 1997, p. 73.

5 Ibid.

6 Hussain, 1976, 6939–6940, 6947–6950, Vol. II, pp. 563–64.

7 Ibid., 1977, 11276–11298, Vol. III, pp. 880–81.

8 Nizami, 1997, pp. 73–74.

9 Hussain, 1891, pp. 316–17; 326–27; Dr A.H. Morton, pers. comm., 1993.

10 Nizami, 1997, p. 74.

11 Hussain, 1976, 2529–2535, Vol. II, p. 252.

12 Ibid., 4876–4894, Vol. II, pp. 428–29.

13 Ibid., 5221–5225, Vol. II, p. 449.

14 Ibid., 5131–5135, Vol. II, pp. 443–44.

15 Ibid., 1977, 11079–11082, Vol. III, p. 866.

16 Ibid., 1977, 10566–10583, 10585–10588, 10589–10594, Vol. III, pp. 832–33.

17 Rangarajan, 1996, p. 141.

CHAPTER 6

THE GREAT MUGHALS GO HUNTING LIONS

1 Beveridge, 1922, pp. 384–85; Thackston, 1996, p. 279.

2 Beveridge, 1922, p. 393; Thackston, 1996, p. 285.

3 Foster, 1926, p. 297.

4 Ibid., p. 324.

5 Rogers and Beveridge, 1909–14, Vol. II, p. 233.

6 Habib, 1982, plates 4B, 6B, 7B, and 8B.

7 Constable, 1934, p. 374.

8 Beveridge, 1904, Vol. II, pp. 422–24; Sen, 1984, pp. 39–40.

9 See Chapter 7, p. 116.

10 Constable, 1934, p. 378.

11 Welch, 1986.

12 Beach and Koch, 1997, p. 18.

13 Ibid., pl. 34.

14 Constable, 1934, p. 379.

15 Thackston, 1999, p. 216; Rogers and Beveridge, 1909–14, Vol. I, p. 369 gives the same figure but identifies the animal as a tiger. We shall come to this matter presently.

16 I am grateful to Dr Asok Kumar Das for bringing this painting from the Maharaja Sawai Man Singh II Museum, Jaipur, Acc. No. 863, to my attention and dating it.

17 Constable, 1934, p. 379.

18 Thackston, 1999, pp. 411, 473.

19 Habib, 1963, p. 368.

20 Thackston, 1999, p. 473.

21 Sunquist and Sunquist, 2002, p. 288.

22 See Appendix 3.

23 Humphreys and Kahrom, 1995, pp. 75, 77.

24 I am grateful to Professor Muzaffar Alam who checked the Sayeed Ahmud text of *Tuzuk-i-Jahangiri* and found the word *shir* in all relevant cases on pp. 65, 78, 80, 89, 92, 117, 140, 175, 179, 182, 185, 221, 366, and 375; Ahmud, 1864.

25 Sunquist and Sunquist, 2002, pp. V–VI.

26 Sen, 1984, plate 20; Divyabhanusinh, 1986 and 1999 for a detailed analysis of the event.

27 Dr Asok Kumar Das, pers. comm., 2003.

28 Thapar, 2004, p. 250.

29 Dr Asok Kumar Das, pers. comm., 2004.

30 Rogers and Beveridge, 1909–14, Vol. I, p. 351.

31 Ibid.; Thackston, 1999, p. 207; Rogers and Beveridge, 1909–14, Vol. I, p. 351.

32 Beveridge, 1904, Vol. II, pp. 294, 482–83. Professor Muzaffar Alam checked the *Akbarnama* text edited by Maulvi Abdul Rahim and found the word to be *shir* in both cases on pp. 189 and 238.

33 Ibid., pp. 482–83.

34 Blochman, 1873, Vol. I, p. 294. Prof. Muzaffar Alam checked the *Ain-i-Akbari* text edited by Saiyad Ahmad Khan and found that the word is *shir* on p. 145.

35 Daljeet, 1999, p. 41.

36 Thackston, 1999, p. 108.

37 Ibid., p. 120.

38 Ibid., p. 91.

39 Ibid., p. 213.

40 Rogers and Beveridge 1909–14, Vol. I, p. 286; Divyabhanusinh, 1999 for a detailed analysis of the incident.

41 Thackston, 1999, pp. 117–18.

42 The description of the painting is based on my discussions with Dr Asok Kumar Das.

43 Thackston, 1999, p. 219.

44 Divyabhanusinh, 1987 for a detailed analysis of the event.

45 Alvi and Rahman, 1968, plate VII.

46 Thackston, 1999, p. 144.

47 Kostioukovitch, 1996, plate 146/folio 72 recto, text pp. 97–98.

48 Ibid., pp. 97–98.

49 Beach and Koch, 1997, plate 30.

50 Das, 1978, frontispiece; Divyabhanusinh, 1999.

51 Constable, 1934, p. 378.

52 Ibid.

53 Beach and Koch, 1997, plate 46.

54 Singh, 1959, plate opp. p. 161; Singh, 1965, pp. 116–19.

55 Robinson, 1976, plates 130–31, p. 264.

56 Koch, 1998, p. 23.

57 Constable, 1934, pp. 182–83.

58 Ibid., p. 379.

59 Blochman, 1873, p. 294, the translated word for *shir* is tiger here.

60 Acc. No. CBL IN 11A.28.

61 Goetz, 1950, plate 77, p. 170.

62 Trivedi, 1998.

63 Habib, 1982, Sheet 7A, p. 25.

64 Guha, 2001, pp. 34, 58. Earlier estimates by Irfan Habib (1982A), which have now been pared down, were a population of 145 million in 1600 and less than 200 million by 1800.

CHAPTER 7

THE BRITISH COME CALLING

1 Kaul, 1979, pp. 424–25.

2 Foster, 1926, p. 176.

3 Ibid., p. 365.

4 Williamson, 1807.

5 Archer, 1969, Vol. I, pp. 162–63.

6 D'Oyly, 1810–15.

7 Dr J.P. Losty, pers. comm., 2002.

8 Ibid.

9 Jerdon, 1867, p. 238.

10 Mundy, 1858, p. 159.

11 Elgood, 1995, p. 157.

12 Anon., 1873, Vol. I, pp. 137–39.

13 Rice, 1884, p. 137.

14 Mehta, 2001, pp. 66–69.

15 Fenton, c. 1924, pp. 6–13.

16 Ibid., p. 13.

17 Kincaid, 1935, pp. 10–11.

18 Fenton, c. 1924, pp. 21–22.

19 M.K. Ranjitsinhji, pers. comm., 2003.

20 Mundy, 1858, p. 159.

21 Rice, 1884, p. 140.

22 Ibid.

23 Edwardes and Fraser, 1907, pp. 179–80.

24 Elgood, 1995, p. 157.

25 Kinnear, 1920.

26 Rice, 1884, p. 138.

27 Newall, 1882–87, Vol. II, p. 445.

28 Rangarajan, 2001.

29 Ibid.

30 Tod, 1832, p. 407.

31 Jacob, 1842, p. 19.

32 Rangarajan, 2001.

33 M.K. Himmatsinhji of Kutch, pers. comm., 1997.

34 Joslin, 1973.

35 Burton, 1959.

36 Prasad, c. 1965.

37 Jepson, 1936, pp. 131–35.

38 Burton, 1931; Burton, 1933.

39 Aflalo, 1904.

40 Joslin, 1973.

41 Rangarajan, 2000, p. 32.

42 Divyabhanusinh, 1995, pp. 196–97, 215–23.

43 Ibid., pp. 222–23.

44 Thapar, 1992, p. 42.

45 Rangarajan, 2000, p. 32.

46 See Chapter 11, p. 178.

47 See Chapter 6, p. 113.

48 Guha, 2001, p. 58.

49 Visaria and Visaria, 1982.

50 See Chapter 8, pp. 141–42.

51 See Appendix 4.

52 Sankhala, 1978, pp. 117–79.

53 See Chapter 6, p. 94.

54 Fox-Davies, 1909, p. 172.

55 Archer, 1962, p. ii.

56 Archer, 1959, pp. 4, 20.

57 Forbes, 1813, Vol. 4, p. 200.

58 Ibid.

59 Archer, 1959, p. 5.

60 Gould, 1971.

61 Joslin et al., 1988, entry no. 38.

62 Ibid., entry no. 75.

63 Ibid., entry no. 96.

64 Nott, 1886, p. 59.

65 Pocock, 1930.

66 Bhavnagar, 1911, opp. p. XIV.

67 Mukherjee, 1990, pp. 87–88, plate IXB.

68 Balachandran, 1998.

69 K.D. Kaur Singh, 2003, pp. 55, 101, 105.

CHAPTER 8

SORUTH SARKAR SAVES LIONS

1 Trautman, 1982.

2 Rajan, 1985, p. 16.

3 Ibid., p. 29.

4 Anon., 1939, pp. 320–21.

5 Shaikh, 1936, p. 1. For general background see Anon., 1903.

6 Wood and Meher, 1998, p. 98.

7 Rangarajan, 2001.

8 Ibid.; Kincaid, 1905 for a detailed account of the outlaws.

9 Rangarajan, 2000.

10 Edwardes and Fraser, 1907, p. 104; Bhavnagar, 1911, Vol. I, p. 385.

11 Shaikh, 1936, p. 8.

12 Joslin, 1973.

13 Wilberforce-Bell, 1916, p. 277.

14 Ratnu, 1934, p. 310; Micklem, 2001, p. 14.

15 Fenton, c. 1924, pp. 1–2.

16 *DUSJ*, Vol. I, No. 4, January 27, 1868.

17 Sanyal, 1892, p. 40.

18 GA, File No. nil, Political Agency Notification No. 22 of May 10, 1879.

19 *DUSJ*, Vol. 13, No. 9, April 1880.

20 Rangarajan, 2001, p. 28.

21 *JRM*, Vol. 3, pp. 1907–08, Notification No. 1683, Resolution No. 1877.

22 Fenton, c. 1924, p. 7.

23 *JAR*, 1907, pp. 1, 21–22.

24 Srivastava and Srivastava, 1999, p. 46.

25 Shri Shambhuprasad Desai, pers. comm., 1996; Edwardes and Fraser, 1907, pp. 92–102; Shaikh, 1936, pp. 11–14.

26 See Chapter 11, p. 178.

27 *JAR*, 1907, pp. 1, 21–22.

28 *JAR*, 1945, p. 112.

29 *JAR*, 1907, pp. 2, 21.

30 *JAR*, 1908–09, pp. 32–33; 1909–10, p. 31.

31 Edwardes and Fraser, 1907, p. 171.

32 Fenton, c. 1924, p. 5.

33 Kincaid, 1905, p. 151.

34 GA, File No. 1, 1900–21.

35 Mosse, 1957.

36 GA, File No. 1, 1900–21.

37 NAI, Home Public, August 1904, No. 15; see Appendix 4.

38 Wynter-Blyth, 1950, pp. 3–5.

39 GA, File No. 1, 1900–21.

40 Fenton, c. 1924, p. 7.

41 GA, File No. 1, 1900–21.

42 Wynter-Blyth, 1950, p. 5.

43 Fenton, c. 1924, p. 7.

44 Wynter-Blyth, 1950, p. 5.

45 Edwardes and Fraser, 1907, pp. 173, 180–82; see Chapter 7, p. 122.

46 Taparia, 1979, p. 220.

47 GA, File No. 1, 1900–21. Junagadh Notification No. 696 of April 29, 1909; Agency Notification No. 25 of June 24, 1909.

48 Shaikh, 1936, pp. 14–15.

49 Sodha, 2002, p. 171.

50 Cadell, 1933.

51 Srivastava and Srivastava, 1999, p. 46.

52 *JAR*, 1911–12, p. 30.

53 Ibid., p. 32.

54 See Chapter 11, p. 179.

55 GA, File No. 37, 1913, Junagadh Notification No. 9 of June 3, 1913; Kathiawar Notification No. 28 of 1913.

56 GA, File No. 60, 1912, letter to Kutch of February 18, 1912; File No. nil of 1912, Letter to Jamnagar of March 22, 1912; File No. 17, 1913, Letters to Bikaner of February 16 and April 10, 1913; File No. 15, 1917, Letter to Poonch of February 23, 1917.

57 GA, File No. 15, 1914 and 1940, letter of December 1914, Rendall's reply of December 9, 1914; Hony. Sec. Zoological Garden, Calcutta's letter of April 5, 1902 and Hony. Sec. BNHS's letter of March 11, 1909.

58 Fenton, c. 1924, p. 7.

59 *JRM*, 1930, p. 1911, Circular no. 118, July 5, 1919.

CHAPTER 9

THE LAST NAWAB BATTLES ON

1   Low, 1947, p. 1342.
2   *JRM*, Vol. III, 1930, p. 1719.
3   *JAR*, 1910–11, p. 3.
4   Shaikh, 1936, pp. 20–22.
5   Menon, 1956, p. 125.
6   Paul and Kapoor, 2003, p. 252.
7   Shri Jaisukhlal P. Sodha, pers. comm., 2002.
8   Sodha, 2002, pp. 32, 82.
9   Shri Shambhuprasad Desai, pers. comm., 1995.
10 This account of the nawab's love of animals is based on several conversations with the late Shri Shambhuprasad Harprasad Desai, as indeed conversations with several members of the princely order and other persons in Junagadh and Kathiawar.
11 Mr E. Joubert van Ingen, pers. comm., 1997.
12 Ibid.
13 Ibid.
14 Cadell, 1933.
15 Shaikh, 1936.
16 Watson, 1884, frontispiece.
17 Gee, 1964, p. 87.
18 Wood and Meher, 1998, p. 95.
19 Anon., 1959, p. 842.
20 Wood and Meher, 1998, p. 98.
21 Anon., 1980, p. 768.
22 Jain, 1999, p. 3.
23 GA, 1922, File No. nil, Letter No. 2713 of September 30, 1922. GA, Shikar Daftar, 1921, File No. nil, Letter from Navanagar to Junagadh of May 31, 1921; Letter from Junagadh to Navanagar of June 1, 1921; Letter of Navanagar to Junagadh of June 5, 1921; Letter of Bikaner to Junagadh of June 5, 1921; Letter of Junagadh to Bikaner of June 6, 1921.
24 Rodrigues, 2003, p. 54.
25 M.K. Ranjitsinhji, pers. comm., 2003.
26 MA, 1921, File No. 1438 Pol. Dept., Junagadh's letter to A.G. of June 29, 1921.
27 MA, File No. 1438, Pol. Dept., June 29, 1921. AG's letter to Sec. to Govt. of July ..., 1921.
28 MA, File No. 1438, Pol. Dept., Sec. to Govt's letter to A.G. Kathiawar of September 8, 1921.
29 Cadell, 1933.

30 GA, File No. 5, 1917–25, letter dated September 30, 1922.
31 GA, File No. 10.8 circular no. 22 of V.S. 1984 (1928).
32 GA, File no. 6, 1914–18; *JRM* Vol. 3, p. 1312, Memo No. 1675/77 from M.J. Vasavda, Revenue Commissioner.
33 GA, File No. 17, 1921. Letter from Junagadh to Agent to Governor, Kathiawar, February 1921.
34 GA, File No. 60, 1913, letter of Administrator to Diwan of Manavadar.
35 GA, File No. 13, 1935, letter of Junagadh to Manavadar of February 5, 1935.
36 M.K. Ranjitsinhji, pers. comm., 2003; Rangarajan, 2001, p. 32.
37 *JRM*, Vol. 3, pp. 1910–11, Firman no. 62 of September 29, 1925.
38 Dalip Singh, pers. comm., March 28, 1997.
39 Mr E. Joubert van Ingen, pers. comm., May 14, 1997.
40 Wankaner, 1952.
41 M.K. Ranjitsinhji, pers. comm., 1997; Darbar Saheb Jaswantsinhji of Bilkha, pers. comm., 1997.
42 GA, File No. 76, Note dated November 4, 1937.
43 Darbar Saheb Jaswantsinhji of Bilkha, pers. comm., 1997.
44 Ibid.
45 Shaikh, 1936, p. 17; photographic record of Viceroy's shoot with Joshi Studio, Rajkot.
46 Wynter-Blyth, 1949; Caldwell, 1938.
47 *JAR*, 1914–15, p. 57; 1915–16, p. 69; 1916–17, p. 56; 1918–19, p. 45; 1920–21, p. 39; 1921–22, p. 50; 1922–23, p. 62; 1923–24, p. 53; 1924–25, p. 59; 1925–26, p. 48; 1926–27, p. 54; 1927–28, p. 66; 1928–29, p. 51; 1929–30, p. 82; 1930–31, p. 70; 1931–32, p. 67; 1932–33, pp. 73–74; 1933–34, p. 63; 1934–35, p. 75; 1935–36, p. 79; 1936–37, p. 78; 1937–38, p. 76; 1938–39, p. 80; 1939–40, p. 82; 1940–41, p. 76; and 1942–43, p. 85.
48 See Chapter 11, p. 182.

CHAPTER 10

THE DOMINION OF INDIA INHERITS LIONS

1   Mohan, 1990, p. 1.

2   Menon, 1956, p. 177; Low, 1947, p. 1342.
3   *JAR*, 1936–37 to 1944–45; Low, 1947, p. 1342.
4   Wolpert, 1984, p. 347; Wolpert, 1993, pp. 25–26. The description in the chapter of the event in 1947 is based on Menon, 1956, pp. 125–50, as also the stories heard by the author while at school at Rajkot in the early 1950s.
5   Maharana Raj Saheb Pratapsinhji of Wankaner, pers. comm., 2002.
6   Ibid.
7   Shri Mahesh Singh, D.F.O. Sasan, pers. comm., 1999.
8   Shri Shambhuprasad Desai, pers. comm., 1996; Darbar Saheb Jaswantsinhji of Bilkha, pers. comm., 1997; stories heard by the author in the early 1950s.
9   Gee, 1964, p. 94.
10 Wynter-Blyth, 1949.
11 M.K. Pushpendrasinhji Lunawada, pers. comm., 1997.
12 Anon., 1948, p. 20; Anon., 1950, pp. 49–50, 239–51.
13 Wynter-Blyth, 1949.
14 Wynter-Blyth, 1950.
15 Ibid.
16 Ibid.
17 Rao, et al., 1966, pp. 496–97.
18 *CAD*, Vol. IV, 1947, pp. 761–93.
19 See Appendix 5.
20 Mr Ashok H. Desai, pers. comm., April 14, 2001.
21 Ibid.
22 Guha, 2000, p. 42.
23 Ibid., p. 43.

CHAPTER 11

THE GREAT NUMBERS GAME

1   Ranjitsinh, 1997, pp. 97–99.
2   Ibid., p. 97; Gee, 1964, p. 153.
3   Divyabhanusinh, 1995.
4   Gee, 1964, p. 87; Ranjitsinh, 1997, p. 22; Sankhala, 1978, p. 176.
5   Ranjitsinh, 1997, p. 25; Sankhala, 1978, p. 177.
6   Rice, 1884, p. 144.
7   Joslin, 1973.
8   Edwardes and Fraser, 1907, p. 172.

9 Watson, 1884, pp. 6–7.

10 Rashid and David, 1992, p. 94; Singh and Kamboj, 1996, p. 64; Singh, 2001, p. 160.

11 Fenton, c. 1924, p. 13.

12 Edwardes and Fraser, 1907, p. 173.

13 GA, File No. 49, 1901.

14 Edwardes and Fraser, 1907, pp. 172–73.

15 Gee, 1964, p. 85.

16 GA, File No. 6, 1913, Letter of May 13, 1913.

17 Wallinger, 1913.

18 Rashid and David, 1992, p. 94; Singh and Kamboj, Vol. I, 1996, p. 64; Singh, 2001, p. 160.

19 Nicholson, 1935.

20 GA, File No. 10/8, 1937.

21 Wynter-Blyth, 1949.

22 Watson, 1884, p. 4.

23 Srivastava and Srivastava, 1999, p. 46.

24 Wynter-Blyth, 1949; Wynter-Blyth and Dharmakumarsinhji, 1950.

25 Wynter-Blyth, 1956.

26 Ibid.; Dharmakumarsinhji, 1969.

27 Ibid.

28 Ibid.

29 Dharmakumarsinhji, 1959, pp. 7–13.

30 Dharmakumarsinhji, 1969; Dalvi, 1969.

31 Singh, 2001.

32 Jain, 2001, p. 191.

33 Jhala, et al., 2002.

CHAPTER 12

A SECOND HOME

1 Singh and Kamboj, 1996, p. 20.

2 Seshadri, 1969, p. 117.

3 Kinnear, 1920.

4 GA, File No. 49, 1901.

5 Dr Mahesh Rangarajan, pers. comm., 2003.

6 Bull and Haksar, 1926, p. 242.

7 Singh, 1965, p. 87; Srivastava, 1969.

8 Singh, 1965, p. 88. He records that another lion was shot near Jhansi. This appears to be questionable as no such record has been found.

9 Stracey, 1963, p. 97.

10 Maharao Brijraj Singh of Kotah, pers. comm., 1977.

11 Minshull, 1937.

12 Thompson, 1999.

13 Smythies, 1942, pp. 108, 115, and 165.

14 Stracey, 1963, p. 97.

15 Lavkumar, 1956.

16 Gee, 1956.

17 Gee, 1962; Negi, 1966 and 1969; Srivastava, 1969; Bachkheti, 1995.

18 Dharmakumarsinhji, et al., 1970.

19 Oza, 1973.

20 Negi, 1969.

21 Ibid.; Joslin, 1985.

22 Humphreys and Kahrom, 1995, p. 77.

23 M.K. Ranjitsinhji, pers. comm., 2003.

24 Humphreys and Kahrom, 1995, pp. 77–78.

25 Ashraf, et al., 1995; Chellam, et al., 1994.

26 Sharma, et al., 2002.

27 Ibid.; Mr P.K. Sen, pers. comm., 2002.

28 PH, January 24 and February 15, 1995.

29 PH, April 14, 1994; April 20, 1997.

30 PH, July 30, 2002.

31 The Times of India, Jaipur, August 3, 2002.

32 Ranjitsinh, 2001.

CHAPTER 13

LIFE IN THE REPUBLIC: THE LION IN WINTER

1 COI, 2003, Seventh Schedule, State List Nos. 18 and 19, p. 226.

2 Rangarajan, 2001.

3 Ibid.

4 Vaidya, 1958, pp. 125, 130; Ylla, 1958, pp. 32–33.

5 Gee, 1964, p. 90.

6 M.K. Ranjitsinhji, pers. comm., 2003.

7 For a detailed description of tracking lions see Dharmakumarsinhji, 1992, pp. 74–75.

8 Jamkhandikar, 2000, p. 48.

9 Ranjitsinh, 1997, p. 51.

10 Dharmakumarsinhji, et al., 1970, pp. 37–38.

11 Ghorpade, 1983, pp. 88–98.

12 Ranjitsinh, 1997, p. 52.

13 Stracey, 1963, p. 98.

14 Joslin, 1973; Rangarajan, 2001.

15 Rangarajan, 2001.

16 Singh, 2001, p. 69.

17 Anon., 1972, p. 14.

18 Ibid., p. 11.

19 Ibid., pp. 12–14.

20 Ibid., pp. 22–24; Singh, 2001A, p. 69.

21 Anon., 1972, p. 16.

22 Singh and Kamboj, 1996, Vol. II, pp. 54–56.

23 Ibid., p. 57.

24 Ibid., pp. 60–61. More recently the number of livestock has been put at approximately 13,000 heads (Mr Bharat J. Pathak, pers. comm., 2004).

25 Singh and Kamboj, 1996, Vol. I, p. 54.

26 Sinha, 1987.

27 Singh and Kamboj, 1996, Vol. I, p. 54.

28 Chellam, 1993.

29 Dharmakumarsinhji, 1979.

30 COI, 2003, Seventh Schedule, Concurrent List No. 17A and 17B, p. 229; Directive Principles of State Policy Article 48A, p. 29.

31 Singh, 2001A.

32 Singh, 1997; 1998; 2001A; Lal, 2000.

33 Singh, 2001A.

34 PH, January 5 and 7, and February 1, 2003.

35 Maharana Raj Saheb Pratapsinhji of Wankaner, pers. comm., 2001.

36 Proverbs 26:13.

37 Singh, 2001A.

38 Mr Bharat Pathak, pers. comm., 2004.

39 Lal, 2000; Singh, 2001A.

40 PH, April 21, 2003.

41 Singh, 2001, p. 77.

42 Singh, 2001A.

43 Anon., 2000.

44 Ibid.

45 Mukhopadhyaya and Aiyar, 2002, p. 32.

46 Mahesh Singh to Nagendra Singh Hada, pers. comm., 1999.

47 Saberwal, et. al., 1994.

48 Wynter-Blyth and Dharmakumarsinhji, 1950.

49 Singh and Kamboj, 1996, Vol. I, p. 88.

50 Ibid, Vol. II, pp. 56–61.

51 Ibid., p. 59.

52 Sharma and Johnsingh, 1996, pp. 77–78.

53 Singh and Kamboj, 1996, Vol. II, p. 53.

54 Ibid., p. 87.

55 Ibid., p. 66.

56 PH, March 21, 27, and 29, 2003.

57 Singh and Kamboj, 1996, Vol. II, p. 65.

58 PH, May 30 and 31, June 1, 7, 8, 11, 12, and 13, 1996.

59 Mukhopadhyaya and Aiyar, 2002, p. 33.

APPENDIX 1

Glossary

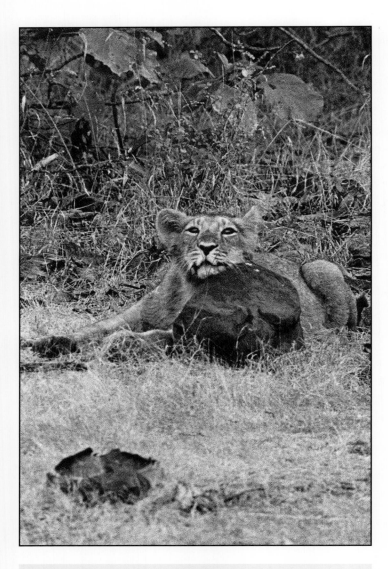

Flora

Ber or Bor	*Zizyphus mauritiana*
Corindah or Karvanda	*Carissa carandas*
Dudhalo	*Wrightia tinctoria*
Jambudo or Jamun	*Eugenia jambolana*
Khakhro or Palas, Flame	
of the Forest	*Butea monosperma*
Khadira or Khair	*Acacia catechu*
Sawar or Semal, Silk Cotton	*Bombax malabaricum*
Sag, Teak	*Tectona grandis*
Udumbara	*Ficus glomerata*
Vad, Banyan	*Ficus benghalensis*

Fauna

Antelope, Indian (Blackbuck)	*Antilope cervicapra*
Four-horned (Chowsingha)	*Tetracerus quadricornis*
Ass, Indian Wild	*Equus hemionus khur*
Persian Wild (Onager)	*Equus hemionus onager*
Boar, Wild	*Sus scrofa*
Buffalo, Wild	*Bubalus bubalis*
Bustard, Great Indian	*Ardeotis nigriceps*
MacQueen's (Houbara)	*Chlamydotis macqueeni*
Caracal	*Caracal caracal*
Cat, Jungle	*Felis chaus*
Rusty-spotted	*Prionailurus rubiginosus*
Cheetah	*Acinonyx jubatus*
Chinkara	*Gazella bennettii*
Crane, Sarus	*Grus antigone*
Crocodile, Marsh (Mugger)	*Crocodylus palustris*
Deer, Hog	*Axis porcinus*
Spotted (Chital)	*Axis axis*
Swamp (Barasingha)	*Cervus duvauceli*
Dog, Indian Wild (Dhole)	*Cuon alpinus*
Eagle, Crested Serpent	*Spilornis cheela*
Elephant, Indian	*Elephas maximus*
Syrian	*Elephas maximus asurus*
Falcon, Peregrine	*Falco peregrinus*
Red-headed or Barbary	*Falco peregrinus babylonicus*
Shahin	*Falco peregrinus peregrinator*
Florican, Lesser	*Sypheotides indica*
Fox, Indian	*Vulpes bengalensis*
Gaur	*Bos gaurus*
Gharial	*Gavialis gangeticus*
Goshawk	*Accipiter gentilis*
Hangul	*Cervus elaphus*
Hare	*Lepus nigricollis*
Hippopotamus	*Hippopotamus amphibius*
Hornbill, Grey	*Ocyceros birostris*
Hyena, Spotted	*Crocuta crocuta*
Striped	*Hyaena hyaena*
Jackal	*Canis aureus*
Kite, Pariah	*Milvus migrans*
Leopard	*Panthera pardus*
Lion	*Panthera leo*
Merlin, Red-headed	*Falco chicquera*

Mongoose, Common	*Herpestes edwardsi*
Nilgai (Blue Bull)	*Boselaphus tragocamelus*
Partridge, Grey	*Francolinus pondicerianus*
Peacock	*Pavo cristatus*
Pigeon, Green	*Treron phoenicoptera*
Quail, Common	*Coturnix coturnix*
Rhinoceros, Great Indian	
one-horned	*Rhinoceros unicornis*
Asian one-horned	*Rhinoceros sondaicus*
Asian two-horned	*Dicerorhinus sumatrensis*
Sambar	*Cervus unicolor*
Sandgrouse, Painted	*Pterocles indicus*
Sangai	*Cervus eldii*
Shrew, Musk	*Suncus murinus*
Sparrowhawk	*Accipiter nisus*
Sunbird, Purple	*Nectarinia asiatica*
Tiger	*Panthera tigris*
Turkey	*Meleagris gallopavo*
Urial	*Ovis orientalis*
Vulture, King	*Sarcogyps calvus*
Wolf	*Canis lupus*
Zebra, Burchell's	*Equus burchelli*

Indian Words

arti	prayer performed with a lamp lit with clarified butter waved before the deity
arzi hakumat	government in exile
ashrafi	gold coin
baharvatia	outlaws
chakravartin	universal ruler
Charan	bard community
chhattra	umbrella over the head of a king sitting on a throne or carried over his head by a bearer, a traditional Indian insignia of royalty
dang	staff of a pastoralist
darbar	court of a ruler; often Darbar is used to denote a Rajput or Kathi
dhamma/dharma	teachings of the Buddha, religion, right behaviour
dharna	form of peaceful protest
hukk	right or entitlement
Kathi	caste of people who ruled many small principalities in Saurashtra, after whom the peninsula was called Kathiawar

Kathiawar; Kathiawari	Saurashtra; Gujarati dialect spoken in Saurashtra
Koli	tribe of hunters and food gatherers
kos or koss, kuroh	measure of length, approximately 2½ miles or 4 kilometres
machan	covered platform usually in a tree erected for shikar
Maldhari	cattle graziers of Saurashtra and elsewhere
mehmandari	hospitality
moongiya	colour of moong, a lentil, dull green or yellow, used in shikar for camouflage
ness	cattle pen of Maldharis
pagi	tracker
prant	administrative unit
Qamargah	mode of encircling and trapping game for hunting by an ever-decreasing circle of men, a procedure made famous by the Mughals
Rabari	cattle herders who make a living out of selling milk and its products
safa	turban of a type popularized in the 20th century, usually worn by Rajputs
Sidi	person of African descent
swapado	savage, ferocious, wild beast
tasu	measure of length, about 1.33 inches or 3.5 centimetres
thikana	fiefdom within a princely state
tilak	mark worn on forehead by a practising Hindu
zortalbi	tribute collected by Junagadh state from other states in Kathiawar

APPENDIX 2

Kathiawari Words Relating to the Lion

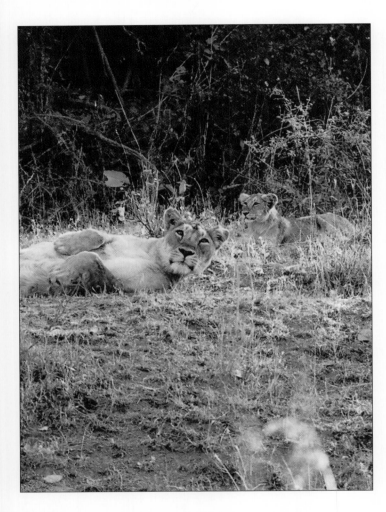

sawaj/hawaj, sinh	male lion, lions
sinhan	lioness
janawar	in Gir the word is usually used for lions; in general usage: animals
pathdo, pathadi	immature lion, lioness
belad	pair of male lions
tolu	pride of lions; in general usage: group of animals, people
bhurio	lion with a light brown mane
danak	lion's roar
daro	lion's warning grunt or growl; in general usage: to frighten
dhodvun	lion's charge; in general usage: to run
gadhio	short-bodied/stockily built lion
ghamak	low grunt used by a lioness to call her cubs
ghor	lioness in oestrus
ghoro	mating of a pair of lions
huk	lion's roar
jamwo	male lion whose mane is very dark but not necessarily black, the body being a shade of grey; usually an old animal
kalo, kalio, kamho	black-maned lion; in general usage: black
kesarisinh	lion with a luxuriant mane
keshwari	mane of a lion; also of a horse
maran	kill of a lion; also of other carnivores such as leopard
pilo	lion with a light coloured mane; in general usage: yellow
radiyo	noisy lion given to roaring very often; in general usage: noisy person
sagad	footprint/spoor of a lion; also of other animals
untio	tall mangy lion, camel coloured lion, scantily maned
velar	long-bodied lion

WITH THE DECREASING numbers of wildlife, most of the vocabulary concerning wild animals has disappeared from common usage. Even dictionaries do not always give the correct meaning. There is an urgent need to record such words before some of them vanish forever. Given here are the words used for lions/lionesses, followed by terms used to describe them and their behaviour.

I have not come across a word for a maneless lion such as the common Gujarati words *taklo, bodo*, or *ganjo* which mean bald. The nearest word is *untio* used for a mangy lion. The word *untio wagh* (camel coloured tiger) is described as the word for a lion in use in Kutch and elsewhere in Gujarat in the literature of the British period (Rice, 1884, p. 138; Russell, 1900, p. 196). It is not in use in the Gir today. Rice also mentions that in the Gir the word *sooee* was used for a lioness. However, this name too is not in use today.

APPENDIX 3

The Size of Asiatic Lions

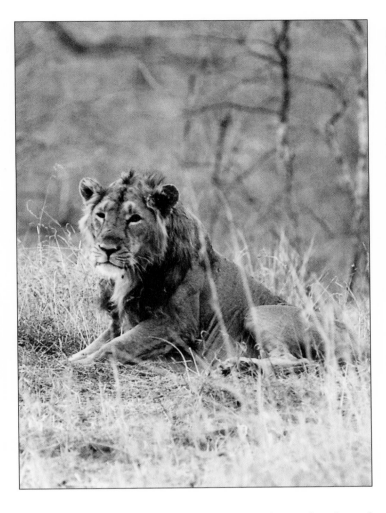

THE SIZE OF the Asiatic lion has been a subject of prolonged discussion during the British period particularly in comparison with the lions from Africa. For a long time it was believed that the animals from Africa were bigger. The present list was compiled with the sizes in descending order to compare it with records from Africa to arrive at a conclusion based on records of hunting trophies which were until recently the single most extensive source available. Usually, the length of the animal was considered.

The tenth edition of *Rowland Ward's Records of Big Game, African and Asiatic Sections* published in 1935, the ultimate authority on the subject, has twelve entries on the length of the trophies from Africa but only four for India (Dollman and Burlace, 1935, pp. 365–67). In order to expand the information base I undertook an extensive search through the shikar literature of the period since 1807, unpublished shikar diaries, personal interviews, etc. to produce the present list which has 77 entries for India. Such a compilation cannot ever be complete.

Measurements of large carnivores were of four kinds. Field measurements of the length were taken by the sportsman from the tip of the nose to the tip of the tail. The measurement was either taken along the curves of the body of the animal, or the animal would be suspended by its feet, pegs would be driven into the ground at the extremities of the nose and the tail, and then the distance between the pegs would be measured. The second method naturally gave a shorter length – the difference varying between 2 and 5 inches (M.K. Ranjitsinhji, pers. comm., 2003). This method appears to have come into vogue after the first world war though a definite date cannot be assigned. The third method was to measure the pegged down pelt after the animal was skinned. Such measurements could exceed the "along the curve" measurements by up to a foot (Ranjitsinhji, pers. comm.). This method appears to have gone out of use early in the 20th century. The last method was to measure the cured and dressed skin of the rug or trophy, which was usually done by the taxidermist. It may be noted here that since field measurements were taken by the sportsman himself, there was a tendency to maximize the length of the trophy so that it would look good in a record book or shikar diary. Which of the first two methods was used by a sportsman in a particular instance, is difficult to ascertain unless specifically noted by him.

Recently there has been a change in the approach, and now only skull measurements are taken. The 22nd edition of *Rowland Ward's Records of Big Game* published in 1989 has 325 entries for lions of Africa and only two for lions from Asia (Smith, et al., 1989). With such a dearth of information from India, the matter was not pursued further as it is now not possible to obtain such measurements from trophies of old.

S. No.	Sportsman	Year	Sex	Size		Locality	Source
				LENGTH	SKIN LENGTH		
1.	Major General William Rice	circa 1850	Male	Over 10' 6" (length of mane 18")	11' 6"	Near Rajkot	Rice, 1884, p. 136; Newall, 1882–87, Vol. II, p. 445.
2.	Unknown	–	Male	–	11' 5"(tail 2' 10", height 3' 3")	Central India	Burke, 1920, pp. 11–12.
3.	"Collector"	1832	Male	–	11' 3"[A]	Banas, Gujarat	Anon., 1873A, p. 132.
4.	J.H. Du Boulay	1905	Male	–	11' 0"	Gir	Edwardes and Fraser, 1907, p. 176; Fenton, c. 1924, p. 9.
5.	Darbar Saheb Imammuddin Khanji Babi of Pajod	circa 1949	Male	–	11' 0" (dressed skin)	Waghania	K.S. Ayaz Khanji of Pajod, pers. comm., 1997.
6.	Colonel W.P. Kennedy	1905	Male	–	10' 10"	Gir	Edwardes and Fraser, 1907, p. 176; Fenton, c. 1924, p. 9.
7.	Lord Lamington	-do-	Male	–	10' 4"	-do-	-do- Stracey, 1963, p. 136; Dollman and Burlace, 1935, p. 367.
8.	M.K. Bhim Singh of Kotah	1935	Male	9' 2"	10' 4" (dressed skin)	Amrithal, Sasan Gir	Maharao Brijraj Singh of Kotah, pers. comm., 1997; Dollman and Burlace, 1935, p. 367.
9.	Princess Rajendrakunverba of Palitana	circa 1950	Male	10' 2"	–	Jamwala, Gir	Princess Rajendrakunverba of Palitana, pers. comm., 1997.

TABLE I: SIZE OF ASIATIC LIONS FROM HUNTING RECORDS

10.	H.H. Maharaja Sayaji Rao Gaekwad of Baroda	circa 1914	Male	About 10' 0"	–	Ghatwad, Amreli district	Carruthers, et al., 1915.
11.	Lieutenant [later Maj. Gen.] W. Rice	circa 1850	Male	9' 11"	–	Gir	Stracey, 1963, p. 136.
12.	Lieutenant Percy Hancock	–	Male	9' 10"	–	Gir	Burke, 1920, p. 11.
13.	Unknown[B]	–	Male	9' 0"	9' 11" (body 6' 10", tail 2' 10", mane 11")	Allahabad	Pocock, 1930.
14.	"Ignotus"	1830	Male	–	9' 6"	Pattan, Khandesh	Burton, 1933, p. 277.
15.	Lord Harris	1893	Male	9' 7"	–	Gir	Pocock, 1930; Dollman and Burlace, 1935, p. 367.
16.	H.H. Maharaja Ganga Singh of Bikaner	1942	Male	9' 7"	–	Gatraliadhar, Sasan Gir	Thakur Dalip Singh, pers. comm., 1997.
17.	Captain Habbert	circa 1900	Male	–	9' 6"	Gir	Edwardes and Fraser, 1907, p. 176.
18.	H.H. Maharaja Ganga Singh of Bikaner	1940	Male	9' 5½"	–	Billiat, Sasan Gir	Thakur Dalip Singh, pers. comm., 1997.
19.	Lieutenant Colonel L.L. Fenton	1886	Male	9' 5" (tail 2' 11")	–	Gir	Fenton, circa 1924, p. 9; Pocock, 1930.
20.	H.H. Maharaja Ganga Singh of Bikaner	1940	Male	9' 4½"	–	Gatraliadhar, Sasan Gir	Thakur Dalip Singh, pers. comm., 1997.
21.	Emperor Jahangir	1623	Male	9' 4"	–	Rahimabad near Agra	Thackston, 1999, p. 411.
22.	Governor General Lord Hastings' party	1815	Female	9' 4"	–	Hansi	Kothari and Chhapgar, 1996, p. 74.
23.	Lieutenant Colonel Sir Montague Gerrard	1872	Male	9' 4" (tail 2' 11", girth 48", around neck 32")	–	Cheen Hills, near Guna	Gerrard, 1903, p. 133.

24.	R.S. Nirmalkumarsinhji of Bhavnagar	1933	Male	9' 4" (height 38", girth 60")	–	Andhania, Gir	Dharmakumar-sinhji and Wynter-Blyth, 1951.
25.	Darbar Rawatwala of Bilkha	circa 1940	Female	9' 4"	–	Bilkha	Darbar Jaswantsinhji of Bilkha, pers. comm., 1997.
26.	Yuvraj Brijraj Singh of Kotah	1946	Male	9' 4"	–	Devalia, Gir	Maharao Brijraj Singh of Kotah, pers. comm., 1997.
27.	Unknown	–	Male	9' 3"	–	–	Burke, 1920, p. 12.
28.	H.H. Maharaja Ganga Singh of Bikaner	1941	Male	9' 3"	–	Booh Badli, Sasan Gir	Thakur Dalip Singh, pers. comm., 1997.
29.	-do-	1941	Male	9' 3"	–	Gatraliadhar, Sasan Gir	-do-
30.	R.K. Pushpendrasingh of Panna	1942	Male	9' 3"	–	Gir	Narayansingh Bhayal, pers. comm., 1997.
31.	Count F. Scheibler	–	Male	9' 3"	–	-do-	Pocock, 1930.
32.	Captain Leathers	Circa 1900 (?)	Male	–	9' 2"	-do-	Edwardes and Fraser, 1907, p. 176.
33.	H.H. Maharaja Ganga Singh of Bikaner	1916	Male	9' 2½"	–	Nana Mano Ness, Sasan Gir	Thakur Dalip Singh, pers. comm., 1997; Dollman and Burlace, 1935, p. 367.
34.	Colonel J.W. Watson	Circa 1890 (?)	Male	–	9' 1"	Gir	Edwardes and Fraser, 1907, p. 176.
35.	Lieutenant Colonel L.L. Fenton	Circa 1895	Male	9' 1"	–	Talala, Gir	Fenton, c. 1924, p. 9.
36.	A.S. Vernay	1929	Male	9' 1"	–	Gir	Pocock, 1930.

37.	Governor General Lord Hastings' party	1815	Female	9' 0"	–	Hansi	Kothari and Chhapgar, 1996, p. 74.
38.	"Quondam's" party	1833	Male	9' 0" (height 3' 0", mane 0' 9")	–	Hansi	Kothari and Chhapgar, 2005, p. 74.
39.	Lieutenant Colonel L.L. Fenton	Circa 1895	Male	9' 0"	–	Khokhra, Gir	Fenton, c. 1924, p. 9.
40.	Colonel J.W. Watson	-do-	Male	9' 0"	–	Mytiala, Bhavnagar	Dharmakumarsinhji and Wynter-Blyth, 1951.
41.	H.H. Maharaja Krishnakumarsinhji of Bhavnagar	1941	Male	9' 0" (tail 3' 1", girth 45 3/4", height 40")	–	-do-	-do-
42.	H.H. Maharaja Raj Mayurdhwajsinhji of Dhrangadhra	1950	Male	9' 0" (along curves) 8' 8" (between pegs)	–	-do-	Maharaja Raj Megrajji of Dhrangadhra, pers. comm., 1995.
43.	Presented to British Museum by H.H. Nawab of Junagadh	1934	Male	–	9' 0" (tail 2' 8", dressed skin)	Gir	Pocock, 1936.
44.	Major H.G. Carnegie	1905	Female	–	9' 0"	Gir	Edwardes and Fraser, 1907, p. 176.
45.	Colonel Founthorpe	1929	Male	–	8' 11" (dressed skin)	-do-	Pocock, 1930.
46.	M.K. Chandrabhanusinhji of Wankaner	1934	Male	8' 11" (girth 45")	–	Ranithav, Mendarda portion of Gir	Wankaner, 1952.
47.	R.S. Dharmakumarsinhji of Bhavnagar	1938	Male	8' 10½" (height 39")	–	Mytiala, Bhavnagar	Dharmakumarsinhji and Wynter-Blyth, 1951.
48.	Captain Trother	1871	Male	8' 10" (tail 35", height 40")	–	Shane, Mytiala, Bhavnagar	-do-

49.	H.H. Maharaja Krishnakumarsinhji of Bhavnagar	1931	Male	8' 10"	–	-do-	-do-
50.	Captain W. Smee	Circa 1830	Male	8' 9½"	–	Ahmedabad	Pocock, 1930.
51.	H.H. Maharani Vijayakumari of Bhavnagar	1938	Male	8' 8½" (tail 37", height 37", girth 38")	–	Mytiala, Bhavnagar	Dharmakumar-sinhji and Wynter-Blyth, 1951.
52.	H.H. Maharaja Krishnakumarsinhji of Bhavnagar	1934	Male	8' 7½" (height 39")	–	Sasan Gir	-do-
53.	W. Kelsey and party	1866	Male	8' 7" (height 3' 3", girth 3' 10")	–	Putna near Allahabad	Burton, 1933, p. 274.
54.	R.S. Nirmalkumarsinhji of Bhavnagar	1935	Male	8' 7" (height 39")	–	Mytiala, Bhavnagar	Dharmakumar-sinhji and Wynter-Blyth, 1951.
55.	Colonel J.W. Watson	Circa 1895	Female	8' 6"	–	-do-	-do-
56.	Lieutenant Colonel A.H. Mosse	1930	Male	8' 6"	–	-do-	-do-
57.	R.S. Dharmakumarsinhji of Bhavnagar	1935	Male	8' 6"	–	-do-	-do-
58.	Thakore Shree Surendrasinhji of Wadhwan	1940	Male	8' 6" (height 40")	–	-do-	-do-
59.	Captain W. Smee	Circa 1830	Male	–	8' 6" (tail imperfect, 2' 7", dressed skin)	Ahmedabad	Pocock, 1930.
60.	M.K. Sadul Singh of Bikaner	1922	Male	8' 5"	–	Sasan, Gir	M.K. Sadulsingh of Bikaner, 1928.
61.	H.H. Maharaja Krishnakumarsinhji of Bhavnagar	1931	Male	8' 5"	–	Mytiala, Bhavnagar	Dharmakumar-sinhji and Wynter-Blyth, 1951.
62.	Presented to British Museum by H.H. Nawab of Junagadh	1934	Female	–	8' 5" (tail 2' 7", dressed skin)	Gir	Pocock, 1936.

63.	R.S. Nirmalkumarsinhji of Bhavnagar	1933	Male	8' 4"	–	-do-	Dharmakumar-sinhji and Wynter-Blyth, 1951.
64.	M. Chandrabhanusinhji of Wankaner	1949	Male	8' 4"	–	Andhania, Gir	Wankaner, 1952.
65.	H.H. Maharaja Krishnakumarsinhji of Bhavnagar	1945	Male	8' 3" (height 35")	–	Mytiala, Bhavnagar	Dharmakumar-sinhji and Wynter-Blyth, 1951.
66.	-do-	1946	Male	8' 3" (tail 28½")	–	-do-	-do-
67.	Yuvraj Pratapsinhji of Wankaner	1939	Male	8' 2" (between pegs, height 3' 3")	–	Mytiala, Bhavnagar	Wankaner, 1971.
68.	Thakore Shree Dharmendrasinhji of Chuda	1950	Female	8' 2"	–	Amreli, Baroda	Thakur Shree Dharmendrasinhji of Chuda, pers. comm., 1995.
69.	H.H. Raja Dhiraj Sudershan Deo of Shahpura	1950	Male	8' 1" (between pegs) 8' 5" (round the curves)	–	Mytiala, Bhavnagar	Maharaja Raj Meghrajji of Dhrangadhra, pers. comm., 1995.
70.	M. Chandrabhanusinhji of Wankaner	1934	Female	8' 0" (girth 34")	–	Chataria, Mendar-da portion of Gir	Wankaner, 1952.
71.	H.H. Maharaja Krishnakumarsinhji of Bhavnagar	1946	Male	8' ⅓" (tail 3')	–	Mytiala, Bhavnagar	Dharmakumar-sinhji and Wynter-Blyth, 1951.
72.	Unknown	–	Female	–	8' 0" (tail 2' 8" dressed skin)	Gujarat	Pocock, 1930.
73.	H.H. Maharaja Raj Mayurdhwajsinhji of Dhrangadhra	1950	Male	7' 11" (between pegs) 8' 2½" (round the curves)	–	Mytiala, Bhavnagar	Maharaja Raj Meghrajji of Dhrangadhra, pers. comm., 1995.
74.	-do-	-do-	Female	7' 8½" (between pegs) 7' 9½" (round the curves)	–	-do-	-do-

75.	M. Chandrabhanusinhji of Wankaner	1934	Female	7' 6" (girth 34")	–	Chataria, Mendarda portion of Gir	Wankaner, 1952.
76.	-do-	-do-	-do-	7' 4" (girth 31")	–	-do-	-do-
77.	"E.L."	1828	Male	6' 3¼" (tip of nose to stump of tail)^C	–	Deesa, Gujarat	Anon., 1873, p. 138.

Notes

A – Though not specified, the length indicates that it was a dressed skin measurement.

B – The length was estimated by W.T. Blanford according to R.I. Pocock.

C – It would appear that the lion's tail was damaged or was not measured.

Rowland Ward's compilation of 1935 (table II) has only one animal from Africa measured by the owner which was over 10 feet, as against two instances from India (table I). On the other hand there are nine entries from Africa of dressed skins above 10 feet whereas only two of Ward's four entries for India show skins above 10 feet.

A critical look at the compilation of the records of Indian trophies reveals that the lion shot by Major General William Rice circa 1850 was by far the largest even if we were to knock off 3 inches from his estimate of minimum length of the animal before skinning since he does not record the exact figure. If one were to discard this record, though Rice was a renowned hunter and would have been careful of his measurements, then the largest lion shot in India and recorded, came a hundred years later circa 1950, by Princess Rajendrakunverba of Palitana whose lion measured 10 feet 2 inches. This conclusion is based on the lengths recorded before skinning as the lengths of skins depend on several factors and this would lead to many more inaccuracies. The lengths are recorded here exactly as they were in various sources, not converted to the metric measures. Only the measurement of Emperor Jahangir's lion has been converted into feet and inches in order to make it uniform with other trophies listed here.

It will be seen that almost all the lions from India for which we have measurements here are of the Gir forest and its environs, a very small geographical area when compared with the African continent. However, if one assumes that the levels of accuracy in measurements are similar, one may conclude that the sizes of lions from Asia and from Africa are more or less equal.

TABLE II: SIZE OF AFRICAN LIONS FROM ROWLAND WARD'S RECORDS OF BIG GAME (AFRICA AND ASIA) 10TH EDITION, 1935

S. No.	Sportsman	Year	Sex	Size		Locality
				LENGTH	LENGTH OF DRESSED SKIN	
1.	Captain J.K. Roberts	–		10' 11"	10' 4" (tail 3' 3")	Sudan
2.	A.S. Vernay	–		9' 10½"	11' 7"	Kalahari
3.	Countess Münster	–		–	10' 8" (tail 3' 2")	Tanganyika
4.	H.H. Prince Youssouf Kamal	–			10' 7" (tail 3' 1")	-do-
5.	F. Edmond Blanc	–		9' 9"	10' 5" (tail 3' 4")	Uganda
6.	Major J.B. Browne	–		9' 8"	10' 9" (tail 3' 4½")	Bahr-el-Arab
7.	H.H. the Heir Apparent [M.K. Sadul Singh] of Bikaner	–		9' 6½"	10' 7½" (tail 3' 2")	Tanganyika
8.	Madame E. Edmond-Blanc	–		–	10' 1" (tail 2' 11")	-do-
9.	Captain C.E. Parker	–			9' 10" (tail 3' 2")	Nyasaland
10.	H.H. the Heir Apparent [M.K. Sadul Singh] of Bikaner	–		–	10' 9" (tail 3' 1")	Tanganyika
11.	D.D. Stewart	–		9' 1"	8' 10" (tail 2' 10")	Darfur
12.	Mrs Hamilton-Leigh	–		–	9' 3½" (tail 3' 1")	Kenya Colony
				8' 2"		

APPENDIX 4

Lord Curzon's Letter of 1902

Letter of H.E. The Rt. Hon'ble George Nathaniel Baron Curzon of Kedleston P.C., G.M.S.I., G.C.I.E., *
Viceroy and Governor-General of India in reply to
The Humble Memorial of The Burma Game Preservation Association of 23rd September 1901 +

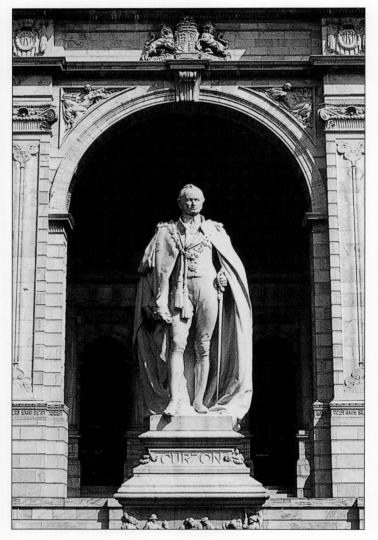

* Privy Councellor, Grand Master of the Star of India, and Extra Knight Grand Commander of the Indian Empire.
+ Source: NAI, Home Public, August 1904, No. 15. In all probability, the letter was written in 1902. It bears no date but at 4.15 pm on January 17, 1902 it was sent for filing by the Personal Secretary to the Viceroy. The file in the NAI bears the date of 1904.

Gentlemen,

Among the many memorials which the enterprising inhabitants of Lower Burma and of Rangoon have showered upon me, and to all of which it has not been possible for me to give a verbal reply, I have selected yours as one of those to which I should be sorry not to return such an answer – owing to the great importance of the subject which it raises.

The question of Game Preservation in India is one that may appeal, in my judgement, not merely to the sportsman, but also to the naturalist and the friend of animal life. It is certainly not through the spectacles of the sportsman only that I would regard it, though I yield to no one in my recognition of the manly attractions of shikar. Such considerations, however, might be suspected of a selfish tinge and I think that in approaching the matter we should as far as possible, put our own predilections in the background, and view it in the public interest at large.

There are some persons who doubt or dispute the progressive diminution of wild life in India. I think that they are wrong. The facts seem to me to point entirely in the opposite direction. Up till the time of the Mutiny lions were shot in Central India. They are now confined to an ever-narrowing patch of forest in Kathiawar. I was on the verge of contribution to their still further reduction a year ago myself: but fortunately I found out my mistake in time, and was able to adopt a restraint which I hope that others will follow. Except in Native States, the Terai, and forest reserves, tigers are undoubtedly diminishing. This is perhaps not an unmixed evil. The rhinoceros is all but exterminated save in Assam. Bison are not so numerous or so easy to obtain as they once were. Elephants have already had to be protected in many parts. Above all deer, to which you particularly allude in the case of Burma, are rapidly dwindling. Every man's hand appears to be against them, and each year thins the herds. Finally many beautiful and innocent varieties of birds are pursued for the sake of their plumage, which is required to minister to the heedless vanity of European fashion.

The causes of this diminution in the wild fauna of India are in some cases natural and inevitable, in others they are capable of being arrested. In the former class I would name the steady increase of population, the widening area of cultivation, and the improvement in means of communication – all of them the sequel of what is popularly termed progress in civilization. Among the artificial and preventable causes I would name the great increase in the number of persons who use firearms, the immense improvement in the mechanism and range of the weapons themselves, the unchecked depredations of native hunters and poachers, and in some cases, I regret to say, a lowering of the standard of sport, leading to the shooting of immature heads, or to the slaughter of females. The result of all these agencies, many of which are found in operation at the same time and in the same place, cannot fail to be a continuous reduction in the wild game of India.

I cannot say that the Government of India have hitherto shown any great boldness in dealing with the matter. But there has been, and still is, in my opinion, very good reason for proceeding cautiously. There are some persons who say that wild animals are as certainly destined to disappear in India as wolves, for instance, have done in England, and that it is of no use to try and put back the hands of the clock. I do not attach much value to this plea, which seems to me rather pusillanimous, as well as needlessly pessimistic. There are others who say that in a continent so vast as India, or – to narrow the illustration – in a province with such extensive forest reserves as Burma, the wild animals may be left to look after themselves. This argument does not impress me either: for the distant jungles are available only to the favoured few, and it is the disappearance of game from the plains and from accessible tracts that is for the most part in question. I do, however, attach great value to the consideration that wild animal life should not be unduly fostered at the expense of the occupations or the crops of the people. Where depredations are committed upon crops or upon flocks and herds, the cultivator cannot be denied, within reasonable limits, the means of self-protection. Similarly, it is very important that any restrictions that are placed upon the destruction of game should not be worked in a manner that may be oppressive or harassing to his interests.

Hitherto the attempts made by Government to deal with the question by legislation, or by rules and notifications based on statute, have been somewhat fitful and lacking in method. In parts, as I have already mentioned, elephants have been very wisely and properly protected. A close season has been instituted for certain kinds of game. An Act has been passed for the preservation of Wild Birds: and I observe from one of the enclosures to your memorial that your ingenuity has not shrunk from the suggestion that a deer may reasonably be considered a wild bird. Under this Act, the possession or sale during the breeding season of the flesh of certain wild birds in Municipal or Cantonment areas is forbidden. Then again rules have been issued under the Forest Act, protecting certain classes of animals in certain tracts.

The general effect of these restrictions has been in the right direction. But I doubt if they have been sufficiently coordinated, or if they have gone far enough: and one of my last acts at Simla, before I had received or read your memorial, was to invite a re-examination of the subject, with the view of deciding whether we might proceed somewhat further than we have already done. We must be very careful not to devise any too stereotyped or Procrustean form of procedures; since there is probably no matter in which a greater variety of conditions and necessities prevails; and the rules or precautions which would be useful in one place might be positively harmful in another. Among the suggestions which will occur to all of us as deserving of consideration, are some greater restriction, by the charge of fees or otherwise, upon the issue of gun licenses, the more strict enforcement of a close season for certain animals; the prohibition of the possession or sale of flesh during the breeding season, penalties upon netting and snaring during the same period, restrictions of the facilities given to strangers to shoot unlimited amounts of game, and upon the sale and export of trophies and skins. I daresay that many other ideas will occur to us in the discussion of the matter, or may be put forward in the press and elsewhere, by those who are qualified to advise. My own idea would be if possible to frame some kind of legislation of a permissive and elastic nature, the provisions of which should be applied to the various provinces of India in so far only as they were adapted to the local conditions. The question of Native States somewhat complicates the matter. But I doubt not that the Government would, where required, meet with the willing cooperation of the Chiefs, many of whom are keen and enthusiastic patrons both of animal life and of sport. The subject is not one that can be hastily taken up or quickly decided; but I have probably said enough to show you that I personally am in close sympathy with your aims: and I need hardly add that if the Government of India finds itself able, after further study, to proceed with the matter, an opportunity will be given to those who are interested in each province to record their opinions.

APPENDIX 5

The Origin and Legal Basis of the Indian National Emblem

Aperusal of various sources relating to the emergence of the Indian Constitution and the coming into being of the Republic of India, in a search for the genesis and the adoption of the capital of the Ashoka pillar at Sarnath as the official seal/emblem of the Union of India, has been illuminating and rewarding but not conclusive.

An obvious start would be to study Indian Constituent Assembly Debates which have been recorded in fourteen volumes and published by the Government of India. The Constituent Assembly Debates are also easily accessible on the Government of India website. It would be noteworthy to remember that the National Flag was adopted after a lengthy debate by the Constituent Assembly and the same has been recorded in Volume 4 of the Constituent Assembly Debates. I have found that there are references to the incorporation of the Ashoka Chakra to replace the charkha in the erstwhile flag of the Indian National Congress. Pandit Jawaharlal Nehru's speech relating to the incorporation of the Ashoka Chakra does not make any reference to the present National Emblem.

I have spent hours on the internet at the Government of India site which hosts the Constituent Assembly Debates and have used various options on the search engines but there appears no mention of the present National Emblem.

Further, I have physically examined the Constituent Assembly Debates from the date of the adoption of the Indian National Flag till June 14, 1948 (the day the Gazette of India changed its emblem from the British signet to the lion capital) and have found no reference to the adoption of the present emblem. I hasten to add that the Constituent Assembly Debates were not held on a day-to-day basis and that I have not examined any debate figuring after June 14, 1948.

The next feature of my research was B. Shiva Rao's multi-volume work, *The Framing of India's Constitution (Select Documents)* published by the Indian Institute of Public Administration, 1966. This work contains working notes of the sub-committee which was formed to decide on the issue of the adoption of the Indian National Flag and National Emblem. There are but two instances in relation to the notes of the sub-committee which are of importance, i.e. the notes dated July 10, 1947, which record the agenda in respect of the National Flag and a possible National Emblem. The notes dated July 18, 1947, crystallize the pattern of the National Flag but put off the National Emblem to a later date, which is not mentioned.

Further, the Gazette of India by a notification dated May 12, 1948 has certain draft amendments in respect of the Indian Pilgrim Ships Rules, 1933. One draft amendment refers to the "new seal" (lion capital) in place of the British signet. It is thus probable that any proposed change in respect of the nation's emblems took place between July 18, 1947 and May 12, 1948.

As this research has originated in Bombay, I also referred to The Bombay Government Gazette and the Gazette of India extraordinary. I found that the last day on which the Bombay Gazette displayed the British signet was Thursday, June 3, 1948. On Friday, June 4, 1948, the Indian emblem was displayed for the first time. Interestingly, the Gazette of India displayed the British signet for the last time on Saturday, June 12, 1948. The first time the Indian emblem was displayed in the Gazette of India extraordinary was Monday, June 14, 1948.

I have found no notification in either of the Gazettes pertaining to the change from the British signet to the [new] National Emblem. Furthermore, it is apparent that there was no uniform notification for the change in display of the National Emblem as the Bombay Gazette moved from the British signet to the Ashoka capital ten days *prior* to the change in the Government of India Gazette.

I therefore find it pertinent to note that the Constituent Assembly Debates do not shed any light on the basis for the choosing of the symbol, its origins, or the reasoning behind the National Emblem. To the best of my knowledge, there is no gazetted notification in the above period pertaining to the adoption of the National Emblem, or any sub-committee notification in respect of the same. As a result, the research on the basis for adoption of the National Emblem or the reasoning behind why the Ashoka capital was chosen is inconclusive and is open to speculation.

Udaybhanusinh
Advocate, High Court, Bombay

Maps

Past and Present Distribution of the Lion in North Africa and Asia

	Boundaries of the lion's historical range
●	Protected area where only remaining population occurs
✳	Sites of potential/unsuccessful reintroduction
▲	Confirmed record
△	Unconfirmed record

SKETCH MAP. NOT TO SCALE.

Courtesy Nowell and Jackson/IUCN 1996.

Past and Present Distribution of the Lion in India,
R.I. Pocock's Map

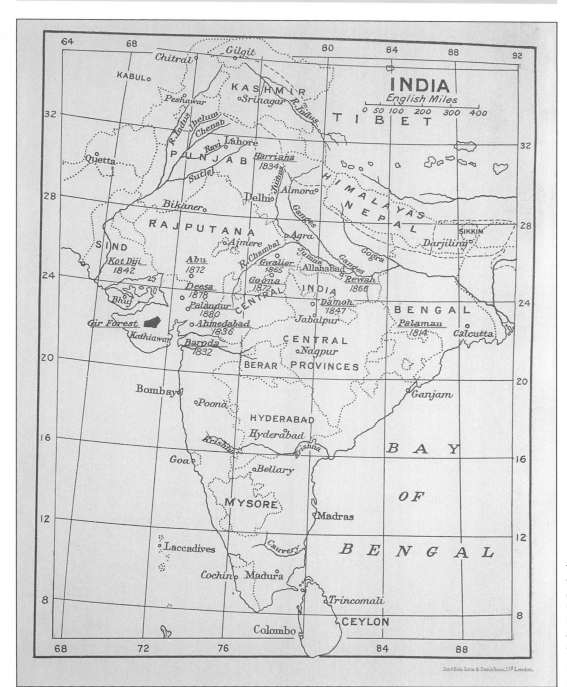

The dates indicate approximately the years when the lion became extinct at the various localities which are underlined in red. From R.I. Pocock, "The Lions of Asia". *Journal, Bombay Natural History Society*, Vol. 34, No. 3, 1930, pp. 638–65. Courtesy Bombay Natural History Society, Mumbai.

Junagadh State
at the Turn of the 20th Century

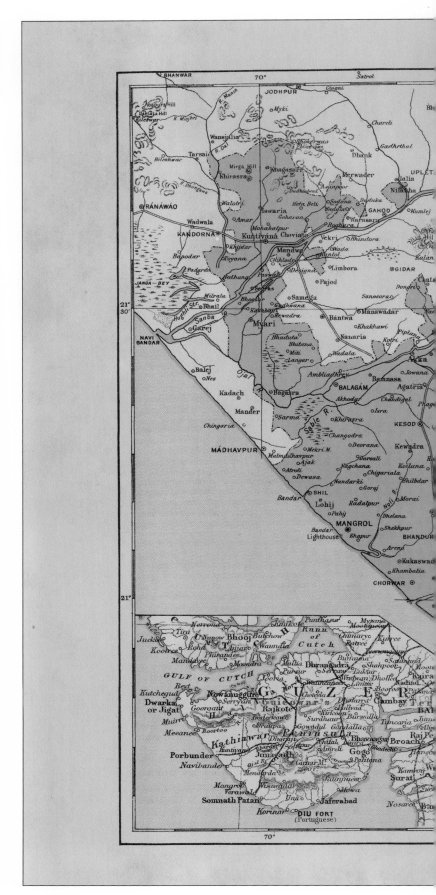

The boundaries of the state remained unchanged until 1947.
From *Ruling Princes of India: Being a Historical, Archaeological,
Political and Statistical Account of the Premier State of Kathiawar*
by S.M. Edwardes and L.G. Fraser, Bombay, The Times of India
Press, 1907.

MAP

OF THE

JUNAGADH STATE

KATHIAWAR

Scale of English Miles.

DIU (Portuguese)

Stanford's Geographical Estab⁵ London.

The Gir National Park and Sanctuary

Courtesy Forest Department, Government of Gujarat.

Current Distribution Range of the Asiatic Lion

Courtesy Forest Department, Government of Gujarat.

epilogue 2008

A LITTLE MORE THAN three years have elapsed since this book was published. It is too short a period to be able to make any substantial additions to the history of a species. However, there is some further information which would be of interest to the reader, and this epilogue brings the story up to date.

In Chapter 2 we had noted Professor Helmut Hemmer's study of the morphological differences between various subspecies of lions. Recent mtDNA analysis carried out at Johannes Gutenberg University, Mainz, Germany, of the materials from specimens of the concerned subspecies, confirms his earlier conclusion that *Panthera leo leo* and *Panthera leo persica*, i.e. the lions of Africa north of the Sahara and the lions of Asia, are phylogenetically closer to each other than to the populations of Sub-Saharan East Africa and South Africa.[1]

In Chapter 6, I had mentioned that I had not come across a painting of a tiger hunt of the Great Mughals. Recently, Dr Asok Kumar Das has drawn my attention to a painting in the National Museum of Pakistan, Karachi, of which only a print is available to us for examination. In his opinion, it shows Emperor Shah Jahan shooting one of two tigers which have obviously been driven out of the jungle. He is using a gun from elephantback and is accompanied by a large retinue. The painting appears to be a copy made at Lucknow circa 1780-90, from a mid-17th-century Mughal original.[2]

It is interesting to note that Emperor Akbar's successors, unlike him, preferred the safety of an elephant and often the support of a retinue while tackling large cats. Lions were usually found in grasslands and scrub jungle. Tigers on the other hand had to be "beaten" out from their preferred habitat of dense jungle in order to shoot them from elephantback. However, the existence of this painting – and possibly others which are not in the public domain – does not change the observation made earlier that lions were central to the Mughal hunt, unlike the tiger.

As is well known, Jahangir took to recording strange occurrences regarding animals in his memoirs. For instance a white cheetah brought to show him or cheetahs breeding in the imperial menagerie, the arrival of a turkey or a Burchell's Zebra or a Barbary Falcon at his court, the courtship display of a pair of Sarus Cranes, and many more incidents, were all meticulously observed and noted by him. Similarly, he recorded some unheard of behaviour of a lion:

> [On November 13, 1609] a lion was brought from the royal lion house to be made to fight an ox. Many people had gathered to watch. There was also a group of yogis, and the lion approached one of the yogis, who was naked, in a playful manner, not in rage, and knocked him to the ground. Then, just as though it were copulating with a female of its own kind, it mounted him and began to hump. It did the same thing the next day. It has acted like this several times. Since before now no such thing has ever been seen, and it is exceedingly strange, it is recorded.[3]

This incident has also been recorded by Mutamad Khan, a *bakshi* (secretary) of the emperor, in his *Iqbalnama-i Jahangiri*, a chronicle of Jahangir's reign. He goes a step further and gives us the name of the errant lion as well, Lal Khan.[4]

The great Mughals maintained huge menageries – a fact noted among others by Ralph Fitch, the English traveller who visited Agra and Fatehpur Sikri during

Landscape with lions and figures
■ Imperial Mughal school, circa 1610. Here Emperor Akbar watches a lion attacking a nilgai. The lioness with three cubs sits near human skeletal remains suggesting man-eating.
Photograph: Christie's Images Ltd.

Akbar's reign. Padarath has left us a painting of a tame lion lightly chained, going for a walk with its keeper, as noted earlier. In the painting above, Akbar witnesses a natural occurrence; however an earlier work attributed to Miskin of circa 1585 and titled "Akbar observing an animal combat while hunting" shows the emperor watching a fight between a bull and a lion. It is obviously a staged affair, the lion has the bull's hump in its mouth while the bull is biting the lion's right thigh. It appears as if the bull has attacked its tormentor rather than the other way round. The painting also has a group of yogis, though their presence is incidental to the event.[5]

This particular incident, recorded by Jahangir himself, finds place in another source as well. The exact date of the occurrence is known, and Mutamad Khan goes on to identify the particular animal by name. Truth has been known to be stranger than fiction; I leave it to the reader to judge the incident's veracity.

There is yet another instance of the strange behaviour of a lion worth noting. Muhammed Hadi who continued to record Jahangir's reign from the 20th regnal year onwards, narrates that a lion presented to the emperor by his grandson, Prince Dawarbaksh, in October 1625, was so friendly with a goat that it lived happily with it in a cage. When another goat of the same colour was introduced in the cage, the lion sniffed and killed it. An ox met the same fate and it was eaten.[6] Compare this with the behaviour of a large cat of another species known for its irascible nature. On the outskirts of a small village, Antoli in Vadodara District, Gujarat, a young wild leopardess regularly visited a tethered cow every evening between October 8 and 22, and November 4 and 29, 2002. They spent hours together, comfortable in each other's company to the extent that the leopardess was observed interacting with the cow without any aggression and was photographed by scores of visitors.[7]

In Chapter 7 I had stated that of the 400 books on shikar and related subjects written during the British period, listed by Kamal Prasad, only three had a chapter on lions. I have subsequently come across an annotated bibliography of books on big game hunting in Asia. It has some 800 entries most of which pertain to India. This anthology lists three more books which deal with shikar of lions.[8] However, this additional information does not change in any way the conclusion I had reached in the text.

In Chapter 9 we looked at the relationship between Junagadh's Nawab Mahbatkhanji III and his brother princes concerning lion shikar, and the altercation between him and Maharaja Ganga Singh of Bikaner over the latter's desire to shoot lions. Bikaner, who maintained a very close relationship with the imperial government had a say in finalizing the itinerary of the Prince of Wales's (later Edward VIII) visit to India in the winter of 1921–22. He had the gall to suggest to

"Modern" hunt
■ Maharaja Rana Natwarsinhji of Porbandar accompanied by Murtaza Khan Saheb of Junagadh with his trophy, circa 1930. The automobile was used extensively for transportation where roads existed in the forest. The numberplate of the Junagadh state car sports a lion.
Author's collection.

John Wood, Political Secretary to the Government of India, that the prince should shoot a lion in the Gir. It would be a "great triumph and honour" for India to give him such a trophy before he went on safari to Africa. Gratuitously he goes on to state that there really were "quite a number of lions there" though it was being said that there were only half a dozen or a dozen of them left.[9] Bikaner had no business to make this suggestion concerning another state. In the event, however, the prince did not go to Kathiawar and the matter ended without the Nawab coming to know of Bikaner's move which, no doubt, would have caused another eruption in Junagadh.

The departure of Nawab Mahbatkhanji III for Karachi in 1947 brought down the curtain on the princely era of Soruth. Did the last Nawab, in his years of self-imposed exile, think of "his" lions and wonder about their condition in India? We don't know, save for one episode that was hitherto unknown to me.

In 1956, Maharana Raj Saheb Digvijaysinhji of Wankaner was an attaché in the Ministry of Commerce and Industry, Government of India, in which capacity he visited Karachi, then the capital of Pakistan, as part of an Indian delegation. With the approval of India's High Commissioner C.C. Desai, i.c.s., he called on the Nawab late one evening. The Nawab, who suffered from night blindness, received him with dignity in spite of his infirmity. They conversed in the Kathiawari dialect of Gujarati. It was obvious to Digvijaysinhji that the Nawab missed his homeland and his brother princes of Kathiawar after whom he enquired with nostalgia. During their conversation Digvijaysinhji praised the Nawab for having protected the lions in his state during his rule. His laconic reply was "I knew that the Asiatic lion was very rare and had to be protected."[10] He said no more. Perhaps he had heard of the free-for-all shoots that had taken place in the aftermath of his departure. The lions, we know, were very close to his heart, and maybe he found the subject too painful to discuss at length. The Nawab died in 1959. To a considerable extent owing to his efforts, the lion survived both his state and himself – this was his unique bequest to his successors in India.

Today, the Gir protected area continues to receive an ever-increasing number of pilgrims who visit Banej, Kankai, and Tulsishyam. Their number has gone up from nearly 50,000 in 1994–95 to over 4,76,000 in 2005–06 and the number of vehicles carrying them has increased from 4,700 to over 66,000, the maximum traffic being to Tulsishyam. Similarly, the number of tourists has increased from over 57,000 to nearly 1,37,000 over the same period. The programme of resettling Maldharis outside the sanctuary is stalled while there is hardly a check on their increasing number as also of their livestock that live in their nesses. Their number has increased from 2,500 in 2004 to over 3,300 in 2005–06 and their livestock has increased from 13,000 to over 14,700 in the same period. Over 11,100 vehicles go to various nesses to collect milk and to remove dung. A similar situation persists in the 14 forest villages where human population has gone up from 4,500 to about 5,200 while livestock heads have increased from 4,200 to about 4,900 in the same period.[11] This in addition to the illegal grazing by livestock in large numbers from surrounding villages. The metre-gauge railway line with four trains running on it daily, vehicular traffic on roads going through the protected area, and unbarricaded wells of the peripheral villages have caused 26 accidental deaths of lions in the five-year period between 2002–03 and 2006–07.[12] In the year 2007–08 a lioness and three cubs were electrocuted on a farm.[13] Uninsulated electric wires are deliberately left by farmers to kill wild boar and other ungulates who raid standing crops. The lions appear to have been unintended victims in this case as has happened in several instances in the past.

To top it all, the Government of India has recently enacted *The Scheduled Tribes and Other Traditional Forest Dwellers (Recognition of Rights) Act* with the laudable intention of conferring rights on these marginalized sections of society. However, this Act does not set aside even the national parks and sanctuaries of the country, which constitute a minuscule area totalling less than 4 per cent of India's landmass, from its purview. The implementation of this Act will adversely affect the Gir. The lion and its habitat will face yet another onslaught.

The poaching of lions for their body parts has until recently been largely an unknown activity. However in March/April 2007, as many as seven lions were killed by poachers' gangs from Central India according to the Government of Gujarat,[14] though the actual figure may have been much higher. Unofficial sources state that nine lions were killed and a total of 31 persons involved in the crime were arrested or rounded up by the state authorities.[15] It is obvious that these attacks were well planned with much wider ramifications than at first meet the eye. The news has sent shockwaves through the country as it has become clear that with the dangerously declining tiger population in India, the pressure has fallen on the other great cat, the lion, for meeting the needs of the traditional Chinese medicine which uses their body parts as well.[16] The Gir forest and its surrounding areas have arguably the largest population of a big cat in Asia – an obviously tempting target for the poachers. This is yet another grave threat to Asia's lions.

On the other hand, the lion census of 2005 has thrown up interesting figures apart from posting an increasing population now at 359 animals. The Gir National Park and Sanctuary and its peripheral areas had 262 lions in 1995, 271 in 2001, and 291 in 2005. Whereas there were 42 lions living permanently outside these areas in 1995, their number had increased to 60 in 2001, and to 68 in 2005 with Mytiala and some nearby areas accounting for as many as 39 of them.[17] These figures indicate that the Gir National Park and Sanctuary can hold about 300 lions in the present state of its protection and management. It also means that the increasing number of lions living outside have to fend for themselves. There is no likelihood of these 68 animals or their descendants returning to the Gir protected area of their own volition, and it is obvious that Gujarat must immediately take steps to protect them.

These old haunts which the lions have re-colonized on their own should be declared sanctuaries and the corridors used by the lions during and after these migrations also need to be protected. So far only Mytiala, with an area of about 19 square kilometres, has been declared a sanctuary in 2004. This is woefully inadequate. A sanctuary with an area of 180 square kilometres of forest around the Girnar hills has been proposed recently.[18] It is home to a breeding population of 17 lions, according to the 2005 census. This forest patch is just a little smaller than the Barda Sanctuary which is 192 square kilometres in area, and which has not been colonized by lions on their own, but is where the Gujarat Government wishes some of them to go either of their own accord or by artificially translocating them. Lions outside protected areas result in constant human-lion interactions and conflicts that are likely to increase with their increasing numbers. According to the state government records, no human deaths have occurred between 2003 and 2005, though there have been reports of a man-eating incident at Sutrapada in 2006.[19]

The vexed issue of a second home for lions outside Gujarat – specifically Kuno

Palpur Sanctuary in Madhya Pradesh – continues to create ripples in the conservation community apart from becoming a problem for the Government of India. Gujarat refuses to part with any of "its" lions for the purpose of relocation. According to a recent report, the Ministry of Environment and Forests of the Government of India proposes to relocate two pairs of captive bred animals to which it has access, in a 15 hectare enclosure in Kuno Palpur. The third generation of these animals would then be released in the wild there.[20]

Successful release and survival of captive bred felines in the wild is not easy at the best of times. One would presume that only those animals which have a clear Asiatic lineage are considered for release. Further, lions being gregarious animals living in prides, it would be advisable to initially release a couple or more of sibling lionesses to whom a male lion could be introduced at an appropriate time. The most difficult though not impossible task would be to teach them or their offspring to hunt in the wild. Expertise in this area must be brought in from wherever it is available as no such experiment has been tried in India. We can only hope that the government has the determination and perseverance to succeed in its endeavour.

REFERENCES

1   Prof. Helmut Hemmer, pers. comm., 2005; Hemmer and Burger, 2005.

2   Dr Asok Kumar Das, pers. comm., 2006.

3   Thackston, 1999, p. 103.

4   Rogers and Beveridge, 1909–14, Vol. II, p. 157.

5   Welch and Masteller, 2004, pp. 86–87.

6   Thackston, 1999, p. 435.

7   Singh, 2003.

8   Czech, 2003: p. 95 (Hall); p. 137 (Maurice); p. 230 (Wilson).

9   NAI, letter dated April 17, 1920 from H.H. Maharaja of Bikaner to John Wood, Political Secretary, Political and Foreign Department in Secret – Reforms Branch, Proceedings, September 1920, Nos. 1–22.

10 Maharana Raj Saheb Digvijaysinhji of Wankaner, pers. comm., 2005.

11 Bharat Pathak, pers. comm., 2005.

12 Pradeep Khanna, Presentation to the Advisory Group for the Conservation of Lions, Gujarat State, April 30, 2007.

13 Kishore Kotecha, pers. comm., 2007.

14 Pradeep Khanna, Presentation, 2007.

15 Kishore Kotecha, pers. comm., 2007.

16 Nowell and Xu Ling, 2007.

17 Bharat Pathak, pers. comm., 2005.

18 *The Times of India*, Ahmedabad, May 24, 2007.

19 Bharat Pathak, pers. comm., 2005; *GS*, May 29, 2006.

20 *The Times of India*, New Delhi, August 5, 2007.

bibliography

This bibliography includes some sources not referred to in the text. The reason for such inclusions is that they may be of relevance to readers interested in the history of Asiatic lions. Such references are identified by an asterisk.

In case of a reprint/revised edition, the original date of publication has been quoted for reference in the endnotes, while the date of the reprint/edition used by this author is also provided here.

The Gujarati sources remain untranslated into English. Quotations in the text from such sources have been translated by the author.

A

Aflalo, F.G. (ed.), 1904, *The Sportsman's Book for India*. Horace Marshall & Son, London.

Ahmud, Syud, 1864, *Toozuk-i-Jehangeeree*. Published by Author, Ally Gurh.

Ait. Br., 1931, *Aitareya Brahmana*, Anandasrama Press, Pune.

Albenda, Pauline, 1974, "Lions on Assyrian Wall Reliefs". *The Journal of the Ancient and Near Eastern Society of Columbia University*, Vol. 6, pp. 1–24. New York.

*Ali, Salim, 1927, "The Mughal Emperors of India as Naturalists and Sportsmen" Part I. *Journal, Bombay Natural History Society*, Vol. 31, No. 4, pp. 833–61. Bombay.

*———, 1928, "The Mughal Emperors of India as Naturalists and Sportsmen" Parts II and III. *Journal, Bombay Natural History Society*, Vol. 32, No. 1, pp. 34–63; No. 2, pp. 264–73. Bombay.

Allaby, Michael (ed.), 1985, *The Oxford Dictionary of Natural History*. Oxford University Press, Oxford.

Allan, John, 1936, *Catalogue of the Coins of Ancient India*. The British Museum, London, 1967.

Alvi, M.A. and A. Rahman, 1968, *Jahangir – The Naturalist*. National Institute of Sciences of India, New Delhi.

Anonymous, 1833, "Capt. Walter Smee on the Maneless Lions of Gujarat". *Proceedings of the Zoological Society*, Vol. I, p. 140. London.

———, 1873, *The Oriental Sporting Magazine From June 1928 to June 1833*, Vol. I, pp. 137–39. Henry S. King & Co., London.

———, 1873A, *The Oriental Sporting Magazine, From June 1928 to June 1833*, Vol. II, pp. 44, 200, 331–32. Henry S. King & Co., London.

———, 1903, *The Babi Rulers of Sorath, with a Short Account of Their Administration*. Junagadh State Press, Junagadh.

———, 1939, *Memorandum on the Indian States*. Government of India, New Delhi.

———, 1948, *White Paper on Indian States*. Ministry of States, Government of India, New Delhi.

———, 1950, -do-

———, 1959, *Stanley Gibbons Simplified Stamp Catalogue, 1960*. Stanley Gibbons Publications Ltd., London.

———, 1972, *The Gir Lion Sanctuary Project*. Revised Edition. Forest Department, Government of Gujarat, Gandhinagar, 1975.

———, 1980, *Stanley Gibbons Stamps of the World, 1981*. Stanley Gibbons Publications Ltd., London.

———, 2000, *India Eco-Development Project: Status Report 1999–2000. Gir National Park and Sanctuary*. Conservator of Forests Wildlife Circle, Junagadh (typescript).

*Ansari, Mohd. Azher, 1960, "The Hunt of the Great Mughals". *Islamic Culture*, Vol. XXXIV, pp. 242–53. Osmania University, Hyderabad.

Apte, Vaman Shivram, 1965, *The Practical Sanskrit–English Dictionary*. Motilal Banarsidass Publishers, Delhi, 1992.

Archer, Mildred, 1959, *Tipoo's Tiger*. Her Majesty's Stationery Office, London.

———, 1962, *Natural History Drawings in the India Office Library*. Her Majesty's Stationery Office, London.

———, 1969, *British Drawings in the India Office Library*, Vols. I and II. Her Majesty's Stationery Office, London.

Ashraf, N.K.V., R. Chellam, S. Molur, D. Sharma, and S. Walker, 1995, *Asiatic Lion: Panthera leo persica. Population and Habitat Assessment P.H.V.A. and Global Animal Survival Plan Workshops, 18–21 October*. Report, Municipal Corporation of Baroda/ Sayaji Baug Zoo, et al., Vadodra.

B

Bachkheti, N.D., 1995, "Introduction of Lions in Chandraprabha Sanctuary". *Cheetal, Journal of the Wildlife Preservation Society of India*, Vol. 34, No. 1, pp. 10–14. Dehra Dun.

Balachandran, G., 1998, *The History of the Reserve Bank of India (1935–51)*. Oxford University Press, Delhi.

Balfour, Surgeon General Edward, 1885, *Encyclopaedia of India, Eastern & Southern Asia*. Third Edition. Bernard Quaritch, London.

Banerjee, S.C., 1980, *Flora and Fauna in Sanskrit Literature*. Naya Prokash, Calcutta.

Basham, A.L., 1954, *The Wonder that Was India; A Survey of History and Culture of the Indian Subcontinent Before the Coming of the Muslims*. Sidgwick & Jackson, London, 1982.

Beach, Milo Cleveland and Ebba Koch, 1997, *King of the World; the Padshahnama An Imperial Mughal Manuscript from the Royal Library, Windsor Castle*. Azimuth Editions/ Sackler Gallery, Washington, DC.

Beveridge, Annette Susannah (tr.), 1922, *Babur Namah (Memoirs of Babur)*, Vols. I and II. Oriental Books Reprint Corporation, New Delhi, 1979.

Beveridge, H. (tr.), 1904, *The Akbar-Nama of*

Abu-l-Fazl, Vol. II. Es Es Publication, New Delhi, 1979.

Bhavnagar, H.H. Sir Bhavsinhji, K.C.S.I., Maharaja of, 1911, *Forty Years of Rajkumar College*, Vol. I. Published by Author, Bhavnagar.

Bikaner, M.K. Sadul Singh of, 1928, *Big Game Diary* (unpublished).

Blochman, H. (tr.), 1873, *The A'in-i Akbari* by Abu'l Fazl, Vol. I. Second Edition, revised and edited by Lt. Col. D.C. Phillot. Oriental Books Reprint Corporation, New Delhi, 1977.

Bodenheimer, Dr F.S., 1960, *Animal and Man in Bible Lands*. E.J. Brill, Leiden.

Bole, P.V. and Yogini Vaghani, 1986, *Field Guide to the Common Trees of India*. World Wildlife Fund – India, Delhi.

Bopearachhi, Osmund, 1998, *Sylloge Nummorum Graecorum, the Collection of American Numismatic Society, Part 9, Graeco-Bactrian and Indo-Greek Coins*. American Numismatic Society, New York.

Bull, H.M. and K.N. Haksar, 1926, *Madhav Rao Scindia of Gwalior, 1876–1925*. Alijah Durbar Press, Gwalior.

Burke, W.S., 1920, *The Indian Field Shikar Book*. Fifth Edition. Thacker Spink & Co., Calcutta.

Burton, Brigadier General R.G., 1931, *A Book of Man-Eaters*. Hutchinson & Co. Publishers, London.

———, 1933, *The Book of the Tiger*. Hutchinson & Co. Publishers, London.

Burton, Lt. Col. R.W., 1959, "The Voice of the Cheetah or Hunting Leopard (*Acinonyx jubatus* EREXLABEN)". *Journal, Bombay Natural History Society*, Vol. 56, No. 2, pp. 317–18. Bombay.

C

CAD, 1947–48, *Constituent Assembly Debates*. Government of India Press, New Delhi.

Cadell, Sir Patrick, 1933, "The Preservation of Wildlife in India, No. 5. The Indian Lion". *Journal, Bombay Natural History Society*, Vol. 37, No. 1, pp. 162–66. Bombay.

Caldwell, Capt. Keith, 1938, "The Gir Lion". *Journal, Society for the Preservation of the Fauna of the Empire*, Vol. 34, pp. 62–65. London.

Campbell, Joseph, 1974, *The Mythic Image*. Princeton University Press, Princeton.

Caputo, Philip, 2002, *Ghosts of Tsavo: Stalking the Mystery Lions of East Africa*. Adventure Press, National Geographic Society, Washington, DC.

Carruthers, D., P.B. Van Der Byl, Lt. Col. R.L. Kenion, J.G. Millains, H. Frank Wallace, and Ford G. Barclay, 1915, *The Gun at Home & Abroad: The Big Game of Asia and North America*. The London & Counties Press Association, London.

*Chavan, Sanat and Dhun Karkaria, 2001, *Gir National Park: Handbook*. Tourism Corporation of Gujarat Limited, Gandhinagar.

Chattopadhyaya, U.C., 2002, "Researches in Archaeology of the Holocene Period (including the Harappan Tradition in India and Pakistan)". *Archaeology and Interactive Disciplines*, Vol. III, pp. 364–422. Indian Council for Historical Research and Manohar Publishers, Delhi.

Chellam, Ravi, 1993, "Ecology of the Asiatic Lion (*Panthera leo persica*)". Ph.D. thesis, University of Saurashtra, Rajkot.

*Chellam, Ravi and A.J.T. Johnsingh, 1993, "Management of Asiatic Lions in the Gir Forest, India". *Mammals as Predators. The Proceedings of a Symposium held by the Zoological Society of London and the Mammal Society, London, 22nd and 23rd November 1991*, No. 65, pp. 409–24. Edited by N. Dunstone and M.L. Gorman. Clarendon Press, Oxford.

Chellam, R., Justin Joshua, Christy A. Williams, and A.J.T. Johnsingh, 1994, *Survey of the Potential Sites for Reintroduction of Asiatic Lions*. Wildlife Institute of India, Dehra Dun (typescript).

COI, 2003, *Constitution of India with Short Notes*. Eighteenth Edition with Supplement. Eastern Book Company, Lucknow.

Constable, Archibald (tr.), 1934, *Travels in the Mughal Empire by Francois Bernier A.D. 1656–1668*. Second Edition, revised by Vincent A. Smith. Oriental Reprint, Delhi, 1983.

Czech, Kenneth P., 2003, *An Annotated Bibliography of Asian Big Game Hunting Books, 1780 to 1980: Including Note of Works Devoted to Pig Sticking and Small Game Shooting*. Land's Edge Press, St Cloud, Minnesota.

D

Dadhimatha, M.M. Pandit Sivadatta (ed.), 1915, *Namalinganusasana alias Amarakosa of Amarasimha*. Chaukhamba Sanskrit Pratishthan, Delhi.

Daljeet, Dr, 1999, *Mughal and Deccani Paintings of the National Museum*. Prakash Book Depot, Delhi.

Dalvi, M.K., 1969, "Gir Lion Census, 1968". *Indian Forester*, pp. 741–52. Forest Research Institute, Dehra Dun.

Daniell, William, 1836, *The Oriental Annual or Scenes in India*. Asian Education Service, New Delhi, 2000.

Das, Asok Kumar, 1978, *Mughal Painting During Jahangir's Time*. The Asiatic Society, Calcutta.

Deekshitar, Raja, 2004, "Discovering the Anthropomorphic Lion in Indian Art", *Marg*, Vol. 55, No. 4 (June), pp. 34–41.

Desai, Shambhuprasad Harprasad, 1983, *Gir*. Prabhas Prakashan, Junagadh.

*———, 1995, *The Forest of Gir*. Prabhas Prakashan, Junagadh.

*Desai, Pradumna Kanchanrai, 1962, *Girna Bhitarma*. Sanskar Sahitya Mandir, Bhavnagar.

Dharmakumarsinhji, R.S., 1959, *A Field Guide to Big Game Census in India*. Ministry of Food and Agriculture, Government of India, New Delhi.

———, 1969, "Story of the Lion Census". *Cheetal, Journal of the Wildlife Preservation Society of India*, Vol. XII, No. 1, pp. 48–56. Dehra Dun.

———, 1979, "The Tiger 'Lionised'". *Swarajya*,

Vol. XXIII, No. 39. Madras.

———, 1992, *Reminiscences of Indian Wildlife* (written late 1970s). Oxford University Press, Delhi, 1998.

Dharmakumarsinhji, R.S. and M.A. Wynter-Blyth, 1951, "The Gir Forest and its Lions" Part III. *Journal, Bombay Natural History Society*, Vol. 49, No. 4, pp. 685–95. Bombay.

Dharmakumarsinhji, R.S., Y.R. Ghorpade, Zafar Futehally, M. Krishnan, Hari Dang, V.B. Singh, and K.S. Sankhala, 1970, *Wildlife Conservation in India. Report of the Expert Committee, Indian Board for Wildlife*. Ministry of Food and Agriculture, Government of India, New Delhi.

Divyabhanusinh, 1986, "Earliest Record of a White Tiger". *Journal, Bombay Natural History Society*, Vol. 83, (Supplement), pp. 163–65. Bombay.

———, 1987, "Record of Two Unique Observations of the Indian Cheetah in Tuzuk-i-Jahangiri". *Journal, Bombay Natural History Society*, Vol. 84, No. 2, pp. 269–74. Bombay.

———, 1995, *The End of a Trail: The Cheetah in India*. Second Edition. Oxford University Press, 2002, Delhi.

———, 1999, "Hunting in Mughal Painting". *Flora and Fauna in Mughal Art*. Edited by Som Prakash Verma, pp. 94–108. Marg Publications, Mumbai.

Dollman, Guy and J.B. Burlace, 1935, *Rowland Ward's Records of Big Game, African and Asiatic Sections*. Tenth Edition. Rowland Ward, London.

D'Oyly, Sir Charles, 1810–15, *Indian Sports*, Vols. I and II. The British Library, OIOC, Acc. No. WD4405–4406 (unpublished album).

DUSJ, 1867 onwards, *Dusturul Umul Surkar Joonagudh*. (The Junagadh State Gazette published from December 1867, issued monthly.) Junagadh.

Dutta, Arun Kumar, 1976, "Occurrence of Fossil Lion and Spotted Hyaena from Pleistocene Deposits of Susania, Bankura District, West Bengal". *Journal of the Geological Society of India*, Vol. 17, No. 3, pp. 386–91. Calcutta.

E

Edwardes, S.M. and L.G. Fraser, 1907, *Ruling Princes of India. Junagadh: Being a Historical, Archaeological, Political and Statistical Account of the Premier State of Kathiwar*. Times of India Press, Bombay.

Elgood, Robert, 1995, *Fire Arms of the Islamic World in the Tareq Rajab Museum, Kuwait*. I.B. Taurus Publishers, London.

F

Falk, Toby and Simon Digby, 1983, *Paintings from Mughal India*. P.D. Colnaghi & Co. Ltd., London.

Falk, Toby, Ellen S. Smart, and Robert Skelton, 1978, *Indian Painting: Mughal and Rajput and a Sultanate Manuscript*. P.D. Colnaghi & Co. Ltd., London.

Fenton, Col. L.L., c. 1924, *The Rifle in India: Being the Sporting Experiences of an Indian Officer*. W. Thacker & Co., London.

Forbes, James, 1813, *Oriental Memoirs Selected from a Series of Familiar Letters Written during Seventeen Years in India*. Gian Publishing House, Delhi, 1988.

Foster, Sir William, 1926, *The Embassy of Sir Thomas Roe to India 1615–19 as narrated in his Journal and Correspondence*. Munshiram Manoharlal Publishers Pvt. Ltd., New Delhi, 1990.

Fox-Davies, Arthur Charles, 1909, *A Complete Guide to Heraldry*. Thomas Nelson and Sons Ltd., London, 1950.

G

GA, Gujarat State Archives, District Record Office, Junagadh. (Prior to 1947 it was called The Central Record Office, Junagadh State.) Records concerning lions are kept in *bastas* – bundles of documents tied in cloth – marked *Jungle Khatanu Daftar* – Forest Department Records.

GS, *Gujarat Samachar*, Gujarati daily newspaper, Ahmedabad.

Gee, E.P., 1956, "The Management of India's Wild Life Sanctuaries and National Parks". *Journal, Bombay Natural History Society*, Vol. 54, No. 1, pp. 1–22. Bombay.

———, 1962, "The Present Status of Four Rare Animals of India". *Cheetal, Journal of the Wildlife Preservation Society of India*, Vol. IV, No. 2, pp. 29–33. Dehra Dun.

———, 1964, *The Wildlife of India*. Collins, London.

Gerrard, Lt. Col. Sir Montague, 1903, *Leaves from the Diary of a Soldier Sportsman During Thirty Years of Service in India, Afghanistan, Egypt and Other Countries*. John Murray, London.

Ghorpade, M.Y., 1983, *Sunlight and Shadows. An Indian Wildlife Photographer's Diary*. Victor Gollancz, London and B.I. Publications, Bombay.

Gida, Bhanabhai, 1999, "Sinhni Dosti". *Gujarati Dhoran* 7, pp. 208–11. Gujarat Rajya Shala Pathyapustak Mandal, Gandhinagar.

Godrej, Pheroza J. and Firoza Punthakey-Mistree, 2002, *A Zoroastrian Tapestry. Art, Religion & Culture*. Mapin Publishing Pvt. Ltd., Ahmedabad.

Goetz, Hermann, 1950, *The Art and Architecture of Bikaner State*. Bruno Cassirer, Oxford.

*Gogate, M.G. (comp.), 1994, *List of References on Lion: Panthera leo Linnaeus* (typescript).

Gould, Brian, 1971, "Mathew Boulton and the Making of the Seringapatam Medal". *Coins*, Vol. 8, No. 9, pp. 23–24. Link House Group, Croydon.

Graves, Robert and Omer Ali-Shah, 1967, *The Rubaiyat of Omar Khayyaam: A New Translation with Critical Commentaries*. Cassell & Co. Ltd., London.

Guggisberg. C.A.W., 1962, *Simba: The Life of the Lion*. Bailey Bros. & Swinfen, London.

Guha, Ramachandra (ed.), 2000, *Nature's Spokesman: M. Krishnan and Indian Wildlife*. Oxford University Press, Delhi.

Guha, Sumit, 2001, *Health and Population in South Asia from Earliest Times to the Present*. Permanent Black, New Delhi.

*Gupta, S.P., 1980, *The Roots of Indian Art*. B.R. Publishing Corporation, Delhi.

H

Habib, Irfan, 1963, *The Agrarian System of Mughal India (1556–1707)*. Aligarh Muslim University, Aligarh and Asia Publishing House, Bombay.

–––, 1982, *An Atlas of Mughal India. Political and Economic Maps with Detailed Notes, Bibliography and Index*. Oxford University Press, Delhi, 1986.

–––, 1982A, "Population". *The Cambridge Economic History of India*. Vol. I: c1200–c1700, edited by Tapan Raychaudhuri and Irfan Habib, pp. 163–71. Orient Longman, Hyderabad and Cambridge University Press, Cambridge, 1984.

Harrington Jr., Fred A., 1977, *A Guide to the Mammals of Iran*. Department of the Environment, Tehran.

Harting, James Edmund, 1883, *Essays on Sport and Natural History*. Horace Cox, "The Field" Office, London.

Hartner, Willy and Richard Ettinghausen, 1964, "The Conquering Lion, The Life Cycle of a Symbol". *Oriens*, Vol. 17, pp. 161–71. E.J. Brill, Leiden.

Hassan, Dr Zaky M., 1937, *Hunting as Practiced in Arab Countries of the Middle Ages*. Ministry of Education, Cairo.

Heaney, Lt. Col. G.F., 1944, "Occurrence of the Lion in Persia". *Journal, Bombay Natural History Society*, Vol. 44, No. 3, p. 407, Bombay.

Hemmer, Helmut, 1974, *Untersuchungen zur Stammesgeschiste der Pantherakatzen (Pantherinae). Teil III, Zur Artgeschiste des Lowen Panthera (Panthera) leo (Linnaeus 1758)*. Veraffenlichungen der Zoologischen Staatssamlung, Munchen. Translated by Uma Iyer (unpublished).

Hemmer, Helmut and Joachim Burger, 2005, "Genetic Confirmation of the Unique Nature of the Zoo Population of the Barbary Lion". *IZN: International Zoo News*, Vol. 52/4, No. 34, pp. 218–23.

Heptner, V.H. and A.A. Sludskii, 1971, *Mammals of the Soviet Union. Vol. III Carnivores*. English translation edited by R.S. Hoffman. Smithsonian Institution and National Science Foundation, Washington, DC, 1992.

Houlihan, Patrick F., 1996, *The Animal World of the Pharaohs*. Thames and Hudson, London.

Humphreys, P.N. and E. Kahrom, 1995, *The Lion and the Gazelle: The Mammals and Birds of Iran*. Comma International Biological Systems, Lower Coed Morgan, Nr. Abergavenney, Gwent, U.K.

Hussain, Agha Mahdi (ed.), 1967, 1976, 1977, *Futuhu's Salatin or Shahnama-i-Hind of 'Isami, Vols. I, II, and III*. Asia Publishing House, Bombay.

Hussain, Maulvi Vilayat, 1891, *Shams Siraj 'Afif, Tarikh-i Firoz Shahi*. The Asiatic Society, Calcutta.

I

Ingalls, Daniel H.H. (tr.), 1965, *An Anthology of Sanskrit Court Poetry: Vidyakara's Subhasitaratnakosa*. Harvard University Press, Cambridge, Mass.

Irwin, John, 1973, " 'Asokan' Pillars: A Reassessment of the Evidence". *The Burlington Magazine*, Vol. CXV, November, pp. 706–20. London.

–––, 1974, " 'Asokan' Pillars: A Reassessment of the Evidence. Part II, Structure". *The Burlington Magazine*, Vol. CXVI, December, pp. 712–27. London.

–––, 1975, " 'Asokan' Pillars: A Reassessment of the Evidence. Part III, Capitals". *The Burlington Magazine*, Vol. CXVII, October, pp. 631–43. London.

–––, 1976, " 'Asokan' Pillars: A Reassessment of the Evidence. Part IV, Symbolism". *The Burlington Magazine*, Vol. CXVIII, November, pp. 734–53. London.

–––, 1983, "The True Chronology of the Asokan Pillars". *Artibus Asiae*, Institute of Fine Arts, New York University. Ascona, Switzerland.

–––, 1985, " 'Asokan Pillars'. Their Mystery and the Explanation" (typescript).

*Islam, Shuja Ul and Col. John H. Roush Jr., 2001, *Hunting Dangerous Game with the Maharajas*. Himalayan Books, New Delhi.

Iyer, K. Bharatha, 1977, *Animals in Indian Sculpture*. D.B. Taraporevala Sons & Co. Pvt. Ltd., Bombay.

J

Jacob, Capt. George Le Grand, 1842, *Report upon the General Condition, in the year 1842 of the Province of Kathiawar*. The Bombay Government, Bombay.

Jain, Manik, 1999, *Phila India 2000 Colour Catalogue: Indian Philately 1852–1998*. Philatelia, Calcutta.

Jain, Pushp (ed. and comp.), 2001, *Project Tiger Status Report*. Ministry of Environment and Forests, New Delhi.

Jamkhandikar, Dr M.M., 2000, *Of Homo sapiens and Panthera leo: A Diary of Experiences in Gir Forest of India*. Tolani Shipping Co. Ltd., Mumbai.

JAR, 1907 and 1908, *Sansthan Junagadh: Administration Report*. Junagadh Sarkari Chapkhana, Junagadh.

–––, 1908–09 to 1924–25 and 1929–30 to 1944–45, *Report on the Administration of Junagadh State*. The State Press, Junagadh.

Jarrige, Jean-Francis and Usman Hassan, 1989, "Funerary Complexes of Baluchistan at the End of the Third Millennium in the Light of Recent Discoveries at Mehrgarh and Quetta". *South Asian Archaeology 1985*. Edited by Karen Frifelt and Per Sorensen. Curzon Press, London.

Jepson, Stanley (ed.), 1936, *Big Game Encounters: Critical Moments in the Lives of Well-known Shikaris*. H.F. & G. Witherby, Ltd., London, 1937.

Jerdon, T.C., 1867, *Mammals of India: A Natural History of all the Animals known to Inhabit Continental India*. John Weldon, London, 1874.

Jha, Amiteshwar and Dilip Rajgor, 1994, *Studies in the Coinage of the Western Kshatrapas*. Indian Institute of Research in Numismatic Studies, Nashik.

Jhala, Y.V., Shoman Mukherjee, Nita Shah, Kartikeya Singh Chauhan, Chitaranjan Dave, and Yogendra Singh Jhala, 2002, "Monitoring Lions". *Impact Monitoring of Gir. A Technical

Consultancy Report submitted to the Gujarat Forest Department under the GEF – India Eco-Development Programme. Final Draft Report, pp. 55–72. Edited by Y.V. Jhala. Wildlife Institute of India, Dehra Dun (unpublished).

*Johnsingh, A.J.T., Ravi Chellam, and Diwakar Sharma, 1998, "Prospect for Conservation of the Asiatic Lion in India". *Biosphere Conservation, Journal of the Society for Conservation Biology,* Vol. 1, No. 2, pp. 81–90. Blackwell Scientific Publications, Malden, MA.

Jones, Horace Leonard (tr.), 1966, *The Geography of Strabo.* Harvard University Press, Cambridge, Mass.

Joslin, E.C., A.R. Litherland, and T.B. Simpkin, 1988, *British Battles and Medals.* Spink, London.

Joslin, P., 1973, *The Asiatic Lion: A Study of Ecology and Behaviour.* Ph.D. thesis, University of Edinburgh.

–––, 1985, *Reintroduction Sites for Indian Lion* (typescript).

JRM, 1930, *Swasthan Junagadh: Revenue Manual. Vol. 3. Junagadh Rajyana Upayog Mate.* Compiled by Dalpatram Govardhan Vyas. State Press, Junagadh.

K

K.D. Kaur Singh, Amrit and Rabindra, 2003, *Images of Freedom.* Indialog, New Delhi.

*Kamboj, R.D., Mahesh Singh, and P.P. Raval, 1997, "Analysis of Threats to Gir Ecosystem". *Indian Forester,* Vol. 123, No. 10, pp. 964–72, Forest Research Institute, Dehra Dun.

Kangle, R.P., 1963, *The Kautilya Arthasastra,* Part II. Motilal Banarsidass, Delhi.

Kaul, H.K., 1979, *Travellers' India. An Anthology.* Oxford University Press, Delhi.

Khan, Saiyad Ahmad, 1882, *Ain-i Akbari.* Nawal Kishore, Lucknow.

Kincaid, C.A., 1905, *The Outlaws of Kathiawar and Other Stories.* The Times Press, Bombay.

–––, 1935, *Indian Lions.* The Times of India Press, Bombay.

Kinnear, N.B., 1920, "The Past and Present Distribution of the Lion in South Eastern Asia". *Journal, Bombay Natural History Society,* Vol. 27, No. 1, pp. 34–39. Bombay.

*Klum, Mattias and Monika, 2000, *Den Sköra Träden: Berättelsen om de Sista Asiatika Lejonen.* Bokförlaget Prisma, Stockholm. (A pictorial book on the lion in Swedish.)

Kosambi, D.D. and V.V. Gokhale (eds.), 1957, *The Subhasitaratnakosa compiled by Vidyakara.* Harvard University Press, Cambridge, Mass.

Koch, Ebba, 1998, "Dara-Shikoh Shooting Nilgais: Hunt and Landscape in Mughal Painting". *Occasional Papers,* Vol. 1. Freer Gallery of Art/Arthur M. Sackler Gallery, Smithsonian Institution, Washington, DC.

Kossak, Steven, 1997, *Indian Court Painting 16th–19th century.* The Metropolitan Museum of Art, New York.

Kostioukovitch, Elena (ed.), 1996, *The St Petersburg Muraqqa: Album of Indian and Persian Miniatures from the 16th through the 18th Century and Specimens of Persian Calligraphy by 'Imad Al-Hasani.* Lenardo Arte srl, Milano & ARCH Foundation, Lugano.

Kothari, Ashok S. and B.F. Chhapgar (eds.), 1996, *Sálim Ali's India.* Bombay Natural History Society, Mumbai.

–––, 2005, *Treasures of Indian Wildlife.* Bombay Natural History Society, Mumbai.

Krishnadasa, Rai, 1999, *Anwar-e-Suhaili: Iyari-Danish.* Bharat Kala Bhavan, Banaras Hindu University, Varanasi.

L

Lal, Bharat, 2000, "Greater Gir Ecosystem: Ecorestoration of Girnar Forest & Recapture of Lost Territory by *Panthera leo persica* (Asiatic Lion)" (typescript).

Lavkumar, K.S., 1956, "Transferring of the Indian Lion to an Additional Locality". *Journal, Bombay Natural History Society,* Vol. 54, No. 1, pp. 173–75. Bombay.

Layard, Austen H., 1853, *Discoveries in the Ruins of Nineveh and Babylon.* John Murray, London.

Leipziger, E. von, 1888, *Sechs Monate Indien.* Adelbert Fischer's Verlag, Leipzig.

Liebert, Gosta, 1976, *Iconographic Dictionary of the Indian Religions: Hinduism-Buddhism-Jainism.* E.J. Brill, Leiden.

Low, Sir Francis (ed.), 1947, *The Indian Year Book 1947,* Volume XXXIII. Bennett, Coleman & Co. Ltd., Bombay.

Luckenbill, Daniel David, 1927, *Ancient Records of Assyria and Babylonia, Vol. II, Historical Records of Assyria from Sargon to the End.* The University of Chicago Press.

M

MA, Maharashtra State Archives, Mumbai.

Macdonald, David, 1992, *The Velvet Claw: A Natural History of the Carnivores.* BBC Books, London.

*Mahesh Singh; Punil P. Gajjar, and Badrish P. Mehra, 2002, *Gir National Park and Sanctuary: Bibliography.* Bishen Singh Mahendra Pal Singh, Dehra Dun.

Mahadevan, Iravatham, 1977, *The Indus Script, Texts, Concordance and Tables.* Archaeological Survey of India, New Delhi.

Mbh., 1936–1966, *Mahabharata.* 19 Volumes, Bhandarkar Oriental Research Institute, Pune.

McCrindle, John Watson, 1877, *Ancient India as described by Megasthenes and Arrian.* Today & Tomorrow Printers & Publishers, New Delhi, 1975.

*–––, 1892, *The Invasion of India by Alexander the Great.* Today & Tomorrow Printers & Publishers, New Delhi (year of publication of this edition not mentioned).

–––, 1901, *Ancient India as described in Classical Literature.* Philo Press, Amsterdam, 1971.

Meghani, Jhaverchand, 1997, *Saurashtrani Rasdhara.* Prasar, Bhavnagar, 2000.

–––, 1997A, *Sona-Navdi.* Prasar, Bhavnagar.

Mehta, Mahruq, 2001, *Cultural Mosaic of Gujarat.* Tourism Corporation of Gujarat Ltd., Gandhinagar.

Menon, V.P., 1956, *The Story of the Integration of Indian States*. Orient Longman, Bombay.

Micklem, James, 2001, *Sidis in Gujarat*. Occasional Papers, Centre for African Studies, University of Edinburgh, Edinburgh.

Minshull, Mrs E., 1937, "The Mysterious Man-Eater of Pachwara. Baby Seized from the Bed and Dropped". *Big Game Encounters: Critical Moments in the Lives of Well-Known Shikaris*, edited by Stanley Jepson, pp. 37–41. M.F. & G. Witherby Ltd., London.

Misra, Shiva Shekhar, 1966, *Somesvarakrta Manasollasa: Ek Sanskrtika Adhyayana*. Choukhambha Vidyabhavan, Varanasi.

Misra, V.N., 2000, "Climate as Factor in the Rise and Fall of the Indus Civilization – Evidence from Rajasthan and Beyond". *Decline and Fall of the Indus Civilization*, edited by Nayanjot Lahiri, pp. 239–51. Permanent Black, New Delhi.

Modi, Dr Sir Jivanji Jamshedji, 1932, "A Few Notes on Persian, African and Indian Lions in the First Century after Christ". *Journal, Bombay Natural History Society*, Vol. XXXV, No. 3., pp. 496–504. Bombay.

Mohan, Arun, 1990, *Princely States and the Reform in Hindu Law*. N.M. Tripathi, Bombay.

Monier-Williams, Sir Monier, 1851, *English-Sanskrit Dictionary*. Munshiram Manoharlal, New Delhi, 1985.

———, 1899, *Sanskrit-English Dictionary*. Munshiram Manoharlal, New Delhi, 1988.

Mosse, Lt. Col. A.H., 1957, "The Lion of the Gir". *Journal, Bombay Natural History Society*, Vol. 54, No. 3, pp. 568–76, Bombay.

Moscati, Sabastino, 1960, *The Face of the Ancient Orient: Near Eastern Civilization in Pre-Classical Times*. Dover Publications, Inc., Miniola, New York, 2001.

Mukherjee, B.N., 1969, *Nana on Lion: A Study in Kushana Numismatic Art*. The Asiatic Society, Calcutta.

Mukherjee, B.N. and T.N. Raychaudhuri, 1990, *The Indian Gold: An Introduction to the Cabinet of Gold Coins in the Indian Museum*. Indian Museum, Calcutta.

Mukhopadhyaya, Jiban K. and Saritha Aiyar (eds.), 2002, *Statistical Outline of India: 2002–2003*. Tata Services Ltd., Mumbai.

Mundy, General Godfrey Charles, 1858, *Pen and Pencil Sketches in India. Journal of a Tour in India*. Third Edition, Asian Educational Services, New Delhi, 1995.

N

NAI, National Archives of India, New Delhi.

Negi, S.S., 1966, "Introduction of the Indian Lion in Uttar Pradesh". *Cheetal, Journal of the Wildlife Preservation Society of India*, Vol. 8, No. 2, pp. 49–52, Dehra Dun.

———, 1969, "Transplanting of Indian Lion in Uttar Pradesh". *Cheetal, Journal of the Wildlife Preservation Society of India*, Vol. 12, No. 1, pp. 98–101, Dehra Dun.

Newall, Maj. Gen. D.J.F., 1882–87, *The Highlands of India. Being a Chronicle of Field Sports and Travel in India*. Vol. II. Logos Press, New Delhi, 1984.

Nicholson, J.W., 1935, *A Census in Tigerland*. Typescript from the Working Plan of the Palamau Division, Forest Department, Bihar Province.

Nizami, Khaliq Ahmad, 1997, *Royalty in Medieval India*. Munshiram Manoharlal, Delhi.

Nott, J. Fortune, 1886, *Wild Animals Photographed and Described*. Sampson Low, Marston, Searle & Rivington, London.

Nowell, Kristin and Peter Jackson (comp. and ed.), 1996, *Status Survey and Conservation Action Plan: Wild Cats*. IUCN World Conservation Union, Gland, Switzerland.

Nowell, Kristin and Xu Ling, 2007, *Taming the Tiger Trade: China's Market for Wild and Captive Tiger Products Since the 1999 Domestic Trade Ban*. Traffic East Asia, Hong Kong, China.

O

O'Brien, Stephen J., 2003, *Tears of the Cheetah and Other Tales from the Genetic Frontier*. Thomas Dunne Books, St Martin's Press, New York.

Oza, G.M.,1973, "Ban Experiments of Introduction of Asiatic Lions". *Indian Forester*, pp. 471–72, Forest Research Institute, Dehra Dun.

P

Pal, Pratapaditya (ed.), 1991, *Master Artists of the Mughal Court*. Marg Publications, Bombay.

Parpola, Asko, 1994, *Deciphering the Indus Script*. Cambridge University Press, Cambridge, 2000.

*Patel, Chandrakant, 1997, *Sinh-Darshan*. Pravin Prakashan, Rajkot.

*Patel, Suleman, circa 1990, *Gir Lions*. Published by author.

Pathan, A.R., 1921, *Kolahpur Shikar Album: containing Beautiful Illustrations of Wild Beasts and Birds*. Pathan, Kolahpur.

Patterson, Lieut. Col. J.H., 1907, *The Man-Eaters of Tsavo and Other East African Adventures*. Macmillan and Co., London, 1952.

Paul, E. Jaywant and Pramod Kapoor, 2003, *The Unforgettable Maharajas: One Hundred and Fifty Years of Photography*. Lustre Press/ Roli Books, New Delhi.

PH, Phulchchab. Gujarati daily newspaper, Rajkot.

Pilgrim, G.E., 1910, "Preliminary Note on a Revised Classification of the Tertiary Freshwater Deposits of India". *Records of the Geological Survey of India*, Vol. V, No. 40, Pt. 3, p. 199. Calcutta.

———, 1938, *The Fossil Carnivora of India*. *Palaeontologia Indica*, New Series, Vol. 18, pp. 138, 199. Geological Survey of India, Calcutta.

Pocock, R.I., 1930, "The Lions of Asia". *Journal, Bombay Natural History Society*, Vol. 34, No. 3, pp. 638–65. Bombay.

———, 1936, "A Pair of Indian Lions presented to the British Museum by H.H. Nawab of Junagadh". *Journal, Bombay Natural History Society*, Vol. 38, No. 2, pp. 382–84. Bombay.

———, 1936A, "The Lion in Baluchistan". *Journal, Bombay Natural History Society*, Vol. 38, No. 2, pp. 381–82. Bombay.

*–––, 1939, *The Fauna of British India including Ceylon and Burma,* Vol. I. Today & Tomorrow Printers & Publishers, New Delhi, 1985.

Possehl, Gregory L., 1999, *The Indus Age: The Beginnings.* University of Pennsylvania Press, Philadelphia.

*Prakash, Ishwar, 1994, *Mammals of the Thar Desert.* Scientific Publishers, Jodhpur.

Prasad, Kamal, c. 1965, *A Preliminary Bibliography of Shikar and Wildlife in India and the Neighbouring Countries* (typescript).

Prater, S.H., 1948, *The Book of Indian Animals.* Bombay Natural History Society, Bombay, 1980.

Q

*Qammen, David, 2003, *Monster of God: The Man-Eating Predator in the Jungles of History and the Mind.* W.W. Norton & Company, New York.

R

RV, 1972–76, *Rgveda Samhita.* 4 Volumes. Vaidika Samsodhana Mandala, Pune.

Raghuvamśa, 1915, *Raghuvamśa of Kalidasa.* Edited by M.R. Kale. The Oriental Publishing Company, Bombay.

Rahim, Maulvi Abdul (ed.), 1879, *Akbarnama.* Asiatic Society, Calcutta.

Rajan, K.V. Soundera, 1985, *Junagadh.* Archaeological Survey of India, New Delhi.

Rangarajan, Mahesh, 1996, *Fencing the Forest: Conservation and Ecological Change in India's Central Provinces 1860–1914.* Oxford University Press, Delhi.

–––, 2000, *India's Wildlife History: An Introduction.* Permanent Black, Delhi.

–––, 2001, "From Princely Symbol to Conservation Icon: A Political History of the Lion in India". *The Unfinished Agenda: Nation Building in South Asia,* edited by Mushirul Hasan and Nariaki Nakazato, pp. 399–442. Manohar Publishers and Distributors, New Delhi.

Ranjitsinh, M.K., 1997, *Beyond the Tiger:*

Portrait of Asia's Wildlife. Brijbasi, New Delhi.

–––, 2001, "In Search of a Home". *The Express Magazine of the Indian Express.* New Delhi, December 9.

Rao, B. Shiva, V.K.N. Menon, J.N. Khosla, K.V. Padmanabhan, C. Ganesan, P.K. Krishna Mani, 1966, *The Framing of India's Constitution: Select Documents.* Vol. I. The Indian Institute of Public Administration, New Delhi.

Rapson, Edward James, 1908, *Catalogue of the Coins of the Andhra Dynasty, The Western Ksatrapas, the Traikutaka Dynasty and the "Budhi" Dynasty.* The British Museum, London, 1967.

Rashid, M.A. and Reuben David, 1992, *The Asiatic Lion (Panthera leo persica).* Department of Environment, Government of India, New Delhi.

Ratnu, Kavi Mavdanji Bhimjibhai, 1934, *Shri Yaduvamsaprakasa ane Jamnagarno itihas.* Jamnagar.

Rawlinson, George, 1910, *Herodotus: The Histories.* Everyman's Library, David Campbell Publishers Ltd., London, 1997.

Rawlinson, George, 1898, *The Memoir of Major General Henry Creswicke Rawlinson.* Longman Green & Co., London.

Reade, Julian, 1983, *Assyrian Sculpture.* The British Museum Press, London, 1998.

Rice, William, 1884, *"Indian Game" (From Quail to Tiger).* W.H. Allen & Co., London.

Rizvi, S.A.A., 1987, *The Wonder that Was India.* Vol. II: A Survey of the History and Culture of the Indian Sub-Continent from the Coming of the Muslims to the British Conquest, 1200–1700. Sidgwick & Jackson Ltd., London.

Robinson, B.W., 1976, *Islamic Painting and the Arts of the Book.* Faber and Faber, London.

Rodrigues, Mario, 2003, *Batting for Empire. Political Biography of Ranjitsinhji.* Penguin Books, New Delhi.

Rogers, Alexander and Henry Beveridge, 1909–14, *The Tuzuk-i-Jahangiri or the Memoirs of Jahangir.* Munshiram Manoharlal, New Delhi, 1980.

Russell, C.E.M., 1900, *Bullet and Shot in Indian Forest, Plain and Hill.* W. Thacker and Co., London.

S

Saberwal, Vasant K., P. James Gibbs, Ravi Chellam, and A.J.T. Johnsingh, 1994, "Lion-Human Conflict in the Gir Forest, India". *Conservation Biology, The Journal of the Society for Conservation Biology,* Vol. 8, No. 2, pp. 501–07. Blackwell Scientific Publications, Malden, MA, USA.

Sankhala, Kailash, 1978, *Tiger! The Story of the Indian Tiger.* Collins, London.

Sanyal, Ram Brahma, 1892, *A Handbook of the Management of Animals in Captivity in Lower Bengal.* Bengal Secretariat Press, Calcutta.

Sarma, Sreeramula Rejeswara, 1991, "*Gajamuktika:* Poetic Convention and Reality". *Bulletin D'Etudes Indiennes.* Association Francaise Pour Les Etudes Sanskrites, Paris.

Śat. Br., 1940, *Śatapatha Brahmana.* 5 Volumes. "Laksmi Venkatesvara" Steam Press, Kalyan – Bombay.

Saunders, Nicholas J., 1991, *The Cult of the Cat.* Thames and Hudson, London.

Schaller, George B., 1972, *The Serengeti Lion, A Study of Predator-Prey Relations.* The University of Chicago Press, Chicago.

Scholfield, A.F. (tr.), 1959, *Aelian: On Peculiarities of Animals.* Harvard University Press, Cambridge, Mass.

Schwartzberg, Joseph E. (ed.), 1978, *A Historical Atlas of South Asia.* Oxford University Press, New York, 1992.

Sen, Geeti, 1984, *Paintings from the Akbar Nama.* Lustre Press Pvt. Ltd., Varanasi.

*Sen, Sri Sujit Narain, 1985, "Anecdotes of Kamargha and Fauna in Mughal Literature". *Indian Museum Bulletin,* Vol. XV, Nos. 1 and 2, pp. 41–48. Calcutta.

Seshadri, Balakrishna, 1969, *The Twilight of India's Wildlife.* John Baker Publishers, London.

Shaikh, G.A., 1936, *The Mahbat Album.* Junagadh.

Sharma, Arpan, Asmita Kabra, and Rumman Hameed, 2002, *Kuno Project, Madhya Pradesh. Progress Report V (November 2001–April 2002)*. Samrakshan Trust, New Delhi (typescript).

Sharma, Diwakar and A.J.T. Johnsingh, 1996, *Impact of Management Practices on Lion and Ungulate Habitats in Gir Protected Area.* Wildlife Institute of India, Dehra Dun.

Sharma, Dr Ramdatta, c. 1970, *Sanskrit Kavyome Pashu Pakshi.* Devnagar Prakashan, Jaipur.

Shastri, M.M. Harprasad (tr.), 1910, *Syainika Sastram: The Art of Hunting in Ancient India of Raja Rudradeva of Kumaon.* Eastern Book Linkers, Delhi, 1982.

Shrigondekar, G.K. (ed.), 1939, *Manasollasa of King Someswara.* Vol. II. Oriental Institute, Baroda.

Singh, H.S., 1997, "Population Dynamics, Group Structure and Natural Dispersal of the Asiatic Lion *Panthera leo persica*". *Journal, Bombay Natural History Society,*   Vol. 94, No. 1, pp. 65–70. Bombay.

———, 1998, *Gir Lion – Population Dynamics Predation Pattern, Dispersal and Management Issues* (typescript).

*———, 1998, *Wildlife of Gujarat.* Gujarat Ecological and Education Research Foundation, Gandhinagar.

———, 2001, *Natural Heritage of Gujarat (Forests and Wildlife).* Gujarat Ecological Education Research (GEER) Foundation, Gandhinagar.

———, 2001A, "Gir Lion – Present Scenario and Future Conservation Strategy". Paper read at *GEF – India Eco Development Project Initiative National Workshop on Regional Planning for Wild Life Protected Areas, 6th–8th August,* New Delhi (typescript).

———, 2003, "Stranger than Fiction", *Sanctuary Asia,* Vol. XXIII, No. 2, pp. 57–58, Mumbai.

Singh, H.S. and R.D. Kamboj, 1996, *Biodiversity Conservation Plan for Gir (A Management Plan for Gir Sanctuary & National Park).* Vols. I and II. Government of Gujarat, Gandhinagar.

Singh, M.K. Brijraj, 1985, *The Kingdom that was Kotah: Paintings from Kotah.* Lalit Kala Akademi, New Delhi.

Singh, Col. Kesri, 1959, *The Tiger of Rajasthan.* Robert Hale Ltd. London.

———, 1965, *Hints on Tiger Shooting (Tigers by Tiger).* The Hindustan Times, New Delhi.

Sinha, S.P., 1987, *Ecology of Wildlife with Special Reference to the Lion (Panthera leo persica) in Gir Wildlife Sanctuary, Saurashtra, Gujarat.* Ph.D. thesis, University of Saurashtra, Rajkot.

Sivaramamurti, C., 1974, *Birds and Animals in Indian Sculpture.* National Museum, New Delhi.

*Skelton, Robert, 1970, "Two Mughal Lion Hunts". *V & A Year Book,* No. 1, pp. 33–48. London.

Smith, S.J., P. Mcbee, and W.C. Mathews, 1989, *Rowland Ward's Records of Big Game XXII Edition.* Rowland Ward Publications, San Antonio, Texas.

Smythies, E.A., 1942, *Big Game Shooting in Nepal (with leaves from the Maharaja's Sporting Diary).* Thacker Spink & Co. (1933) Ltd., Calcutta.

Sodha, Jaisukhlal P., 2002, *Sorathna Antim Babi Shasak.* Pujam, Junagadh.

Soustiel, Joseph, 1973, *Miniatures Orientales de L'Inde: Les Ecoles et lurs styles Presentation d'un ensemble de peintures musulmanes et rajpoutes.* Librairie Leguettel, Paris.

*Spillett, J. Juan, 1968, "A Report on Wild Life Surveys in South and West India, November–December 1966". *Journal, Bombay Natural History Society,* Vol. 65, No. 1, pp. 1–46, Bombay.

Srivastava, Asheem and Suvira, 1999, *Asiatic Lion on the Brink.* Bishen Singh Mahendra Pal Singh, Dehra Dun.

Srivastava, T.N., 1969, "New Home for Lions in India". *Indian Forester,* pp. 706–10, Forest Research Institute, Dehra Dun.

*Stracey, P.D., 1959, "Lion Implanting in India". *Cheetal, Journal of the Wildlife Preservation Society of India,* Vol. I, No. 2. pp.

16–18, Dehra Dun.

———, 1963, *Wild Life in India: Its Conservation and Control.* Ministry of Food and Agriculture, Government of India, New Delhi.

Śubh., 1985, *Śubhasitaratnabhandagara.* "Shree Venkatesvara" Steam Press, Bombay.

Sunquist, Mel and Fiona, 2002, *Wild Cats of the World.* The University of Chicago Press, Chicago.

Sursinh, 1893, *Kalapino Kekarav.* Pravin Pustak Bhandar, Rajkot, 1982.

Suryakanta, Dr, 1962, *Kumarasambhava of Kalidasa.* Sahitya Akademi, New Delhi.

T

Taparia, Jaswantsinh Harisinh, 1979, *Amar Charitra: Wankaner Maharana Rajsaheb Sir Amarsinhjinu Jeevan Vrutanta.* Wankaner.

Thackston, Wheeler M., 1996, *The Baburnama: Memoirs of Babur Prince and Emperor.* Freer Gallery of Art/Arthur M. Sackler Gallery, Oxford University Press, New York.

———, 1999, *The Jahangirnama: Memoirs of Jahangir, Emperor of India.* Freer Gallery of Art/Arthur M. Sackler Gallery, Washington, DC and Oxford University Press, New York.

Thapar, Romila, 1961, *Asoka and the Decline of the Mauryas.* Oxford University Press, Oxford.

———, 1966, *A History of India.* Vol. I. Penguin Books Ltd., Harmondsworth, Midddlesex, 1985.

Thapar, Valmik, 1992, *The Tiger's Destiny.* Time Books International, New Delhi.

———, 2002, *The Cult of the Tiger.* Oxford University Press, New Delhi.

———, 2004, *Tiger: The Ultimate Guide.* CDS Books/Two Brothers Press, New York.

Thomas, Elizabeth Marshall, 1994, *The Tribe of Tiger: Cats and their Culture.* Simon & Schuster, New York.

Thomas, P.K. and P.P. Joglekar, 1994, "Holocene Faunal Studies in India". *Man and Environment.* Vol. XIX, Nos. 1 and 2, pp. 179–203. Deccan College, Pune.

Thompson, Edward, 1999, "Mainly about Lions". *Oxford Anthology of Indian Wildlife: Watching and Conserving*, edited by Mahesh Rangarajan, Vol. II, pp. 96–99. Oxford University Press, New Delhi.

Titley, Norah M., 1983, *Persian Miniature Painting and its Influence on the Art of Turkey and India*. The British Library, London.

Tod, James, 1832, *Annals and Antiquities of Rajasthan*. Vol. II. K.M.N. Publishers, New Delhi, 1971.

*Tod, Neil B., 1965, "Metrical and Non-metrical Variation in the Skulls of Gir Lions". *Journal, Bombay Natural History Society*, Vol. 62, No. 3, pp. 507–20. Bombay.

Toynbee, J.M.C., 1973, *Animals in Roman Life and Art*. Cornell University Press, Ithaca, New York.

Trautman, Thomas R., 1982, "Elephant and the Mauryas". *India: History and Thought. Essays in Honour of A.L. Basham*, edited by S.N. Mukherji, pp. 254–81. Subernarekha, Calcutta.

Trivedi, K.K., 1998, "Estimating Forests, Wastes and Fields, c 1600". *Studies in History*, Vol. 14, No. 2, pp. 301–11. Sage Publications India Pvt. Ltd., New Delhi.

Turner, Alan, 1997, *The Big Cats and their Fossil Relatives: An Illustrated Guide to their Evolution and Natural History*. Illustrations by Mauricio Anton. Columbia University Press, New York.

V

Vaidya, Suresh, 1958, *Ahead Lies the Jungle*. Robert Hale Ltd., London.

Van Buren, E. Douglas, 1939, *The Fauna of Ancient Mesopotamia as represented in Art*. Pontificum Institutum Biblicum, Roma.

Visaria, Leela and Pravin, 1982, "Population (1757–1947)". *The Cambridge Economic History of India, Vol. II, c1757–c1970*. Edited by Dharma Kumar and Meghnad Desai, pp. 463–532. Orient Longman, Hyderabad and Cambridge University Press, Cambridge, 1984.

*Vyas, Bhaskar N., 1997, *Girni Godma*. Published by author, Una, Gujarat.

*Vyas, Chintamani and Dr Daljeet, 1988, "Hunting Scenes in Indian Miniatures". *Indrama*, Vol. XIII, No. 3. Delhi.

W

Wallinger, W.A., 1913, *Report on Junagadh Forests*. Submitted to the Administrator of Junagadh State (typescript).

Wankaner, M.K. Chandrabhanusinhji of, 1952, *Shikar Diaries (Animals)* (unpublished).

Wankaner, Maharana Raj Saheb Pratapsinhji of, 1971, *Shikar Diary* (unpublished).

Watson, Col. J.W., 1884, *Statistical Account of Junagadh: Being the Junagadh Contribution to the Kathiawar Portion of the Bombay Gazetteer*. Bombay.

Weissert, Elnathan, 1997, "Royal Hunt and Royal Triumph in a Prism Fragment of Ashurbanipal (82-5-22.2)". *Assyria 1995. Proceedings of the 10th Anniversary Symposium of the Neo-Assyrian Text Corpus Project, Helsinki, September 7–11, 1995*, edited by S. Parpola and R.M. Whiting, pp. 339–57. The Neo-Assyrian Text Corpus Project, Helsinki.

Welch, Stuart Carey, 1978, *Imperial Mughal Painting*. George Braziller, New York.

———, 1986, "A Lion-Kings' Lion". *Dimensions of Indian Art: Pupul Jaykar Seventy*, edited by Lokesh Chandra and Jyotindra Jain, Vol. I, pp 577–80. Agam Kala Prakashan, Delhi.

Welch, Stuart Cary and Kimberly Masteller, 2004, *From Mind, Heart and Hand: Persian, Turkish and Indian Drawings from the Stuart Cary Welch Collection*. Yale University Press, New Haven, Conn./Harvard University Art Museum, Cambridge, Mass.

Wilberforce-Bell, Capt. H., 1916, *The History of Kathiawad from the Earliest Times*. William Heinemann, London.

Wildt, D.E., K.L. Bush, K.L. Goodrowe, C. Parker, A.E. Pusey, J.L. Brown, P. Joslin, and S.J. O'Brien, 1987, "Reproductive and Genetic Consequences of Founding Isolated Lion Populations". *Nature*, Vol. 329, No. 6137, pp. 328–31, September 24. Macmillan Magazines Ltd., London.

Williamson, Captain Thomas, 1807, *Oriental Field Sports; Being a Complete, Detailed and Accurate Description of the Wild Sports of the East*. Edward Orme, London.

Wolpert, Stanley, 1984, *Jinnah of Pakistan*. Oxford University Press, Delhi.

———, 1993, *Zulfi Bhutto of Pakistan*. Oxford University Press, Delhi, 1994.

Wood, Ron with Meher, Vijay, 1998, *Soruth. Handbook of Indian Philately, Second Series – No. 3*. India Study Circle for Philately, London.

Wynter-Blyth, M.A., 1949, "The Gir Forest and its Lions". *Journal, Bombay Natural History Society*, Vol. 48, No. 3, pp. 493–514. Bombay.

———, 1950, *Report on the Lions of the Gir Forest*. Published by author, Rajkot.

———, 1956, "The Lion Census of 1955". *Journal, Bombay Natural History Society*, Vol. 53, No. 4, pp. 528–36. Bombay.

———, c. 1961, *An Essay on the Geography of Saurashtra*. Rajkumar College, Rajkot.

Wynter-Blyth, M.A. and K.S. Dharmakumarsinhji, 1950, "The Gir Forest and its Lions" Part II. *Journal, Bombay Natural History Society*, Vol. 49, No. 3, pp. 456–70, Bombay.

Y

Ylla, 1958, *Animals in India*. Hamish Hamilton, London and La Guilde du Livre, Lausanne.

Yule, Henry and A.C. Burnell, 1886, *Hobson-Jobson: A Glossary of Colloquial Anglo-Indian Words and Phrases*. Routledge and Kegan Paul, London, 1985.

Z

Zeuner, Frederick E., 1963, *A History of Domesticated Animals*. Hutchinson, London.

Zimmermann, Francis, 1987, *The Jungle and the Aroma of Meats: An Ecological Theme in Hindu Medicine*. University of California Press, Berkeley.

index

Page numbers in bold refer to
illustrations/captions